POWERPOINT®
FOR WINDOWS® 95
FOR
DUMMIES®

POWERPOINT®
FOR WINDOWS® 95
FOR
DUMMIES®

by Doug Lowe

IDG Books Worldwide, Inc.
An International Data Group Company

Foster City, CA ♦ Chicago, IL ♦ Indianapolis, IN ♦ Braintree, MA ♦ Dallas, TX

PowerPoint® For Windows® 95 For Dummies®

Published by
IDG Books Worldwide, Inc.
An International Data Group Company
919 E. Hillsdale Blvd.
Suite 400
Foster City, CA 94404

Library of Congress Catalog Card No.: 95-81441

ISBN: 1-56884-931-1

Printed in the United States of America

10 9 8 7 6 5 4 3 2 1

1A/SZ/RS/ZV

Distributed in the United States by IDG Books Worldwide, Inc.

Distributed by Macmillan Canada for Canada; by Computer and Technical Books for the Caribbean Basin; by Contemporanea de Ediciones for Venezuela; by Distribuidora Cuspide for Argentina; by CITEC for Brazil; by Ediciones ZETA S.C.R. Ltda. for Peru; by Editorial Limusa SA for Mexico; by Transworld Publishers Limited in the United Kingdom and Europe; by Al-Maiman Publishers & Distributors for Saudi Arabia; by Simron Pty. Ltd. for South Africa; by IDG Communications (HK) Ltd. for Hong Kong; by Toppan Company Ltd. for Japan; by Addison Wesley Publishing Company for Korea; by Longman Singapore Publishers Ltd. for Singapore, Malaysia, Thailand, and Indonesia; by Unalis Corporation for Taiwan; by WS Computer Publishing Company, Inc. for the Philippines; by WoodsLane Pty. Ltd. for Australia; by WoodsLane Enterprises Ltd. for New Zealand.

For general information on IDG Books Worldwide's books in the U.S., please call our Consumer Customer Service department at 800-762-2974. For reseller information, including discounts and premium sales, please call our Reseller Customer Service department at 800-434-3422.

For information on where to purchase IDG Books Worldwide's books outside the U.S., contact IDG Books Worldwide at 415-655-3021 or fax 415-655-3295.

For information on translations, contact Marc Jeffrey Mikulich, Director, Foreign & Subsidiary Rights, at IDG Books Worldwide, 415-655-3018 or fax 415-655-3295.

For sales inquiries and special prices for bulk quantities, write to the address above or call IDG Books Worldwide at 415-655-3200.

For information on using IDG Books Worldwide's books in the classroom, or ordering examination copies, contact Jim Kelly, Director of Corporate, Education and Government Sales, at 800-434-2086.

For authorization to photocopy items for corporate, personal, or educational use, please contact Copyright Clearance Center, 222 Rosewood Drive, Danvers, MA 01923, or fax 508-750-4470.

 is a trademark under exclusive license to IDG Books Worldwide, Inc., from International Data Group, Inc.

About the Author

Doug Lowe has written more than 20 computer books (including IDG Books Worldwide's *The Microsoft Network For Dummies, Microsoft Office 4 For Windows For Dummies Quick Reference,* the upcoming *MORE Word For Windows 95 For Dummies,* and *Networking For Dummies*) and knows how to present technobabble in a style that is both entertaining and enlightening. He is a contributing editor to *DOS Resource Guide* magazine.

ABOUT IDG BOOKS WORLDWIDE

Welcome to the world of IDG Books Worldwide.

IDG Books Worldwide, Inc., is a subsidiary of International Data Group, the world's largest publisher of computer-related information and the leading global provider of information services on information technology. IDG was founded more than 25 years ago and now employs more than 7,700 people worldwide. IDG publishes more than 250 computer publications in 67 countries (see listing below). More than 70 million people read one or more IDG publications each month.

Launched in 1990, IDG Books Worldwide is today the #1 publisher of best-selling computer books in the United States. We are proud to have received 8 awards from the Computer Press Association in recognition of editorial excellence and three from Computer Currents' First Annual Readers' Choice Awards, and our best-selling ...For Dummies® series has more than 19 million copies in print with translations in 28 languages. IDG Books Worldwide, through a joint venture with IDG's Hi-Tech Beijing, became the first U.S. publisher to publish a computer book in the People's Republic of China. In record time, IDG Books Worldwide has become the first choice for millions of readers around the world who want to learn how to better manage their businesses.

Our mission is simple: Every one of our books is designed to bring extra value and skill-building instructions to the reader. Our books are written by experts who understand and care about our readers. The knowledge base of our editorial staff comes from years of experience in publishing, education, and journalism — experience which we use to produce books for the '90s. In short, we care about books, so we attract the best people. We devote special attention to details such as audience, interior design, use of icons, and illustrations. And because we use an efficient process of authoring, editing, and desktop publishing our books electronically, we can spend more time ensuring superior content and spend less time on the technicalities of making books.

You can count on our commitment to deliver high-quality books at competitive prices on topics you want to read about. At IDG Books Worldwide, we continue in the IDG tradition of delivering quality for more than 25 years. You'll find no better book on a subject than one from IDG Books Worldwide.

John J. Kilcullen

John Kilcullen
President and CEO
IDG Books Worldwide, Inc.

IDG Books Worldwide, Inc., is a subsidiary of International Data Group, the world's largest publisher of computer-related information and the leading global provider of information services on information technology. International Data Group publishes over 250 computer publications in 67 countries. Seventy million people read one or more International Data Group publications each month. International Data Group's publications include: **ARGENTINA:** Computerworld Argentina, GamePro, Infoworld, PC World Argentina; **AUSTRALIA:** Australian Macworld, Client/Server Journal, Computer Living, Computerworld, Digital News, Network World, PC World, Publishing Essentials, Reseller; **AUSTRIA:** Computerwelt, PC TEST; **BELARUS:** PC World Belarus; **BELGIUM:** Data News; **BRAZIL:** Annuário de Informática, Computerworld Brazil, Connections, Super Game Power, Macworld, PC World Brazil, Publish Brazil, SUPERGAME; **BULGARIA:** Computerworld Bulgaria, Networkworld/Bulgaria, PC & MacWorld Bulgaria; **CANADA:** CIO Canada, ComputerWorld Canada, InfoCanada, Network World Canada, Reseller World; **CHILE:** Computerworld Chile, GamePro, PC World Chile; **COLUMBIA:** Computerworld Colombia, GamePro, PC World Colombia; **COSTA RICA:** PC World Costa Rica/Nicaragua; **THE CZECH AND SLOVAK REPUBLICS:** Computerworld Czechoslovakia, Elektronika Czechoslovakia, PC World Czechoslovakia; **DENMARK:** Communications World, Computerworld Danmark, Macworld Danmark, PC World Danmark, PC World Danmark Supplements, TECH World; **DOMINICAN REPUBLIC:** PC World Republica Dominicana; **ECUADOR:** PC World Ecuador, GamePro; **EGYPT:** Computerworld Middle East, PC World Middle East; **EL SALVADOR:** PC World Centro America; **FINLAND:** MikroPC, Tietoverkko, Tietoviikko; **FRANCE:** Distributique, Golden, Info PC, Le Guide du Monde Informatique, Le Monde Informatique, Reseaux & Telecoms; **GERMANY:** Computer Business, Computerwoche, Computerwoche Extra, Computerwoche Focus, Electronic Entertainment, GamePro, I/M Information Management, Macwelt, PC Welt; **GREECE:** GamePro, Macworld & Publish; **GUATEMALA:** PC World Centro America; **HONDURAS:** PC World Centro America; **HONG KONG:** Computerworld Hong Kong, PCWorld Hong Kong, Publish in Asia; **HUNGARY:** ABCD CD-ROM, Computerworld Szamitastechnika, PC & Mac World Hungary, PC-X Magazine; **INDIA:** Computerworld India, PC World India, Publish in Asia; **INDONESIA:** InfoKomputer PC World, Komputek Computerworld, Publish in Asia; **IRELAND:** ComputerScope, PC Live!; **ISRAEL:** PC World 32 BIT, People & Computers; **ITALY:** Computerworld Italia, Computerworld Italia Special Editions, Lotus Italia, Macworld Italia, Networking Italia, PC Shopping, PC World Italia, PC World/Walt Disney; **JAPAN:** Macworld Japan, Nikkei Personal Computing, SunWorld Japan, Windows World Japan; **KENYA:** East African Computer News; **KOREA:** Hi-Tech Information/Computerworld, Macworld Korea, PC World Korea; **MACEDONIA:** PC World Macedonia; **MALAYSIA:** Computerworld Malaysia, PC World Malaysia, Publish in Asia; **MEXICO:** Computerworld Mexico, GamePro, Macworld, PC World Mexico; **MYANMAR:** PC World Myanmar; **NETHERLANDS:** Computable, Computer! Totaal, LAN Magazine, Macworld, Net Magazine; **NEW ZEALAND:** Computer Buyer, Computerworld New Zealand, MTB, Network World, PC World New Zealand; **NICARAGUA:** PC World Costa Rica/Nicaragua; **NIGERIA:** PC World Africa; **NORWAY:** Computerworld Norge, Computerworld Privat, CW Rapport Klient/Tjener, CW Rapport Nettverk & Telecom, CW Rapport Offentlig Sektor, IDG's KURSGUIDE, Macworld Norge, Multimedia World, PC World Ekspress, PC World Nettverk, PC World Norge, PC World's Produktguide, Windows Spesial; **PAKISTAN:** Computerworld Pakistan, PC World Pakistan; **PANAMA:** GamePro, PC World Panama; **PARAGUAY:** PC World Paraguay; **P. R. OF CHINA:** China Computerworld, China Infoworld, Computer & Communication, Electronic Product World, Electronics Today, Game Camp, PC World China, Popular Computer Week, Software World, Telecom Product World; **PERU:** Computerworld Peru, GamePro, PC World Profesional Peru, PC World Peru; **POLAND:** Computerworld Poland, Computerworld Special Report, Macworld, Networld, PC World Komputer; **PHILIPPINES:** Computerworld Philippines, PC Digest, Publish in Asia; **PORTUGAL:** Cerebro/PC World, Correio Informático/Computerworld, Mac•In/PC•In Portugal; **PUERTO RICO:** PC World Puerto Rico; **ROMANIA:** Computerworld Romania, PC World Romania, Telecom Romania; **RUSSIA:** Computerworld Rossiya, Network World Russia, PC World Russia; **SINGAPORE:** Computerworld Singapore, PC World Singapore, Publish in Asia; **SLOVENIA:** MONITOR; **SOUTH AFRICA:** Computing S.A., Network World S.A., Software World; **SPAIN:** Computerworld España, COMUNICACIONES WORLD, Dealer World, Macworld España, PC World España; **SWEDEN:** CAP&Design, Computer Sweden, Corporate Computing, MacWorld, Maxi Data, MikroDatorn, Nätverk & Kommunikation, PC/Aktiv, PC World, Windows World; **SWITZERLAND:** Computerworld Schweiz, Macworld Schweiz, PCtip; **TAIWAN:** Computerworld Taiwan, Macworld Taiwan, PC World Taiwan, Publish Taiwan, Windows World; **THAILAND:** Thai Computerworld, Publish in Asia; **TURKEY:** Computerworld Monitör, MACWORLD Turkiye, PC WORLD Turkiye; **UKRAINE:** Computerworld Kiev, Computers & Software Magazine, PC World Ukraine; **UNITED KINGDOM:** Acorn User, Amiga Action, Amiga Computing, Amiga, Appletalk, CD Powerplay, CD-ROM Now, Computing, Connexion, GamePro, Lotus Magazine, Macaction, Macworld, Open Computing, Parents and Computers, PC Home, PC Works, The WEB; **UNITED STATES:** Cable in the Classroom, CD Review, CIO Magazine, Computerworld, Computerworld Client/Server Journal, Digital Video Magazine, DOS World, Electronic, InfoWorld, I-Way, Macworld, Maximize, MULTIMEDIA WORLD, Network World, PC World, PUBLISH, SWATPro Magazine, Video Event, WebMaster; **URUGUAY:** PC World Uruguay; **VENEZUELA:** Computerworld Venezuela, GamePro, PC World Venezuela; and **VIETNAM:** PC World Vietnam
10/17/95

Dedication

To Debbie, Rebecca, Sarah, and Bethany

Acknowledgments

Thanks to Pam Mourouzis for whipping this book into shape and not yelling at me when I was a day or two late, and to Leah Cameron and Jim McCarter for their editorial and technical prowess. Oops, gotta run, another deadline coming up. . . .

(The Publisher would like to give special thanks to Patrick J. McGovern, without whom this book would not have been possible.)

Credits

**Senior Vice President
and Publisher**
Milissa L. Koloski

Associate Publisher
Diane Graves Steele

Brand Manager
Judith A. Taylor

Editorial Managers
Kristin A. Cocks
Mary C. Corder

Product Development Manager
Mary Bednarek

Editorial Executive Assistant
Richard Graves

Editorial Assistants
Constance Carlisle
Chris Collins
Kevin Spencer

Production Director
Beth Jenkins

Production Assistant
Jacalyn L. Pennywell

**Supervisor of
Project Coordination**
Cindy L. Phipps

Supervisor of Page Layout
Kathie S. Schnorr

Production Systems Specialist
Steve Peake

Pre-Press Coordination
Tony Augsburger
Patricia R. Reynolds
Theresa Sánchez-Baker

Media/Archive Coordination
Leslie Popplewell
Michael Wilkey

Project Editor
Pamela Mourouzis

Editor
Leah P. Cameron

Technical Reviewer
Jim McCarter

Associate Project Coordinator
J. Tyler Connor

Graphics Coordination
Shelley Lea
Gina Scott
Carla Radzikinas

Production Page Layout
Brett Black
Cameron Booker
Angela F. Hunckler
Jill Lyttle

Proofreaders
Jenny Kaufeld
Christine Meloy Beck
Gwenette Gaddis
Dwight Ramsey
Carl Saff
Robert Springer

Indexer
David Heiret

Cover Design
Kavish + Kavish

Contents at a Glance

Introduction 1

Part I: Basic PowerPoint 95 Stuff 7

Chapter 1: PowerPoint 101 9
Chapter 2: Editing Slides 35
Chapter 3: Doing It in Outline View 55
Chapter 4: Doing It with Style 67
Chapter 5: Printing Your Presentation 77
Chapter 6: Help! 85

Part II: Looking Mahvelous 93

Chapter 7: Fabulous Text Formats 95
Chapter 8: Masters of the Universe Meet the Templates of Doom 109
Chapter 9: When I Am Old, I Shall Make My Slides Purple 127
Chapter 10: Using Clip Art 141
Chapter 11: Drawing on Your Slides 157

Part III: Neat Things You Can Add to Your Slides 177

Chapter 12: Graphs 179
Chapter 13: Organization Chart (Or, Who's in Charge Here?) 193
Chapter 14: Equations, WordArt, and Other Ornaments 205
Chapter 15: Lights! Camera! Action! (Adding Sound and Video) 217
Chapter 16: Transitions and Animation Effects 225

Part IV: Cool PowerPoint 95 Features 233

Chapter 17: Using AutoCorrect 235
Chapter 18: Creating Notes Pages 239
Chapter 19: Making 35mm Slides 247
Chapter 20: Show Time! 251

Part V: Working with Files 261

Chapter 21: Juggling Multiple Presentations and Stealing Slides 263
Chapter 22: Sharing Information with Other Programs 273
Chapter 23: Managing Your Files 279

Part VI: The Part of Tens 287

Chapter 24: Ten PowerPoint Commandments 289
Chapter 25: Ten Things That Often Go Wrong 293
Chapter 26: Ten PowerPoint Shortcuts 297
Chapter 27: Ten Tips for Creating Readable Slides 301
Chapter 28: Ten New Features in PowerPoint 95 305
Chapter 29: Ten Cool Things on the PowerPoint Multimedia CD-ROM 309
Chapter 30: Ten Ways to Keep Your Audience Awake 315

Appendix: Installing PowerPoint 319

Index 323

Reader Response Card .... Back of Book

Cartoons at a Glance

By Rich Tennant

page 233

page 287

page 177

page 156

page 322

page 93

page 261

page 7

page 76

page 300

Table of Contents

Introduction **1**

About This Book 1
How to Use This Book 2
What You Don't Need to Read 3
Foolish Assumptions 3
How This Book Is Organized 4
    Part I: Basic PowerPoint 95 Stuff 4
    Part II: Looking Mahvelous 4
    Part III: Neat Things You Can Add to Your Slides 4
    Part IV: Cool PowerPoint 95 Features 4
    Part V: Working with Files 5
    Part VI: The Part of Tens 5
Icons Used in This Book 5
Where to Go from Here 6

Part I: Basic PowerPoint 95 Stuff **7**

Chapter 1: PowerPoint 101 .... **9**

What in Sam Hill Is PowerPoint? 10
Introducing PowerPoint for Windows 95, Version 7! 12
Starting PowerPoint 12
    How much should I tip? 14
    Choices, choices 15
    Help me, Mr. Wizard! 17
    What is all this stuff? (Making sense of the PowerPoint screen) 22
I Can't See the Whole Slide! 25
Editing Text 25
Moving from Slide to Slide 26
50 Ways to Add a New Slide 26
Outline That for Me! 28
Printing That Puppy 29
Saving Your Work 30
Retrieving a Presentation from a Disk 31
Closing a Presentation 32
Exiting PowerPoint 33

Chapter 2: Editing Slides **35**

Moving from Slide to Slide 36
Working with Objects 36
    Selecting objects 38
    Resizing or moving an object 38
Editing a Text Object: The Baby Word Processor 40
    Using the arrow keys 41
    Moving around faster 42
    Deleting text 43
    Marking text for surgery 43
Using Cut, Copy, and Paste 44
    Cutting or copying a text block 45
    Pasting text 45
    Cutting, copying, and pasting entire objects 46
Oops! I Didn't Mean It (the Marvelous Undo Command) 47
Deleting a Slide 47
Finding Text 48
Replacing Text 50
Rearranging Your Slides in Slide Sorter View 51

Chapter 3: Doing It in Outline View **55**

Switching to Outline View 55
Understanding Outline View 56
Selecting and Editing an Entire Slide 57
Selecting and Editing One Paragraph 58
Promoting and Demoting Paragraphs 58
    Promoting paragraphs 59
    Demoting paragraphs 59
    Dragging paragraphs to new levels 60
Adding a New Paragraph 60
Adding a New Slide 61
Moving Text Up and Down 62
    Moving text up or down by using the keyboard 62
    Dragging text up or down 62
Expanding and Collapsing the Outline 63
    Collapsing an entire presentation 63
    Expanding an entire presentation 63
    Collapsing a single slide 63
    Expanding a single slide 64
Showing and Hiding Formats 64

Chapter 4: Doing It with Style **67**

Checking Your Spelling 67
Capitalizing Correctly 70

To Period or Not to Period. Period. 71
Using the Style Checker 72

Chapter 5: Printing Your Presentation **77**

The Quick Way to Print 77
Using the Print Dialog Box 78
    Changing printers 79
    Printing part of a presentation 80
    Printing more than one copy 80
    What do you want to print? 81
    What are all those other check boxes? 82
Printing Boo-Boos 83

Chapter 6: Help! **85**

Several Ways to Get Help 85
Finding Your Way Around in Help 86
Take-You-by-the-Hand Help 89
Searching for Lost Help Topics 89
Using the Answer Wizard 91
Getting Help on The Microsoft Network 92

Part II: Looking Mahvelous .... _93_

Chapter 7: Fabulous Text Formats **95**

Changing the Look of Your Characters 95
    To boldly go 97
    Italics 98
    Underlines 98
    Big and little characters 99
    Text fonts 99
    The color purple 100
    The shadow knows 101
    Embossed text 101
Biting the Bullet 102
Lining Things Up 104
    Centering text 104
    Flush to the left 104
    Flush to the right 105
    Stand up, sit down, justify! 105
Messing with Tabs and Indents 105
Spacing Things Out 107

Chapter 8: Masters of the Universe Meet the Templates of Doom 109

Working with Masters 110
Changing the Slide Master 110
    Adding recurring text 112
    Changing the Master color scheme 113
    Changing the Title Master 113
Changing the Handout and Notes Masters 114
    Changing the Handout Master 115
    Changing the Notes Master 116
Using Masters 116
    Overriding the Master text style 117
    Changing the background for just one slide 117
Using Headers and Footers 119
    Adding a date, number, or footer to slides 119
    Adding a header or footer to notes or handout pages 120
    Editing the header and footer placeholders directly 121
Thank Heavens for Templates 121
    Applying a different template 122
    Creating a new template 123
    Creating a new default template 124

Chapter 9: When I Am Old, I Shall Make My Slides Purple 127

Using Color Schemes 127
    Using a different color scheme 129
    Overriding the color scheme 130
    Changing colors in a color scheme 131
    Shading the slide background 133
    Using other background effects 135
Coloring Text and Objects 136
    Applying color to text 137
    Changing an object's fill color 138
    Creating a semi-transparent object 139
    Copying color from an existing object 139

Chapter 10: Using Clip Art 141

Free Pictures! 141
Dropping In Some Clip Art 142
Moving, Sizing, and Stretching Pictures 144
Boxing, Shading, and Shadowing a Picture 146
Editing a Clip Art Picture 147
Colorizing a Clip Art Picture 150
Adding Your Own Pictures to the ClipArt Gallery 151

Adding Pictures from the PowerPoint CD-ROM 153
Inserting Pictures without Using the ClipArt Gallery 153

Chapter 11: Drawing on Your Slides 157

Some General Drawing Tips 157
Zoom in 158
Activate the Drawing+ toolbar 158
Display the ruler 158
Stick to the color scheme 159
Save frequently 159
Don't forget Ctrl+Z 160
Drawing Simple Lines and Shapes 160
Drawing straight and curved lines 162
Drawing rectangles, squares, and circles 162
Drawing a polygon or freeform shape 163
Using the AutoShapes button 165
Setting the Fill Color, Line Style, and Shadow 167
Flipping and Rotating Objects 169
Flipping an object 169
Rotating an object 90 degrees 169
Using the Free Rotate button 169
Drawing a Complicated Picture 170
Changing layers 172
Line 'em up 172
Group therapy 174

Part III: Neat Things You Can Add to Your Slides 177

Chapter 12: Graphs 179

Understanding Microsoft Graph 180
Creating a Graph 181
Inserting a new slide with a graph 181
Inserting a graph in an existing slide 185
Moving and Resizing a Graph 185
Working with the Datasheet 186
Changing the Graph Type 187
Embellishing a Graph 189
Adding graph titles 189
Adding a label 190
Adding a legend 190
Applying an AutoFormat 191

Chapter 13: Organization Chart (Or, Who's in Charge Here?) 193

Creating an Organizational Chart 194
  Inserting a new slide with an organizational chart 195
  Inserting an organizational chart in an existing slide 198
Adding Boxes to a Chart 198
Rearranging the Chart 199
  Selecting boxes 199
  Deleting chart boxes 200
  Moving a box 200
  Using group styles 201
Formatting Chart Boxes 203

Chapter 14: Equations, WordArt, and Other Ornaments 205

Using Equation Editor 205
  Adding an equation to a slide 206
  Editing an equation 209
  Typing text 209
Using WordArt 210
Adding a Word Table or Excel Worksheet 213
  Inserting a Word table 214
  Inserting an Excel worksheet 216

Chapter 15: Lights! Camera! Action! (Adding Sound and Video) 217

Adding Sound to a Slide 217
  All about sound files 218
  Inserting a sound in PowerPoint 219
  Playing an embedded sound 220
  Removing a sound 220
  Using transition sounds 220
Working with Video 221
  Adding a movie to a slide 221
  Playing a movie 221
  Hiding the video controls 223
  Setting a movie to play automatically 223

Chapter 16: Transitions and Animation Effects 225

Using Slide Transitions 225
  Slide transitions the easy way 226
  Slide transitions the hard way 227
Using Builds 228
  Build effects the easy way 228
  Build effects the hard way 229

Animating Other Slide Objects 230
Using the Predefined Animation Effects 230
Setting Up a Presentation That Runs by Itself 232

Part IV: Cool PowerPoint 95 Features 233

Chapter 17: Using AutoCorrect 235

Doing the AutoCorrect Thing 235
    Correct TWo INitial CApitals 236
    Capitalize Names of Days 236
    Replace Text as You Type 237
Creating AutoCorrect Entries 237
Deleting AutoCorrect Entries 238

Chapter 18: Creating Notes Pages 239

Understanding Notes Pages View 240
Adding Notes to a Slide 241
My Notes Don't Fit! 241
    Increasing the size of the text area on a notes page 241
    Adding an extra notes page for a slide 243
Adding a New Slide from Notes Pages View 244
Printing Notes Pages 244
Random Thoughts about Speaker Notes 245

Chapter 19: Making 35mm Slides 247

Using a Local Photo Lab 247
Using Genigraphics 248

Chapter 20: Show Time! 251

Starting a Slide Show 251
    Keyboard tricks during a slide show 252
    Mouse tricks during a slide show 253
    The John Madden effect 253
Taking Your Show on the Road 254
    Using the Pack and Go Wizard 254
    Loading a packed presentation on another computer 257
    Running a slide show by using the Viewer 257
The Meeting Minder 259
Running a Presentation over a Network 259

Part V: Working with Files 261

Chapter 21: Juggling Multiple Presentations and Stealing Slides 263

Editing More Than One Presentation at a Time 263
Stealing Slides from Other Presentations 267
    Stealing a whole presentation 267
    Stealing just a few slides 269
Document Properties 269

Chapter 22: Sharing Information with Other Programs 273

Importing a Foreign File 273
    Creating a presentation from a foreign file 274
    Inserting slides from an outline 276
Exporting an Outline 276
Saving Slides as Graphic Files 277

Chapter 23: Managing Your Files 279

Organizing Your Files 279
    Using filenames that you can remember 280
    Using folders wisely 280
Using the File⇨Open Command 282
    Changing views 282
    Deleting and renaming files and folders 283
    Playing favorites 283
Finding Lost Files 284
Copying Files 285
Creating a New Folder 285
Deleting Files 285
Backing Up Your Files 286

Part VI: The Part of Tens 287

Chapter 24: Ten PowerPoint Commandments 289

I. Thou Shalt Frequently Saveth Thy Work 289
II. Thou Shalt Storeth Each File in Its Proper Folder 289
III. Thou Shalt Not Abuseth Thy Programs' Formatting Features 290
IV. Thou Shalt Not Stealeth Thy Neighbor's Clip Art 290
V. Thou Shalt Not Departeth from the Way of Thy Color Scheme; Neither
    Shalt Thou Departeth from the Pattern of Thine AutoLayout 290

VI. Thou Shalt Not Fondle Thy INI and Registry Files 290
VII. Remember Thy Computer Gurus, to Keep Them Happy 291
VIII. Thou Shalt Backeth Up Thy Files Day by Day 291
IX. Thou Shalt Fear No Evil, for Ctrl+Z Is Always with Thee 291
X. Thou Shalt Not Panic 291

Chapter 25: Ten Things That Often Go Wrong 293

I Can't Find My File! 293
I've Run Out of Memory! 293
I've Run Out of Disk Space! 294
PowerPoint Has Vanished! 294
I Accidentally Deleted a File! 294
It Won't Let Me Edit That! 294
Something Seems to Be Missing! 295
What Happened to My Clip Art? 295
One of the Toolbars Is Missing! 295
All the Text Is the Same! 295

Chapter 26: Ten PowerPoint Shortcuts 297

Shift+Click the View Buttons to Display Masters 297
Right-Click Anywhere to Get a Quick Menu 297
Ctrl+X, Ctrl+C, or Ctrl+V to Cut, Copy, or Paste 298
Ctrl+Z to Undo a Mistake 298
Ctrl+B or Ctrl+I for Bold or Italics 298
Ctrl+S to Save a File 299
Ctrl+G to Show the Guides 299
Shift While Drawing to Constrain Objects 299
Alt+Esc, Alt+Tab, or Ctrl+Esc to Switch to Another Program 299
F1: The Panic Button 299

Chapter 27: Ten Tips for Creating Readable Slides 301

Try Reading the Slide from the Back of the Room 301
Five Bullets, Tops 301
Avoid Small Text 301
Avoid Excessive Verbiage Leading to Excessively Lengthy Text That Is
    Not Only Redundant but Also Repetitive and Reiterative 302
Use Consistent Wording 302
Stick to the Color Scheme 302
Stick to the AutoLayouts When You Can 303
Keep the Background Simple 303
Use Only Two Levels of Bullets 303
Keep Graphs Simple 303

Chapter 28: Ten New Features in PowerPoint 95 .... **305**

Long Filenames 305
The Style Checker 305
AutoCorrect 305
AutoClipArt 306
Title Masters 306
New Fill Options 306
Simpler Transitions and Animations 307
Meeting Minder 307
Presentation Conferencing 308
Genigraphics Wizard 308
Customizable Toolbars 308

**Chapter 29: Ten Cool Things on the PowerPoint
Multimedia CD-ROM** **309**

Sounds 309
Clip Art 309
Microsoft Imager 309
Photos 310
Samples 311
More Templates 311
Videos 312

Chapter 30: Ten Ways to Keep Your Audience Awake **315**

Don't Forget Your Purpose 315
Don't Become a Slave to Your Slides 315
Don't Overwhelm Your Audience with Unnecessary Detail 316
Don't Neglect Your Opening 316
Be Relevant 316
Don't Forget the Altar Call 317
Practice, Practice, Practice 317
Don't Panic 317
Expect the Unexpected 317
Above All Else, Don't Be Boring 318

Appendix: Installing PowerPoint **319**

System Requirements 319
Installing PowerPoint 320

Index **323**

Reader Response Card .... *Back of Book*

Introduction

· ·

Welcome to *PowerPoint For Windows 95 For Dummies,* the book written especially for those who are forced to use PowerPoint at gunpoint and want to learn just enough to save their necks.

Do you ever find yourself in front of an audience, no matter how small, flipping through flip charts or shuffling through a stack of handwritten transparencies? You need PowerPoint! Have you always wanted to take your notebook computer with you to impress a client at lunch, but you don't know what to do with it between trips to the salad bar? You need PowerPoint! Are you H. Ross Perot and you just spent $5 million for a 30-minute commercial, and you want to use some flip charts? You *really* need PowerPoint!

Or maybe you're one of those hapless chaps who bought Microsoft Office because it was such a bargain and you needed a Windows word processor and spreadsheet anyway and hey, you're not even sure what PowerPoint is, but it was free. Who can resist a bargain like that?

Whichever way, you're holding the perfect book right here in your magic-marker-stained hands. Help is here, within these humble pages.

This book talks about PowerPoint in everyday — and often irreverent — terms. No lofty prose here; the whole thing checks in at about the fifth-grade reading level. I have no Pulitzer expectations for this book. My goal is to make an otherwise dull and lifeless subject at least tolerable, if not kind of fun.

About This Book

This isn't the kind of book that you pick up and read from start to finish as though it were a cheap novel. If I ever see you reading it at the beach, I'll kick sand in your face. This book is more like a reference, the kind of book you can pick up, turn to just about any page, and start reading. It has 30 chapters, each one covering a specific aspect of using PowerPoint — such as printing, changing colors, or using clip art. The appendix tells you how to install PowerPoint on your computer.

Each chapter is divided into self-contained chunks, all related to the major theme of the chapter.

For example, the chapter on using clip art contains nuggets like these:

- ✔ Dropping in some clip art
- ✔ Moving, sizing, and stretching pictures
- ✔ Boxing, shading, and shadowing a picture
- ✔ Editing a clip art picture
- ✔ Adding your own pictures to the ClipArt Gallery
- ✔ Inserting pictures without using the ClipArt Gallery

You don't have to memorize anything in this book. It's a "need-to-know" book: You pick it up when you need to know something. Need to know how to create an organization chart? Pick up the book. Need to know how to override the Slide Master? Pick up the book. Otherwise, put it down and get on with your life.

How to Use This Book

This book works like a reference. Start with the topic you want to learn about; look for it in the table of contents or in the index to get going. The table of contents is detailed enough that you should be able to find most of the topics you look for. If not, turn to the index, where you'll find even more detail.

When you've found your topic in the table of contents or the index, turn to the area of interest and read as much or as little as you need or want. Then close the book and get on with it.

This book is loaded with information, of course, so if you want to take a brief excursion into your topic, you're more than welcome. If you want to know all about Slide Masters, read the chapter on templates and masters. If you want to know all about color schemes, read the chapter on color schemes. Read whatever you want. This is *your* book, not mine.

On occasion, this book directs you to use specific keyboard shortcuts to get things done. When you see something like this:

Ctrl+Z

it means to hold down the Ctrl key while pressing the Z key and then release both together. Don't type the plus sign.

Sometimes I tell you to use a menu command, like this:

File⇨Open

This line means to use the keyboard or mouse to open the File menu and then choose the Open command. (The underlined letters are the keyboard *hot keys* for the command. To use them, first press the Alt key. In the preceding example, you press and release the Alt key, press and release the F key, and then press and release the O key.)

Whenever I describe a message or information you see on-screen, it looks like this:

```
Are we having fun yet?
```

Anything you are instructed to type appears in bold like so: Type **b:setup** in the Run dialog box. You type exactly what you see, with or without spaces.

Another nice feature of this book is that the first time I discuss a certain button you need to click to accomplish the task at hand, the button appears in the margin. This way, you can easily locate it on your screen!

This book rarely directs you elsewhere for information — just about everything you need to know about using PowerPoint is right here. On occasion, I suggest that you turn to Andy Rathbone's *Windows 95 For Dummies* (IDG Books Worldwide, Inc.) for more specific information about wildebeests and dilithium mining techniques — oops — I mean Windows 95.

What You Don't Need to Read

Much of this book is skippable. I've carefully placed extra-technical information in self-contained sidebars and clearly marked them so that you can give them a wide berth. Don't read this stuff unless you just gots to know. Don't worry; I won't be offended if you don't read every word.

Foolish Assumptions

I make only three assumptions about you:

- You use a computer.
- You use Windows 95.
- You use or are thinking about using PowerPoint for Windows 95.

Nothing else. I don't assume that you're a computer guru who knows how to change a controller card or configure memory for optimal use. These types of computer chores are best handled by people who *like* computers. Hopefully, you are on speaking terms with such a person. Do your best to stay there.

How This Book Is Organized

Inside this book are chapters arranged in six parts. Each chapter is broken down into sections that cover various aspects of the chapter's main subject. The chapters have a logical sequence, so it makes sense to read them in order if you want. But you don't have to read the book that way; you can flip it open to any page and start reading.

Here's the lowdown on what's in each of the six parts:

Part I: Basic PowerPoint 95 Stuff

In this part, you review the basics of using PowerPoint. This is a good place to start if you're clueless about what PowerPoint is, let alone how to use it.

Part II: Looking Mahvelous

The chapters in this part show you how to make presentations that look good. Most important is the chapter about templates and masters, which control the overall look of a presentation. Get the template right, and everything else falls into place.

Part III: Neat Things You Can Add to Your Slides

The chapters in this part show you how to spice up an otherwise dreary presentation with clip art, graphs, drawings, organization charts, sealing wax, and other fancy stuff. It also shows you how to make your slides grunt like Tim Allen.

Part IV: Cool PowerPoint 95 Features

The chapters in this part cover a handful of miscellaneous PowerPoint for Windows 95 features that I might not have gotten to if I didn't include a part like this.

Part V: Working with Files

Unfortunately, you can't live your entire life hiding under the shadow of PowerPoint's menus. Once in a while, you have to peer out into the real world for some routine housekeeping chores. That's what the three chapters in this part are all about.

Part VI: The Part of Tens

This wouldn't be a ...*For Dummies* book without lists of interesting snippets: ten PowerPoint commandments, ten things that often go wrong, ten PowerPoint shortcuts, and more!

There's also a free bonus appendix that shows you how to install PowerPoint. Sorry, no Ginsu knives.

Icons Used in This Book

As you are reading all this wonderful prose, you'll occasionally see the following icons. They appear in the margins to draw your attention to important information. They are defined as follows:

Watch out! Some technical drivel is just around the corner. Read it only if you have your pocket protector firmly attached.

Pay special attention to this icon — it tells you that some particularly useful tidbit is at hand, perhaps a shortcut or a way of using a command that you may not have considered.

Danger! Danger! Danger! Stand back, Will Robinson!

Did I tell you about the memory course I took?

Pay attention; something interesting is on the way.

You may already know how to do this stuff if you use any of the other programs in Microsoft Office, specifically Word for Windows 7 or Excel 7.

This stuff is new to PowerPoint for Windows 95. Cool!

Where to Go from Here

Yes, you *can* get there from here. With this book in hand, you're ready to charge full speed ahead into the strange and wonderful world of desktop presentations. Browse through the table of contents and decide where you want to start. Be bold! Be courageous! Be adventurous! Above all else, have fun!

Part I
Basic PowerPoint 95 Stuff

In this part...

*I*ust a few short years ago, the term *presentation software* meant poster board and marker pens. But now, programs such as Microsoft's PowerPoint enable you to create spectacular presentations on your computer.

The chapters in this part comprise a bare-bones introduction to PowerPoint. You'll learn exactly what PowerPoint is and how to use it to create simple presentations. More advanced stuff like adding charts or using fancy text fonts is covered in later parts. This part is just the beginning. As a great king once advised, begin at the beginning, and go on 'til you come to the end; then stop.

Chapter 1

PowerPoint 101

- -

In This Chapter

▶ What in Sam Hill is PowerPoint?

▶ Introducing PowerPoint for Windows 95

▶ Starting PowerPoint

▶ How much should I tip?

▶ Help me, Wizard!

▶ What is all this stuff? (Making sense of the PowerPoint screen)

▶ Viewing the whole slide

▶ Editing text

▶ 50 ways to add a new slide

▶ Moving from slide to slide

▶ Outline that for me!

▶ Printing that puppy

▶ Saving and closing your work

▶ Retrieving a presentation from disk

▶ Exiting PowerPoint

- -

*T*his chapter is sort of the kindergarten of PowerPoint. It takes your hand and walks you around, showing you some really basic stuff like how to start PowerPoint, how to save your work in a file, and how to print. It even explains what PowerPoint is, just in case you're starting at the very beginning. If you get tired midway through this chapter, feel free to have some milk and graham crackers and maybe even take a nap.

What in Sam Hill Is PowerPoint?

PowerPoint is the oddball program that comes with Microsoft Office. Most people buy Microsoft Office because it's a great bargain: You get Microsoft Word and Excel for less than it would cost to buy them separately. As an added bonus, you get Schedule+, PowerPoint, a complete set of Ginsu knives, and a Binford VegaPneumatic Power Slicer and Dicer (always wear eye protection).

You know what Word is — a word processor, like WordPerfect but trendier. Excel is a spreadsheet kind of like Lotus 1-2-3, but with more ambition. But what the heck is PowerPoint? Does anybody know or care?

PowerPoint is a *desktop presentation* program, and it's one of the coolest programs I know. If you've ever flipped a flip chart, headed over to an overhead projector, or slipped on a slide, you're going to love PowerPoint. With just a few clicks of the mouse, you can create presentations that bedazzle your audience and instantly sway them to your point of view, even if you're selling real estate on Mars, Ruble futures, or season tickets for the Mets.

PowerPoint is kind of like a word processor, except that it's geared toward producing *presentations* rather than *documents.* In PowerPoint lingo, a presentation consists of a sequence of *slides.* Once you've created the slides, you can print them on plain paper or on transparencies for overhead projection, or you can have them made into glorious 35mm color slides. You can print handouts with two, three, or six slides on each page, notes on the pages to help you bluff your way through your presentation, and a complete outline of your presentation.

Here are a few important features of PowerPoint:

- ✔ PowerPoint is a great time-saver for anyone who makes business presentations, whether you've been asked to speak in front of hundreds of people at a shareholders' convention, to a group of sales reps at a sales conference, or one-on-one with a potential client.

- ✔ PowerPoint is also great for teachers or conference speakers who want to back up their lectures with slides or overheads.

- ✔ You can also use PowerPoint to create fancy on-computer presentations, where the slides are displayed on-screen one at a time. You can embellish an on-computer presentation with all sorts of jazzy effects like slides, wipes, dissolves, sound effects, and even rudimentary animations. This process can get a bit theatrical, but it's loads of fun. It is an especially popular feature with insurance reps who own laptop computers.

✔ Okay, not everybody buys PowerPoint as part of Microsoft Office. Some people buy it separately. I figured that if you bought PowerPoint by itself, you probably did it on purpose, so it's safe to assume that you already know what PowerPoint is (at least sort of). Heck, you didn't need to read this section anyway. I wrote this little section for the millions of innocent people who bought Microsoft Office just to get Word and Excel and have no idea what to do with PowerPoint other than to use it as a bookend.

✔ Who in Sam Hill was Sam Hill?

PowerPoint lingo you can't escape

Sorry, but if you're going to use PowerPoint, you have to get used to its own peculiar lingo. Here's a quick spin through the PowerPoint lexicon:

Body text: Most slides also have a text object called the body text. The body text usually (but not always) consists of a series of main points set off by bullets. The main points can have subpoints that are indented under the main points. (The subpoints can have sub-subpoints and sub-sub-subpoints, but let's not get ridiculous.) The format of body text is also controlled by the Slide master.

Object: An element on a slide. Objects can contain text, clip art pictures, charts, organization charts, or other types of graphics. You cannot place text directly on a slide; instead, a slide must contain at least one text object if you want text to appear on the slide.

Presentation: All of the supporting materials you need to present information to an audience. The audience may be small (just one person) or large (63 million people tuned in to watch you in a presidential debate). In PowerPoint, a presentation consists of slides, presenter notes, handouts, and an outline.

Presentation file: A PowerPoint file that contains the presentation materials, the PowerPoint equivalent of a Microsoft Word document file or an Excel spreadsheet file. The three-character extension part of a PowerPoint filename is PPT.

Slide: One page of a PowerPoint presentation. You can set up the slide page to fit the dimensions of an overhead transparency, a 35mm film slide, or the actual computer screen.

Slide Master: Sets up elements that appear on all slides, such as a background design, your name, the date, and so on.

Slide show: Displays slides in sequence on your computer screen. You can use slide show to preview the appearance of your slides before you print them, or you can use it to actually present your slides to your audience.

Title: Most slides have a text object called the title. The format of the title text is governed by the Slide Master.

View: How you look at your presentation while working in PowerPoint. There are four views: Slide view, Outline view, Notes Pages view, and Slide Sorter view. Each view is best at a particular editing task.

Introducing PowerPoint for Windows 95, Version 7!

Microsoft released its latest and greatest version of Windows, called Windows 95, in August 1995. Windows 95 sports many new features, most of which are actual improvements over the older and clunkier Windows 3.1. One of the most important of these improvements is that Windows 95 frees you from the tyranny of eight-character file names. With Windows 95, you can create long filenames such as "Letter to my Mom.doc" or "Presentation for Spacely Sprockets.ppt."

At the same time, Microsoft released a new Windows 95 version of Microsoft Office, called Office 95. All programs that make up Microsoft Office — including PowerPoint — have been updated to work with Windows 95. Thus, the new PowerPoint for Windows 95 allows you to use long filenames and takes advantage of other new features in Windows 95.

Microsoft also took the opportunity to cram a bunch of flashy new features — some of them useful — into PowerPoint for Windows 95. These features are covered throughout this book. In addition, PowerPoint comes with a CD-ROM disk that contains bonus clip art, sound, and video files that you can incorporate into your presentations. These multimedia goodies are described in Chapter 29.

Starting PowerPoint

Here's the procedure for starting PowerPoint:

1. **Get ready.**

   Light some votive candles. Take two Tylenol and an allergy pill if you are allergic to banana slugs. Sit in the lotus position facing Redmond, WA and recite the Windows creed three times:

   I will use Windows and I will like it. Click click.
   I will use Windows and I will like it. Click click.
   I will use Windows and I will like it. Click click.

2. **Start your engines.**

   Turn your computer on. Hopefully, you have to flip only one switch to do that. But if your computer, monitor, and printer are plugged in separately, you have to turn each one on separately.

What's in a name?

Up until a few months before the release of Windows 95, everyone assumed that the newest version of Windows would be called *Windows 4.0,* the natural successor to Windows 3.1. Then the marketing geniuses at Microsoft decided that instead of version numbers, Microsoft should switch to model years like Ford or Honda. Hence the name of the new Windows version: *Windows 95.*

Unfortunately, Microsoft got itself tied up into knots when trying to decide exactly what to call the new versions of its application programs that run under Windows 95. Each of the programs that made up the old Office suite of applications — Word, Excel, and PowerPoint — had a different version number: Word was at version 6, Excel was at version 5, and PowerPoint was at version 4. Microsoft decided that all of the version numbers for the new Office programs should be brought into sync. Because Word was already at version 6, Microsoft decided that all of the new Office programs would be labeled *Version 7.* So the new version of PowerPoint can be called *PowerPoint 7.* And because Microsoft went straight from PowerPoint 4 to PowerPoint 7, there is no PowerPoint 5 or PowerPoint 6. Go figure.

To be consistent with the new model year product labeling, Microsoft prefers to call the new version *Microsoft PowerPoint for Windows 95,* without the Version 7 designation. The title appears without this designation on the PowerPoint manual (if you can seriously call a 116-page picture book a *manual*) and on the 12 installation diskettes.

On the other hand, the PowerPoint installation CD and the product box itself refer to the program as *Microsoft PowerPoint Designed for Windows 95.* The label *Version 7.0* appears on the box only once, in what looks like 6-point type. Hmph.

Well, who cares what Microsoft wants to call their program. I'll just call it *PowerPoint.* And when it's important to know which version I'm referring to — such as when I'm pointing out a new feature — I'll call it *PowerPoint 7* or *PowerPoint 95,* depending on my mood. I'll have none of this Microsoft-PowerPoint-Designed-for-Windows-95 stuff in my book!

By the way, the "What's in a name?" passage is one of the most often misquoted passages in all of Shakespeare. Juliet didn't say "a rose by any other *name* would smell as sweet." What Juliet actually said was, "What's in a name? That which we call a rose by any other *word* would smell as sweet."

3. Click the Start button.

The Start button is ordinarily found at the lower-left corner of the Windows 95 display. After you click it, a menu magically appears out of nowhere.

If you can't find the Start button, try moving the mouse pointer all the way to the bottom edge of the screen and holding it there a moment. With luck on your side, you see the Start button appear. If not, try moving the mouse pointer to the other three edges of the screen: top, left, and right. Sometimes the Start button hides behind these edges.

If you're not sure what I mean by *click,* read the sidebar, "The mouse is your friend," later in this chapter.

4. Point to Programs on the Start menu.

Once you've clicked the Start button to reveal the Start menu, move the mouse pointer up to the word Programs and hold it there a moment. Yet another menu appears, revealing a bevy of commands resembling those shown in Figure 1-1.

5. Click Microsoft PowerPoint on the Programs menu.

Your computer whirs and clicks and possibly makes other unmentionable noises while PowerPoint comes to life.

How much should I tip?

When you start PowerPoint, you first see a helpful PowerPoint tip like the one shown in Figure 1-2. You have to click the OK button to dismiss this helpful tipmeister. (It helps if you shove a five-spot its way, too.)

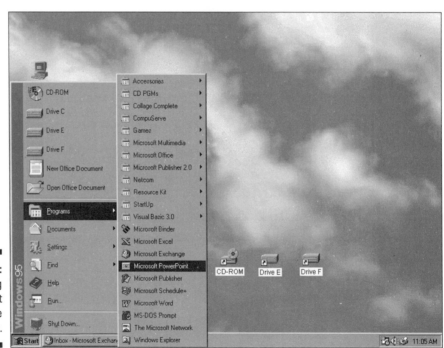

Figure 1-1:
Starting
PowerPoint
from the
Start menu.

Figure 1-2:
PowerPoint
greets you
each day
with a
helpful (or
annoying,
depending
on your
tempera-
ment) tip.

If you're the type who likes to learn a little something every day, you'll appreciate these tips. If the tips serve only as a daily reminder that you don't have a
clue about what you're doing, you may want to throw them over a cliff. Fortunately, you can do that (without breaking any laws) by unchecking the check
box that reads Show Tips at Startup so that the check goes away. Then click the
OK button.

If you disable the tips and then later decide you want to see them again, don't
fret; you can call them up by using the Help⇨Tip of the Day command.
PowerPoint displays a different tip each day. If you don't want to wait all year to
see all the tips, you can click the Next Tip button to look ahead. This is a great
way to avoid doing real work.

Choices, choices

The next thing you see as a result of PowerPoint's ongoing efforts to make you
realize that you need to get a life is the innocent-looking dialog box shown in
Figure 1-3.

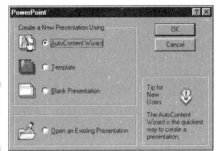

Figure 1-3:
Choose your
weapon.

The mouse is your friend

Remember that scene in *Star Trek IV* when Scotty, having been zapped back into the 1980s and forced to use a primitive computer (it was a Macintosh), picked up the mouse and talked into it like a microphone? "Computer! Hello computer! Hmmph. How quaint."

You don't get very far with PowerPoint (or any other Windows program) until you learn how to use the mouse. You can try picking it up and talking into it if you want, but you don't get any better results than Scotty did.

Most mice have two or three buttons on top and a ball underneath. When you move the mouse, the ball rolls. The rolling motion is detected by little wheels inside the mouse and sent to your computer, which responds to your mouse movements by moving the mouse cursor on-screen. What will they think of next?

A mouse works best when used with a *mouse pad*, a small (7-inch × 9-inch or so) rubbery pad that gives better traction for the rolling ball on the mouse's rump. You can use the mouse directly on a desk surface, but it doesn't roll as smoothly.

Here's the lowdown on the various acts of mouse dexterity you are asked to perform as you use PowerPoint:

✔ To *move* or *point* the mouse means to move it so that the mouse cursor moves to a desired screen location, without pressing any mouse buttons. Remember to leave the mouse on the mouse pad as you move it; if

you pick it up, the ball doesn't roll and your movement doesn't register.

✔ To *click* means to press and release the left mouse button. Usually, you are asked to click something, which means to point to the something, and then click the left button.

✔ To *double-click* means to press and release the left mouse button twice, as quickly as you can.

✔ To *triple-click* means to press and release the left mouse button three times as quickly as you can. Right.

✔ To *right-click* means to click the right mouse button instead of the left. Get used to right-clicking: it's a handy action in PowerPoint.

✔ To *click and drag* something (also called simply *drag*) with the mouse means to point at it, press the left button (or right button, depending on the task), and move the mouse while holding down the button. When you arrive at your destination, you release the mouse button.

✔ To *stay* the mouse means to let go of the mouse and give it the command "Stay!" There is no need to raise your voice; speak in a normal but confident and firm tone. If your mouse starts to walk away, say "No," put it back in its original position, and repeat the command "Stay!" (Under no circumstances should you strike your mouse. Remember, there are no bad mice.)

PowerPoint gives you four options to choose from:

> ✔ **AutoContent Wizard:** This option practically builds a whole presentation for you by asking basic questions about what you want to say. It is designed for true beginners who not only know nothing about PowerPoint but also know nothing about giving presentations. It's pretty limited but can help get you going.

The marketing folks at Microsoft want you to believe that the AutoContent writes your presentation for you, as if you just click the button and then go play a round of golf while PowerPoint does your research, organizes your thoughts, writes your text, and throws in a few good lawyer jokes to boot. Sorry. All the AutoContent Wizard does is create an outline for several common types of presentations. It doesn't do your thinking for you.

✔ **Template:** This option enables you to pick from one of the 150 predefined *templates* supplied with PowerPoint. The template you use governs the basic appearance of each slide in your presentation — things like the background color, text font, and so on.

✔ **Blank Presentation:** This option is useful in two situations: (1) You're a computer whiz who is insulted by the shortcuts provided by the AutoContent or Template options, or (2) You're an incredibly boring person and you *want* your presentations to have a blank sort of look to them.

✔ **Open an Existing Presentation:** You pick this option if you want to work a little more on that presentation you didn't quite finish yesterday, or if the presentation you want to create is so similar to the one you gave last month that there's no point in starting all over again.

To choose one of these options, click the appropriate check box; then click the OK button. You can bail out of this startup dialog box altogether by clicking the Cancel button or pressing the Escape key. Doing so leaves you with a blank screen but enables you to use the menus or toolbars to create a new presentation or open an existing one.

Help me, Mr. Wizard!

The easiest way to create a new presentation, especially for novice PowerPoint users, is to use the AutoContent Wizard. This wizard asks you for some pertinent information, such as your name, the title of your presentation, and the type of presentation you want to create. Then it automatically creates a skeleton presentation, which you can modify to suit your needs.

To create a presentation using the AutoContent Wizard, follow these steps:

1. **Start PowerPoint.**

   Click OK to dismiss the Tip of the Day dialog box (if you haven't disabled it altogether).

2. **Choose AutoContent Wizard from the PowerPoint startup dialog box and click OK.**

   The AutoContent Wizard takes over and displays the dialog box shown in Figure 1-4.

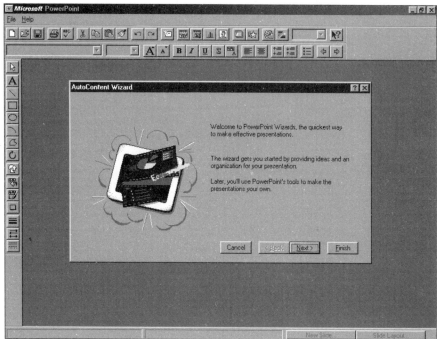

Figure 1-4:
The
AutoContent
Wizard gets
underway.

3. **Click the Next button.**

   The dialog box shown in Figure 1-5 appears.

4. **Type your name, the title of your presentation, and any other information you want to appear on the first slide of your presentation.**

   For example, in Figure 1-5, I typed *Doug Lowe* as my name, *Rent-a-Nerd* as the title, and *The Easy Way to Handle All Your Computer Problems* for the other information.

5. **Click Next.**

   The dialog box shown in Figure 1-6 appears.

6. **Select the type of presentation you want to create by clicking one of the presentation types, and then click Next.**

   If your presentation doesn't fit one of the categories listed in the dialog box, click Other. Selecting Other displays a list of additional predefined presentation types you can choose from. If all else fails, select the General presentation type.

   After you have selected the presentation type and clicked Next, you see a dialog box like the one in Figure 1-7.

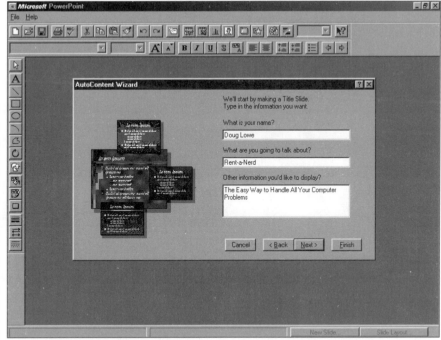

Figure 1-5:
The AutoContent Wizard asks for your name, the presentation title, and other information you want to appear on the first slide.

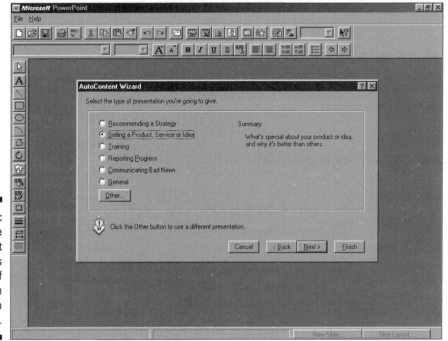

Figure 1-6:
The AutoContent Wizard asks what type of presentation you want to create.

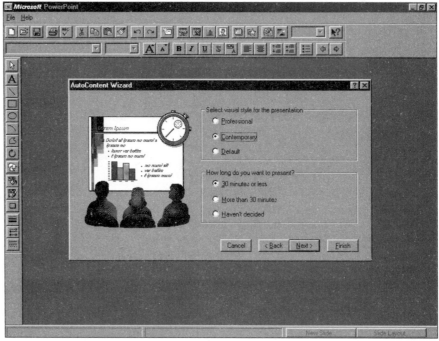

Figure 1-7:
The
AutoContent
Wizard nags
you with
more
questions.

7. Select the visual style for your presentation by clicking Professional, Contemporary, or Default.

The AutoContent Wizard offers three style choices: Professional, Contemporary, or Default. Your choice here isn't really that critical, because you can easily change the visual style later.

8. Indicate how long you expect your presentation to run.

Choose 30 minutes or less, More than 30 minutes, or Haven't decided. If you choose More than 30 minutes, the AutoContent Wizard builds a more detailed outline of your presentation than if you choose 30 minutes or less or Haven't decided.

9. Click Next.

Next, the AutoContent Wizard asks about the format of your presentation, as shown in Figure 1-8.

10. Indicate the type of output you want to create and whether you want to print handouts.

11. Click Next.

The last page of the AutoContent Wizard appears, as shown in Figure 1-9.

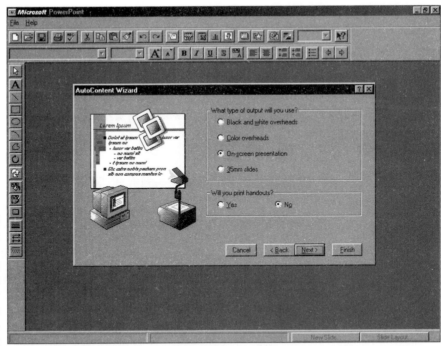

Figure 1-8:
The
AutoContent
Wizard asks
about your
presentation
format.

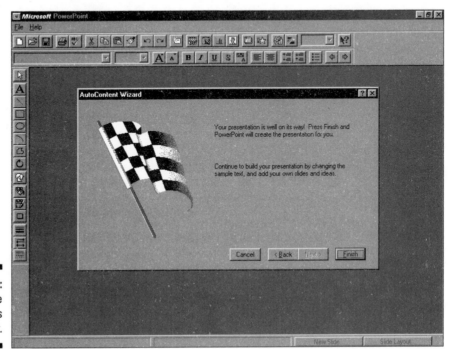

Figure 1-9:
Finally, the
finish line is
in sight.

12. **Click Finish.**

The AutoContent Wizard creates a presentation for you. Once the presentation is finished, you can use the editing and formatting techniques described in the rest of this chapter and throughout the book to personalize the presentation.

What is all this stuff? (Making sense of the PowerPoint screen)

Working with the AutoContent Wizard is easy enough: It presents you with a series of simple, fill-in-the-blank questions and a limited number of buttons you can click. After you finish with the questions, the Wizard creates a skeleton presentation and dumps you into the overly cluttered PowerPoint screen. Now you are free to figure out for yourself how to use the dozens of menu commands and toolbar buttons that make PowerPoint work. Being abandoned like this is maddening enough to drive you to consider newsprint and markers as a viable alternative for your presentation.

Figure 1-10 provides a road map to the PowerPoint screen. Look this map over briefly to get your bearings. North is up.

Five items on the PowerPoint screen are worthy of your attention:

✔ Across the top of the screen, just below the Microsoft PowerPoint title, is the *menu bar.* PowerPoint's deepest and darkest secrets are hidden on the menu bar. Wear a helmet when exploring it.

✔ Just below the menu bar are two of the many *toolbars* PowerPoint offers you in an effort to make its most commonly used features easy to use. Each toolbar consists of a bunch of buttons you can click to perform common functions. The toolbar on the top is the *Standard toolbar;* immediately beneath it is the *Formatting toolbar.* Down the left side of the screen is the *Drawing toolbar.*

You can quickly figure out what any toolbar button does by placing the mouse pointer on it. After a moment, the name of the button appears in a box just below the button, and a brief description of the button's function appears at the bottom of the screen in the status bar.

✔ Right smack in the middle of the screen is the current slide.

✔ At the bottom of the screen is the *status bar,* which tells you which slide is currently displayed (in this example, *Slide 1*). The status bar includes helpful buttons to create a new slide or to change the layout of the slide that's showing in the window.

✔ The *salad bar* is located . . . well, actually there is no salad bar. I lied. There are really only four things worth noticing in Figure 1-10.

Drawing toolbar   Title bar   Menu bar   Slide   Formatting toolbar   Standard toolbar

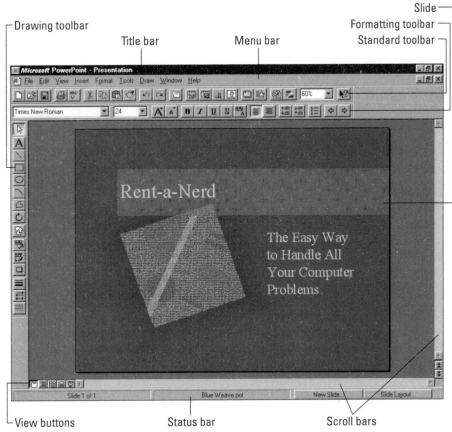

Figure 1-10:
The
PowerPoint
screen.

View buttons   Status bar   Scroll bars

You'll never get anything done if you feel that you have to understand every pixel of the PowerPoint screen before you can do anything. Don't worry about the stuff you don't understand; just concentrate on what you need to know to get the job done and worry about the bells and whistles later.

There's lots of stuff crammed into the PowerPoint screen, enough stuff that the program works best if you let it run in *Full Screen* mode. If PowerPoint doesn't take over your entire screen, look for the boxy-looking maximize button near the top right corner of PowerPoint's window (it's the middle of the three buttons clustered in the top right corner — the box represents a window maximized to its largest possible size). Click it to *maximize* the PowerPoint screen. PowerPoint overtakes your entire screen and the maximize button changes to an icon that represents two smaller windows. Click it again to restore the PowerPoint screen to its smaller size.

On the left bottom edge of the Presentation window is a series of View buttons. These buttons enable you to switch among PowerPoint's various *views*, or ways of looking at your presentation. Table 1-1 summarizes what each of these buttons does.

Table 1-1	View Buttons
Button	*What It Does*
▭	Switches to Slide view, which shows the slides as they appear when printed.
▤	Switches to Outline view, which enables you to focus on the content of your presentation rather than its appearance.
▦	Switches to Slide Sorter view, which enables you easily to rearrange the slides in your presentation.
▣	Switches to Notes Pages view, which enables you to add speaker notes so that you can remember what you want to say.
▢	Switches to Slide Show view, which displays your slides in an on-screen presentation.

Don't read this unless you already know Word for Windows

If you already know how to use Word for Windows, thank your lucky stars because you already know how to use many of PowerPoint's features. Here are a few examples of things you already know how to do:

✔ **Open a file:** Use the File➪Open command or click the Open button on the Standard toolbar.

✔ **Save a file:** Use the File➪Save or File➪Save As command or click the Save button on the Standard toolbar.

✔ **Print a file:** Use the File➪Print command or click the Print button on the Standard toolbar.

✔ **Cut, Copy, or Paste text:** Use the Ctrl+X, Ctrl+C, or Ctrl+V keyboard combinations.

✔ **Check a presentation for spelling errors:** Use the Tools➪Spelling command or click the Spelling button on the Standard toolbar.

✔ **Change the format of selected text:** Use the Format➪Font command or the controls on the Formatting toolbar, which work just as they do in Word 6. The keyboard shortcuts for formatting text — such as Ctrl+B for bold or Ctrl+I for italic — work the same way, too.

This list can go on and on. When in doubt about how to do something, try it the way you would in Word and odds are it will work. On the other hand, you may end up shutting down the power grid for all of San Diego. It just depends.

I Can't See the Whole Slide!

PowerPoint automatically adjusts its zoom factor so that Slide view displays each slide in its entirety. Depending on the size of your computer's monitor and whether you have maximized the PowerPoint window, the slide may end up being too small to see. If this miniaturization happens, you can increase the zoom factor using the View⇨Zoom command or the Zoom control on the Standard toolbar.

On the other hand, if you set the zoom so high that the entire slide doesn't fit in the window, PowerPoint calls up the scroll bars at the right and the bottom of the window. You can use these scroll bars to scoot the slide around so you can see the slide parts that don't fit in the window.

Editing Text

In PowerPoint, slides are blank areas that you can adorn with various types of objects. The most common type of objects are *text objects,* which are rectangular areas that are specially designated for holding text. Other types of objects include shapes such as circles or triangles, pictures imported from clip-art files, and graphs.

Most slides contain two text objects: one for the slide's title, the other for its body text. However, you can add additional text objects if you wish, and you can remove the body text or title text object. You can even remove both to create a slide that contains no text.

Whenever you move the mouse cursor over a text object, the cursor changes from an arrow to what's lovingly called the *I-beam,* which you can use to support bridges or build aircraft carriers. Seriously, when the mouse cursor changes to an I-beam, you can click the mouse button and start typing text.

When you click a text object, a box appears around the text and an *insertion pointer* appears right at the spot where you clicked. PowerPoint then becomes like a word processor. Any characters you type on the keyboard are inserted into the text at the insertion pointer location. You can use the Delete or Backspace keys to demolish text, and you can use the arrow keys to move the insertion pointer around in the text object. If you press the Enter key, a new line of text begins within the text object.

When a text object contains no text, a *placeholder* message appears in the object. For a title text object, the message `Click to add title` appears. For other text objects, the placeholder message reads `Click to add text`. Either way, the placeholder message magically vanishes when you click the object and begin typing text.

If you start typing without clicking anywhere, the text you type is entered into the title text object — assuming that the title text object doesn't already have text of its own. If the title object is not empty, any text you type (with no text object selected) is simply ignored.

When you're done typing text, press the Esc key or click the mouse anywhere outside the text object.

In Chapter 2, you find many details about playing with text objects. So hold your horses. You have more important things to attend to first.

Moving from Slide to Slide

There are several ways to move forward and backward through your presentation, from slide to slide:

- ✔ Click one of the double-headed arrows at the bottom of the vertical scroll bar. Doing this moves you through the presentation one slide at a time.

- ✔ Use the Page Up and Page Down keys on your keyboard. Using these keys also moves one slide at a time.

- ✔ Drag the scroll box (the box that appears in the middle of the scroll bar) up or down. As you drag the scroll box, you see a text box that indicates which slide PowerPoint will display when you release the mouse button. Dragging the scroll box is the quickest way to move directly to any slide in your presentation.

50 Ways to Add a New Slide

In all likelihood, the slides created by the AutoContent Wizard will not be adequate for your presentation. Although you may be able to adapt some of the prebuilt slides by editing their titles and text objects, eventually you'll need to add slides of your own.

You're in luck! PowerPoint gives you about 50 ways to add new slides to your presentation. You see only three of them here:

New Slide...

- ✔ Click the New Slide button on the status bar (shown in the margin).
- ✔ Click the Insert New Slide button in the Standard toolbar (shown in the margin).
- ✔ Choose the Insert⇨New Slide command.
- ✔ Press Ctrl+M.

In all three cases, PowerPoint displays the New Slide dialog box shown in Figure 1-11. This dialog enables you to pick from 21 different types of slide layouts. Just click the mouse on the one you want to use and click OK. PowerPoint inserts the new slide into your presentation immediately *after* the slide currently shown on-screen.

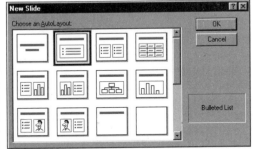

Figure 1-11:
The New
Slide dialog
box.

Notice that each slide layout has a name. The one that's highlighted in Figure 1-11 is called *Bulleted List.* The layout name tells you which types of objects are included in the layout. For example, *Bulleted List* includes a text object that contains a bulleted list. *Text & Clip Art* layout includes two objects: one for text, the other for a picture from the PowerPoint clip art gallery. You'll probably use the *Bulleted List* layout most. It's the best format for presenting a topic along with several supporting points. For example, Figure 1-12 shows a bulleted list slide that may be included in the Rent-a-Nerd presentation; the bullet items in this slide explain why computer consultants from Rent-a-Nerd are better than other consultants.

Figure 1-12:
The slide
with a
bulleted list.

One of the layouts available in the AutoLayout section of the New Slide dialog box is named *Blank*. This layout doesn't include any objects; it is a blank slate you can use to create a slide that doesn't fit any of the predefined layouts. All slide layouts except *Blank* include a single line text object that serves as a title for the slide. This title is formatted consistently from slide to slide in order to give your presentation a professional look.

Outline That for Me!

So far, you've been working with PowerPoint in *Slide view,* the view mode that shows your presentation slides one at a time, exactly as they appear when you print them. Slide view is useful for tinkering with each slide's appearance, but it's not exactly the most efficient way to dump a bunch of text into PowerPoint for a whole series of slides. To make a series of slides, you need to switch PowerPoint to *Outline view.*

Figure 1-13 shows the Rent-a-Nerd presentation as displayed in Outline view. Gone are the glamorous graphics, the fancy fonts, and the cheery colors. Instead, all you get is the text that shows up on each slide, in that most boring of all formats: the good old-fashioned outline. The view is not pretty, but it frees you from the tyranny of appearances and enables you to concentrate on your presentation's content, which is what you should be concentrating on. (Unless your audience is so gullible that they'd buy the Brooklyn Bridge if your slides were dazzling enough.)

There are two ways to flip PowerPoint to Outline view:

 ✔ Click the Outline View button on the status bar.

 ✔ Choose the View➪Outline command.

Once in Outline view, you can zip back to Slide view using either of these methods:

 ✔ Click the Slide View button on the status bar.

 ✔ Choose the View➪Slides command.

A few hints on using Outline view:

 ✔ Once in Outline view, press the Enter key to create a new line. Then use the Tab key at the beginning of a line to indent the line or use the Shift+Tab key to reduce the line's indent.

 ✔ You can find loads of other tricks to work with in Outline view. If you're totally confused but think that Outline view sounds like the greatest thing since sliced bread, you can find more about it in Chapter 3.

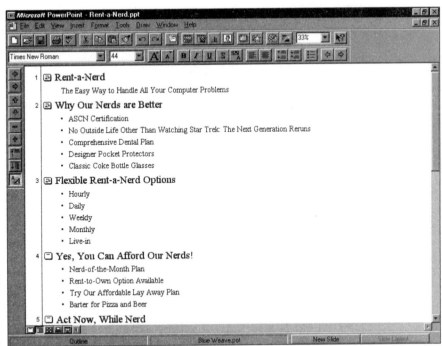

Figure 1-13:
Outline
view.

Printing That Puppy

Once you've finished your masterpiece, you'll probably want to print it. Here's the procedure for printing all the slides in your presentation:

1. Make sure your printer is turned on and ready to print.

Make sure that the *select* or *on-line* light is on. If it isn't, press the *select* or *on-line* button to make it so. Check the paper while you're at it.

2. Click the Print button on the Standard toolbar.

If you prefer, use the File⇒Print command, or press Ctrl+P or Ctrl+Shift+F12. Whichever way you do it, you see the Print dialog box. The Print dialog box has myriad options that you can fiddle with to print your presentation just so, but you can leave them alone if you want to print all the slides in your presentation.

3. Click the OK button or press the Enter key.

Make sure that you say "Engage" in a knowing manner, pointing at your printer as you do so. The main idea is to fool your printer into thinking that you know what you're doing.

Printed pages should soon appear on your printer. Check the pages to make sure that they look the way you want. Depending on how complex your slides are and how fast your printer is, your slides may pop right out of your printer before you can say "I love this program"; or you may be able to take a family vacation to Disneyland while your slides print.

If you are using overhead transparencies, you can load them directly into your laser printer provided that you get transparencies that are designed for laser printers — ordinary transparencies may melt and leave gooey stuff all over your printer's guts and possibly spread radioactive dust throughout the entire tri-state area. Bad idea. Laser transparencies are expensive, though, so it's a good idea to print a proof on plain paper before printing on the transparencies.

Tune in to Chapter 5 if you want to more know about printing. If you want your output printed on 35mm slides, check out Chapter 19.

Saving Your Work

Now that you've spent hours creating the best presentation since God gave Moses the Ten Commandments, you can just turn your computer off, right? Wrong-o! All your precious work is held in your computer's fleeting RAM (*random access memory*) until you save your work to a disk file. Turn off your computer before you save your work and *Poof!* your work vanishes as if David Copperfield were in town.

Like everything else in PowerPoint, there are at least four ways to save a document:

- ✔ Click the Save button on the Standard toolbar.
- ✔ Choose the File⇨Save command.
- ✔ Press Ctrl+S.
- ✔ Press Shift+F12.

If you haven't yet saved the file to disk, the magical Save As dialog box appears. Type the name you want to use for the file in the Save As dialog box and click the OK button to save the file. After you save the file once, subsequent saves update the disk file with any changes you made to the presentation since the last time you saved it.

Some notes to keep in mind when saving files:

- ✔ Use your noggin when assigning a name to a new file. The filename is how you can recognize the file later on, so pick a meaningful name that suggests the file's contents.

✔ When you save a document, PowerPoint displays a bar graph at the bottom of the screen to prove that it's really doing something. See how PowerPoint saves. Save, PowerPoint, save!

✔ After you save a file for the first time, the name in the presentation window's title area changes from *Presentation* to the name of your file. Still more proof that the file has been saved.

✔ Don't work on your file for hours at a time without saving it. I've learned the hard way to save my work every few minutes. After all, the earth may be hit by a giant asteroid any time now. Get into the habit of pressing Ctrl+S every few minutes, especially after making a significant change to a presentation, like adding a covey of new slides or making a gaggle of complicated formatting changes.

When you save a file for the first time, you may get a dialog box asking you for a title, author, and other useful information about the presentation. Type away; then click OK or press Enter to save the file. If you try to save a file using a filename you've already used for another presentation, PowerPoint asks whether you're sure you want to replace the existing disk file. Assuming you made a mistake and didn't really mean to assign a filename that's already in use, click No and save the file under a different name. Consult Chapter 23 for more information about filenames and file management.

Retrieving a Presentation from a Disk

After you save your presentation to a disk file, you can retrieve it later when you want to make additional changes or to print it. As you may guess, PowerPoint gives you about 40 ways to accomplish the retrieval. Here are the four most common:

✔ Click the Open button on the Standard toolbar.

✔ Use the File⇨Open command.

✔ Press Ctrl+O.

✔ Press Ctrl+F12.

All four retrieval methods pop up the Open dialog box, which gives you a list of files to choose from. Click the file you want; then click the OK button or press the Enter key. PowerPoint reads the file from disk and puts it into your computer's RAM where you can work on it.

The Open dialog box has controls that enable you to rummage through the various folders on your hard disk in search of your files. If you know how to open a file in any Windows 95 application, you know how to do it in PowerPoint (because the Open dialog box is pretty much the same in any Windows program). If you seem to have lost a file, rummage around in different folders to see whether you can find it. Sometimes you can save a file in the wrong folder by accident. Also, check the spelling of the filename. Maybe your fingers weren't on the home row when you typed the filename, so instead of BRODART.PPT, you saved the file as NTPFSTY.PPT. I hate it when that happens.

The fastest way to open a file from the Open dialog box is to double-click the file you want to open. Point to the file and click the mouse twice, as fast as you can. This spares you from having to click the file once and then clicking the OK button. Double-clicking also exercises the fast-twitch muscles in your index finger.

PowerPoint keeps track of the last few files you've opened and displays them on the File menu. To open a file you've recently opened, click the File menu and inspect the list of files at the bottom of the menu. If the file you want is in the list, click it to open it.

Closing a Presentation

Having finished your presentation and printed it just right, you have come to the time to close it. Closing a presentation is kind of like gathering up your papers, putting them neatly in a file folder, and returning the folder to its proper file drawer. The presentation disappears from your computer screen. Don't worry: It's tucked safely away on your hard disk where you can get to it later if you need to.

To close a file, use the File⇨Close command. You also can use the keyboard shortcut Ctrl+W, but you'd need to have a mind like a steel trap to remember that Ctrl+W stands for Close.

You don't have to close a file before exiting PowerPoint. If you exit PowerPoint without closing a file, PowerPoint graciously closes the file for you. The only reason you may want to close a file is when you want to work on a different file and you don't want to keep both files open at the same time.

If you've made changes since the last time you saved the file, PowerPoint offers to save the changes for you. Click Yes to save the file before closing or click No to abandon any changes you've made to the file.

If you close all the open PowerPoint presentations, you may discover that most of PowerPoint's commands have been rendered useless (they are *grayed* on the menu). Fear not. Open a presentation or create a new one and the commands return to life.

Exiting PowerPoint

Had enough excitement for one day? Use any of these techniques to shut PowerPoint down:

✔ Choose the File⇨Exit command.

✔ Click the X box at the top right corner of the PowerPoint window.

✔ Press Alt+F4.

Bammo! PowerPoint is history.

There are a few things you should know about exiting PowerPoint (or any application):

✔ PowerPoint doesn't enable you to abandon ship without first considering to save your work. If you've made changes to any presentation files and haven't saved them, PowerPoint offers to save the files for you. Lean over and plant a fat kiss right in the middle of your monitor — PowerPoint just saved you your job.

✔ Never, never, never, ever, never turn off your computer while PowerPoint or any other program is running. You may as well pour acid into the keyboard or run over the motherboard with a truck. Always exit PowerPoint and all other programs that are running before you turn off your computer.

✔ In fact, you'd best get clean out of Windows before shutting down your computer. Exit all your programs the same way you exited PowerPoint. Then click the Windows 95 Start button and choose the Shut Down command. Select the Shut down your computer option and click Yes. Then wait for Windows to display the message `It's now safe to turn off your computer` before turning off your computer.

Chapter 2
Editing Slides

● ●

In This Chapter

▶ Moving around in a presentation
▶ Working with objects
▶ Editing text
▶ Undoing a mistake
▶ Deleting slides
▶ Finding and replacing text
▶ Rearranging slides

● ●

*I*f you're like Mary Poppins ("Practically Perfect in Every Way"), you can skip this chapter. Perfect people never make mistakes, so everything they type in PowerPoint comes out right the first time. They never have to press Backspace to erase something they typed wrong by mistake, go back and insert a line to make a point they left out, or rearrange their slides because they didn't add them in the right order to begin with.

If you're more like Jane ("Rather Inclined to Giggle; Doesn't Put Things Away") or Michael ("Extremely Stubborn and Suspicious"), you probably make mistakes along the way. This chapter shows you how to go back and correct those mistakes.

Reviewing your work and correcting it if necessary is called *editing*. It's not a fun job, but it has to be done. A spoonful of sugar usually helps.

This chapter focuses mostly on editing text objects. Many of the techniques apply to editing other types of objects, such as clip art pictures or drawn shapes. For more information about editing other object breeds, see Part III, "Neat Things You Can Add to Your Slides."

Moving from Slide to Slide

The most common way to move around in a PowerPoint presentation is to press the Page Up and Page Down keys on your keyboard:

  ✓ **Page Down:** Moves forward to the next slide in your presentation
  ✓ **Page Up:** Moves backward to the preceding slide in your presentation

Alternatively, you can move forward or backward through your presentation by clicking the double-headed arrows at the bottom of the vertical scroll bar on the right edge of the presentation window. You also can use the vertical scroll bar on the right edge of the presentation window to move forward or backward through your presentation.

Another way to move quickly from slide to slide is to click the scroll box within the vertical scroll bar on the right side of the window and drag it up or down by holding down the left mouse button. As you drag the box, a little text box pops up next to the slide bar to tell you which slide will be displayed if you release the button at that position.

Microsoft made a subtle improvement in this scrolling feature for PowerPoint 7 that makes the feature much more usable: Instead of just showing the slide number as it did in PowerPoint 4, PowerPoint for Windows 95 now shows the slide number and the slide's title text. With the title text as a reference, you can now easily identify the slide you want to display.

Dragging the scroll box to move from slide to slide is just one example of the many Windows tasks that are much harder to explain than to actually do. After you read this, you probably will say to yourself, "Huh?" But after you try it, you'll say, "Oh, I get it! Why didn't he just say so?"

Working with Objects

In the beginning, the User created a slide. And the slide was formless and void, without meaning or content. And the User said, "Let there be a Text Object." And there was a Text Object. And there was evening and there was morning, one day. Then the User said, "Let there be a Picture Object." And there was a Picture Object. And there was evening and there was morning, a second day. This continued for forty days and forty nights, until there were forty objects on the slide, each after its own kind. And the User was laughed out of the auditorium by the audience who could read the slide not.

I present this charming little parable solely to make the point that PowerPoint slides are nothing without objects. Objects are the lifeblood of PowerPoint. Objects give meaning and content to otherwise formless and void slides.

Most slide objects are simple text objects, which you don't have to worry much about. If you're interested, read the following sidebar about other types of objects. Otherwise, just plow ahead.

When you add a new slide to your presentation, the slide layout you choose determines which objects are initially placed on the new slide. For example, if you choose the Title layout, PowerPoint creates a new slide with two text objects. You can add more objects to the slide later; or you can delete objects, move them around, or resize them if you want. Most of the time, though, you can be content to leave the objects where they are.

Each object occupies a rectangular region on the slide. The contents of the object may or may not visually fill the rectangular region, but you can see the outline of the object when you select it (see the section "Selecting objects," later in this chapter).

Objects can overlap. Usually, you don't want them to, but sometimes doing so creates a jazzy effect. You may lay some text on top of some clip art, for example.

I object to this meaningless dribble about PowerPoint objects

I don't really want to do this to you, but I feel compelled to point out that you can use several distinct types of objects on a PowerPoint slide. They're shown in this list:

✔ **Text object:** The first and most common type of object. Most of the objects you create are probably text objects. Text objects contain, uh, text.

✔ **Shape objects:** Contain shapes such as rectangles, circles, and arrowheads. Odd as it may seem, shape objects can also contain text. To confuse the issue even more, PowerPoint uses the term *text object* to refer to both text objects and shape objects.

✔ **Line objects:** Lines and free-form drawing objects made up of line segments. Unlike shapes, lines cannot contain text.

✔ **Embedded objects:** Beasties created by some other program. Embedded objects can be clip art pictures, organization charts, graphs, sounds, movies, or other types of ornaments. PowerPoint comes with a handful of programs for creating embedded objects, and it can also work with Microsoft Word and Excel to create embedded tables and spreadsheets in a slide.

Forget about everything except text objects for now. All these other types of objects are covered in later chapters.

Selecting objects

Before you can edit anything on a slide, you have to *select* the object that contains whatever it is you want to edit. For example, you cannot start typing away to edit text on-screen. Instead, you must first select the text object that contains the text you want to edit. Likewise, you must select other types of objects before you can edit their contents.

Here are some guidelines to keep in mind when selecting objects:

- ✔ Before you can select anything, make sure that the cursor is shaped like an arrow. If it isn't, click the arrow button on the Drawing toolbar. (This button is officially called the *selection button,* but it sure looks like an arrow to me.)

- ✔ To select a text object so that you can edit its text, move the arrow pointer over the text you want to edit and click the left button. A rectangular box appears around the object, and the background behind the text changes to a solid color to make the text easier to read. A text cursor appears so that you can start typing away.

- ✔ Other types of objects work a little differently. Click an object, and the object is selected. The rectangular box appears around the object to let you know that you have hooked it. After you have hooked the object, you can drag it around the screen or change its size, but you cannot edit it. To edit a nontext object, you must double-click it. (Selecting the object first is not necessary. Just point to it with the arrow pointer and double-click.)

- ✔ Another way to select an object — or more than one object — is to use the arrow pointer to drag a rectangle around the objects you want to select. Point to a location above and to the left of the object or objects you want to select, click and drag the mouse down and to the right until the rectangle surrounds the objects. When you release the button, all the objects within the rectangle are selected.

- ✔ Also, you can press the Tab key to select objects. Press Tab once to select the first object on the slide. Press Tab again to select the next object. Keep pressing Tab until the object you want is selected.

Pressing Tab to select objects is handy when you cannot easily point to the object you want to select. This problem can happen if the object you want is buried underneath another object or if the object is empty or otherwise invisible and you're not sure of its location.

Resizing or moving an object

When you select an object, an outline box appears around it, as shown in Figure 2-1. If you look closely at the box, you can see that it has love handles, one on each corner and one in the middle of each edge. You can use these love handles to adjust the size of an object. And you can grab the box between the love handles to move the object around on the slide.

To change the size of an object, click it to select it and then grab one of the love handles by clicking it with the arrow pointer. Hold down the mouse button and move the mouse to change the object's size.

The love handles on a text object don't appear unless you click directly on the text object's outline box or press the Tab key.

Why so many handles? To give you different ways to change the object's size. The handles at the corners allow you to change both the height and the width of the object. The handles on the top and bottom edge allow you to change just the object's height, and the handles on the right and left edges change just the width.

Changing a text object's size does not change the size of the text in the object; it changes only the size of the "frame" that contains the text. Changing the width of a text object is equivalent to changing margins in a word processor: It makes the text lines wider or narrower. To change the size of the text within a text object, you must change the point size. Chapter 7 has the exciting details.

Love handles ⌐

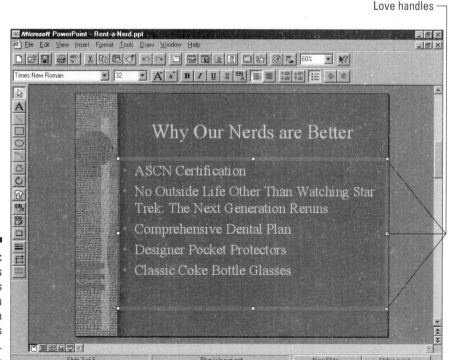

Figure 2-1:
PowerPoint's
love handles
let you
adjust an
object's
size.

If you hold down the Ctrl key while you drag one of the love handles, the object stays centered at its current position on the slide. Try it and you can see what I mean. Also, try holding down the Shift key as you drag an object using one of the corner love handles. This combination maintains the object's proportions as you resize it.

To move an object, click anywhere on the outline box except on a love handle; then drag the object to its new locale.

The outline box can be hard to see if you have a fancy background on your slides. If you select an object and have trouble seeing the outline box, try squinting or cleaning your monitor screen. Or, in severe weather, try clicking the B&W View button in the Standard toolbar. This button switches to Black and White view, in which the slide is displayed without its colors. Viewing the slide in this mode may make the love handles easier to spot. To switch back to full-color view, click the B&W View button again.

Editing a Text Object: The Baby Word Processor

When you select a text object for editing, PowerPoint transforms itself into a baby *word processor*. If you're familiar with just about any other Windows word processor, including Microsoft Word or even WordPad (the free word processor that comes with Windows 95), you will have no trouble working in baby word processor mode. This section presents some of the highlights, just in case.

PowerPoint automatically splits lines between words so that you don't have to press the Enter key at the end of every line. Press Enter only when you want to begin a new paragraph.

Text in a PowerPoint presentation is usually formatted with a *bullet character* at the beginning of each paragraph. The default bullet character is usually a simple square box, but you can change it to just about any shape you can imagine (see Chapter 7). The point to remember here is that the bullet character is a part of the paragraph format, not a character you have to type in your text.

Most word processors enable you to switch between *insert mode* and *typeover mode* by pressing the Insert key on the right side of your keyboard. In insert mode, characters you type are inserted at the cursor location; in typeover mode, each character you type replaces the character at the cursor location. However, PowerPoint always works in insert mode, so any text you type is inserted at the cursor location. Pressing the Insert key has no effect on the way text is typed.

Using the arrow keys

You can move around within a text object by pressing the *arrow keys*. I looked at my computer's keyboard and saw that 13 of the keys have arrows on them — 16, if you count the greater-than (>) and less-than (<) signs and the ubiquitous caret (^), which look sort of like arrows. So I have included Figure 2-2, which shows you the arrow keys I'm talking about.

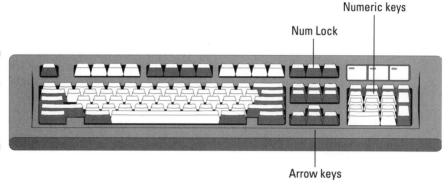

Figure 2-2:
The arrow keys I'm talking about.

The arrow keys are sometimes called the *cursor keys* because they move the cursor around the screen. Each key moves the cursor in the direction in which the arrow points, as shown in Table 2-1.

Table 2-1	The Arrow Keys
Keystroke	*Where the Cursor Moves*
↑	Up one line
↓	Down one line
←	One character to the left
→	One character to the right

The arrow keys are duplicated on the 2, 4, 6, and 8 numeric keys on the right side of the keyboard. The function of these keys alternates between numeric keys and cursor-control keys, depending on whether you have pressed the Num Lock key. When you press Num Lock once, the Num Lock light comes on, indicating that the numeric keys will create numerals when you press them. When you press Num Lock again, the Num Lock light goes off, which indicates that these keys control the cursor.

Using the mouse can be the fastest way to get somewhere. Point at the exact spot in the text where you want the cursor to appear and click the left button. The cursor magically jumps to that spot.

The left-arrow key looks just like the Backspace key. This evil plot is designed to fool computer novices into fearing that the arrow keys will erase text, just as the Backspace key does. Not so! Pay no attention to those fearmongers! The arrow keys are completely docile. All they do is move the cursor around; they do not destroy text.

Moving around faster

The arrow keys can get you anywhere within a text object, but sometimes they're as slow as molasses. Table 2-2 shows a few tricks for moving around faster.

For the Ctrl+key combinations listed in Table 2-2, first press and hold the Ctrl key and then press the arrow key, the End key, or the Home key. Then release both keys.

Table 2-2	Keyboard Tricks for Moving around Faster
Keystroke	*Where the Cursor Moves*
Ctrl+↑	Up one paragraph
Ctrl+↓	Down one paragraph
Ctrl+←	Left one word
Ctrl+→	Right one word
End	To end of line
Home	To beginning of line
Ctrl+End	To end of text object
Ctrl+Home	To beginning of text object

Your keyboard has two Ctrl keys, a lefty and a righty. Either one works. I usually press the one on the left with my little finger and press the arrow key with my right hand. Whatever feels good is okay by me.

As long as the Ctrl key is pressed, you can press any of the arrow keys repeatedly. To move three words to the right, for example, hold down the Ctrl key and press the right-arrow key three times. Then release the Ctrl key. If the cursor is in the middle of a word, pressing Ctrl+← moves the cursor to the beginning of that word. Pressing it again moves the cursor to the beginning of the preceding word.

Deleting text

You delete text by pressing the Delete or Backspace key, both of which work as shown in Table 2-3.

Table 2-3	Deleting Text
Keystroke	*What It Deletes*
Delete	The character immediately to the right of the cursor
Backspace	The character immediately to the left of the cursor
Ctrl+Delete	Characters from the cursor all the way to the end of the current word
Ctrl+Backspace	Characters from the cursor all the way to the beginning of the current word

You can press Ctrl+Delete to delete an entire word by first pressing Ctrl+→ or Ctrl+← to move the cursor to the beginning of the word you want to delete. Then press Ctrl+Delete.

If you first select a block of text, the Delete and Backspace keys delete the entire selection. If you don't have a clue about what I'm talking about, skip ahead to the following section, "Marking text for surgery."

Another way to delete a word is to double-click anywhere in the middle of the word and then press the Delete key. The double-click marks the entire word and then the Delete key deletes the marked word.

You can also use the Edit⇨Clear command to delete text permanently. The Delete key is simply a keyboard shortcut for the Edit⇨Clear command.

Marking text for surgery

Some text-editing operations — such as amputations and transplants — require that you first mark the text on which you want to operate. This list shows you the methods for doing so:

✔ When you use the keyboard, hold down the Shift key while you press any of the cursor-movement keys to move the cursor.

✔ When you use the mouse, point to the beginning of the text you want to mark and then click and drag the mouse over the text. Release the button when you reach the end of the text you want to mark.

PowerPoint's Automatic Word Selection option tries to guess when you intend to select an entire word. If you use the mouse to mark a block of text, you will notice that the selected text jumps to include entire words as you move the mouse. If you don't like this feature, you can disable it by using the Tools➪Options command (click the Edit tab and then uncheck the Automatic Word Selection check box).

- ✔ To mark a single word, point the cursor anywhere in the word and double-click. Click-click.

- ✔ To mark an entire paragraph, point anywhere in the paragraph and triple-click. Click-click-click.

- ✔ To delete the entire block of text you have marked, press the Delete key or the Backspace key.

- ✔ To replace an entire block of text, mark it and then begin typing. The marked block vanishes and is replaced by the text you are typing.

- ✔ You can use the Cut, Copy, and Paste commands from the Edit menu with marked text blocks. These commands are described in the following section.

Using Cut, Copy, and Paste

Like any good Windows program, PowerPoint uses the standard Cut, Copy, and Paste commands. These commands work on the *current selection.* When you're editing a text object, the current selection is the block of text you have marked. But if you select an entire object, the current selection is the object itself. In other words, you can use the Cut, Copy, and Paste commands with bits of text or with entire objects.

Cut, Copy, and Paste all work with one of the greatest mysteries of Windows, the Clipboard. The *Clipboard* is where Windows stashes stuff so that you can get to it later. The Cut and Copy commands add stuff to the Clipboard, which you can later retrieve by using the Paste command. After you place something on the Clipboard, it stays there until you replace it with something else by using another Cut or Copy command or until you exit Windows.

The keyboard shortcuts for Cut, Copy, and Paste are the same as they are for other Windows programs: Ctrl+X for Cut, Ctrl+C for Copy, and Ctrl+V for Paste. Because these three keyboard shortcuts work in virtually all Windows programs, it pays to learn them.

The Copy and Paste commands are often used together to duplicate information. If you want to repeat an entire sentence, for example, you first copy the sentence to the Clipboard and then place the cursor where you want the sentence duplicated and use the Paste command.

The Cut and Paste commands are used together to move stuff from one location to another. To move a sentence to a new location, for example, select the sentence and cut it to the Clipboard. Then place the cursor where you want the sentence moved and choose the Paste command.

Cutting or copying a text block

When you cut a block of text, the text is removed from the slide and placed on the Clipboard, where you can retrieve it later if you want. Copying a text block stores the text in the Clipboard but doesn't remove it from the slide.

To cut a block, first mark the block you want to cut by using the keyboard or the mouse. Then conjure up the Cut command by using any of these three methods:

✔ Choose the Edit⇨Cut command from the menu bar.

✔ Click the Cut button on the Standard toolbar (shown in the margin).

✔ Press Ctrl+X.

Using any method causes the text to vanish from your screen. Don't worry, though. It's safely nestled away on the Clipboard.

To copy a block, mark the block and invoke the Copy command by using one of these methods:

✔ Choose the Edit⇨Copy command.

✔ Click the Copy button on the Standard toolbar (shown in the margin).

✔ Press Ctrl+C.

The text is copied to the Clipboard, but this time it doesn't vanish from the screen. To retrieve the text from the Clipboard, use the Paste command, as described in the following section.

Every time you cut or copy text to the Clipboard, the previous contents of the Clipboard are lost. If you want to move several blocks of text, move them one at a time: cut-paste, cut-paste, cut-paste, not cut-cut-cut, paste-paste-paste. The latter method pastes the results of the third cut three times; the first two cuts are lost.

Pasting text

To paste text from the Clipboard, first move the cursor to the location where you want to insert the text. Then invoke the Paste command by using whichever of the following techniques suits your fancy:

✔ Choose the Edit⇨Paste command from the menu bar.

 ✔ Click the Paste button on the Standard toolbar.

 ✔ Press Ctrl+V.

Cutting, copying, and pasting entire objects

The use of Cut, Copy, and Paste isn't limited to text blocks; they work with entire objects also. Just select the object, copy or cut it to the Clipboard, move to a new location, and paste the object from the Clipboard.

To move an object from one slide to another, select the object and cut it to the Clipboard. Then move to the slide where you want the object to appear and paste the object from the Clipboard.

To duplicate an object on several slides, select the object and copy it to the Clipboard. Then move to the slide you want the object duplicated on and paste the object.

You can duplicate an object on the same slide by selecting the object, copying it to the Clipboard, and then pasting it. The only glitch is that the pasted object appears exactly on top of the original object, so you cannot tell that you now have two copies of the object on the slide. Never fear! Just grab the newly pasted object with the mouse and move it to another location on the slide. Moving the object uncovers the original so that you can see both objects.

An easier way to duplicate an object is to use the Edit⇨Duplicate command. It combines the functions of Copy and Paste but doesn't disturb the Clipboard. The duplicate copy is offset slightly from the original so that you can tell them apart. (The keyboard shortcut for the Edit⇨Duplicate command is Ctrl+D.)

If you want to blow away an entire object permanently, select it and press the Delete key or use the Edit⇨Clear command. This step removes the object from the slide but does *not* copy it to the Clipboard. It is gone forever. (Well, sort of — you can still get it back by using the Undo command, but only if you act fast. See the section "Oops! I Didn't Mean It (the Marvelous Undo Command)" later in this chapter.)

To include the same object on each of your slides, you can use a better method than copying and pasting: Add the object to the *master slide,* which governs the format of all the slides in a presentation (see Chapter 8).

Oops! I Didn't Mean It (the Marvelous Undo Command)

Made a mistake? Don't panic. Use the Undo command. Undo is your safety net. If you mess up, Undo can save the day.

There are three ways to undo a mistake:

- ✔ Choose the Edit⇨Undo command from the menu bar.
- ✔ Click the Undo button on the Standard toolbar.
- ✔ Press Ctrl+Z.

Undo reverses whatever you did last. If you deleted text, Undo adds it back in. If you typed text, Undo deletes it. If you moved an object, Undo puts it back where it was. You get the idea.

Undo remembers up to 20 of your most recent actions. However, as a general rule, it's best to correct your mistakes as soon as possible. If you make a mistake, feel free to curse, kick something, or fall on the floor in a screaming tantrum if you must, but *don't do anything else on your computer!* If you use Undo immediately, you can reverse your mistake and get on with your life.

PowerPoint also offers a Redo command, which is sort of like an Undo for Undo. In other words, if you undo what you thought was a mistake by using the Undo command and then decide that it wasn't a mistake after all, you can use the Redo command. Following are three ways to use the Redo command:

- ✔ Choose the Edit⇨Redo command from the menu bar.
- ✔ Click the Redo button on the Standard toolbar.
- ✔ Press Ctrl+Y.

Deleting a Slide

Want to delete an entire slide? No problem. Move to the slide you want to delete and use the Edit⇨Delete Slide command. Zowie! The slide is history.

No keyboard shortcut for deleting a slide exists, nor does the Standard toolbar have a button for it. Sorry — you have to use the menu for this one.

You can also delete a slide in Outline or Slide Sorter view. Outline view is covered in Chapter 3, and Slide Sorter view is covered at the end of this chapter.

Remember those confounded Ctrl+key combinations

Quick — memorize these four keyboard shortcuts:

Ctrl+Z	Undo
Ctrl+X	Cut
Ctrl+C	Copy
Ctrl+V	Paste

Do these Ctrl+key combinations make any sense to you? If not, the following two memory tricks can help you tuck these four key combinations into your frontal lobe for easy access:

✔ Notice that all four keys flank each other on the keyboard. They're the first four keys on the bottom row, just above the spacebar.

✔ At first glance, there's no mnemonic trick for remembering these combinations. Ctrl+C makes sense if you remember C for Copy, but what about the others? Try these tips:

Ctrl+Z	"Zap," as in "Zap the last thing I did. It was a mistake!"
Ctrl+X	How do you mark something you want deleted? By crossing it out — drawing an X through it.
Ctrl+C	Easy. C is for Copy.
Ctrl+V	The standard editing symbol for inserting text is a caret (^), which is an upside-down V.

It pays to memorize these key combinations because they work in just about every Windows program. I hope that they help you.

Finding Text

You know that buried somewhere in that 60-slide presentation is a slide that lists the options available on the Vertical Snarfblat, but where is it? This sounds like a job for PowerPoint's Find command!

The Find command can find text buried in any text object on any slide. These steps show you the procedure for using it:

1. Think of what you want to find.

Snarfblat will do in this example.

2. Summon the Edit⇨Find command.

The keyboard shortcut is Ctrl+F. Figure 2-3 shows the Find dialog box, which contains the secrets of the Find command.

3. Type the text you want to find.

It shows up in the Find What box.

4. Press the Enter key.

Or click the <u>F</u>ind Next button. Either way, the search begins.

Figure 2-3:
The Find
dialog box.

If the text you type is located anywhere in the presentation, the Find command zips you to the slide that contains the text and highlights the text. Then you can edit the text object or search for the next occurrence of the text within your presentation. If you edit the text, the Find dialog box stays on-screen to make it easy to continue your quest.

Here are some facts to keep in mind when using the Find command:

✔ To find the next occurrence of the same text, press Enter or click the <u>F</u>ind Next button again.

✔ To edit the text you found, click the text object. The Find dialog box remains on-screen. To continue searching, click the <u>F</u>ind Next button again.

✔ You don't have to be at the beginning of your presentation to search the entire presentation. When PowerPoint reaches the end of the presentation, it automatically picks up the search at the beginning and continues back to the point at which you started the search.

✔ You may receive the message:

```
PowerPoint has finished searching the presentation. The
search item was not found.
```

This message means that PowerPoint has given up. The text you typed just isn't anywhere in the presentation. Maybe you spelled it wrong, or maybe you didn't have a slide about Snarfblats after all.

✔ If the right mix of uppercase and lowercase letters is important to you, check the Match <u>C</u>ase box before beginning the search. This option is handy when you have, for example, a presentation about Mr. Smith the Blacksmith.

✔ Speaking of Mr. Smith the Blacksmith, use the Find <u>W</u>hole Words Only check box to find your text only when it appears as a whole word. If you want to find the slide on which you talked about Mr. Smith the Blacksmith's mit, for example, type **mit** for the Fi<u>n</u>d What text and check the Find <u>W</u>hole Words Only box. That way, the Find command looks for *mit* as a separate word. It doesn't stop to show you all the *mit*s in Smith and Blacksmith.

✔ If you find the text you're looking for and decide that you want to replace it
with something else, click the Replace button. This step changes the Find
dialog box to the Replace dialog box, which is explained in the following
section.

✔ To make the Find dialog box go away, click the Close button or press the
Esc key.

Replacing Text

Suppose that the Rent-a-Nerd company decides to switch to athletic consulting,
so it wants to change the name of its company to Rent-a-Jock. Easy. Just use the
handy Replace command to change all occurrences of the word *Nerd* to *Jock*.
The following steps show you how:

1. Invoke the Edit⇨Replace command.

The keyboard shortcut is Ctrl+H. I have no idea why. In any case, you see
the Replace dialog box, as shown in Figure 2-4.

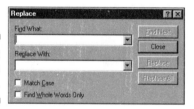

Figure 2-4:
The Replace
dialog box.

2. In the Find What box, type the text you want to find.

Enter the text that you want to replace with something else (*Nerd*, in the
example).

3. Type the replacement text in the Replace With box.

Enter the text that you want to use to replace the text you typed in the
Find What box (*Jock*, in the example).

4. Click the Find Next button.

PowerPoint finds the first occurrence of the text.

5. Click the Replace button to replace the text.

Read the text first to make sure that it found what you were looking for.

6. Repeat the Find Next and Replace sequence until you're finished.

Click Find Next to find the next occurrence, click Replace to replace it, and
so on. Keep going until you have finished.

If you're absolutely positive that you want to replace all occurrences of your Find What text with the Replace With text, click the Replace All button. This step dispenses with the Find Next and Replace cycle. The only problem is that you're bound to find at least one spot where you didn't want the replacement to occur. Replacing the word *mit* with *glove,* for example, results in *Sgloveh* rather than *Smith.*

Don't forget that you can also use the Find Whole Words Only option to find and replace text only if it appears as an entire word.

In previous PowerPoint versions, Undo didn't work for the Replace command, so there was no way to recover from a misguided use of Replace All. As a gesture of good will, Microsoft has decided that the Undo command should now work with the Replace command. As a result, if you totally mess up your presentation by clicking Replace All, you can now use the Undo command to restore sanity to your presentation.

Rearranging Your Slides in Slide Sorter View

Slide view is the view you normally work in to edit your slides, move things around, add text or graphics, and so on. But Slide view has one serious limitation: It doesn't enable you to change the order of the slides in your presentation. To do that, you have to switch to Slide Sorter view or Outline view.

Outline view is useful enough — and complicated enough — to merit its own chapter, so it's covered in Chapter 3. But Slide Sorter view is easy enough to discuss here.

You can switch to Slide Sorter view in two easy ways:

 ✔ Click the Slide Sorter view button in the bottom-left corner of the screen.

 ✔ Choose the View➪Slide Sorter command.

PowerPoint's Slide Sorter view is shown in Figure 2-5.

The following list tells you how to rearrange, add, or delete slides from Slide Sorter view:

 ✔ To move a slide, click and drag it to a new location. Point to the slide and then press and hold down the left mouse button. Drag the slide to its new location and release the button. PowerPoint adjusts the display to show the new arrangement of slides.

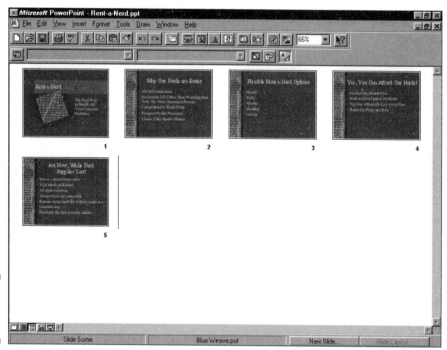

Figure 2-5:
Slide Sorter
view.

✔ To delete a slide, click the slide to select it and then press the Delete key. The Delete key works on an entire slide only in Slide Sorter view. You also can use the Edit⇨Delete Slide command.

✔ To add a new slide, click the slide you want the new slide to precede and then click the New Slide button. The New Slide dialog box appears so that you can choose the layout for the new slide. To edit the contents of the slide, return to Slide or Outline view by using the view buttons (located at the bottom-left corner of the screen) or the View command.

If your presentation contains more slides than fit on-screen at one time, you can use the scroll bars to scroll through the display. Or you can change the zoom factor to make the slides smaller. Click the down arrow next to the zoom size in the Standard toolbar and choose a smaller zoom percentage, or just type a new zoom size into the toolbar's zoom control box. (See Figure 2-6.)

Slide Sorter view may seem kind of dull and boring, but it's also the place where you can add jazzy transitions, build effects, and cool animation effects to your slides. For example, you can make your bullets fall from the top of the screen like bombs and switch from slide to slide by using strips, wipes, or blinds. All this cool stuff is described in Chapter 18.

Figure 2-6:
The
Standard
toolbar's
zoom
control.

Zoom control

Chapter 3

Doing It in Outline View

● ●

In This Chapter

▶ What is Outline view?

▶ Focusing on substance, not form

▶ Adding a slide in Outline view — the many ways

▶ Promoting, demoting, and the lateral arabesque

▶ Collapsing and expanding the outline

● ●

You probably have already noticed that most presentations consist of slide after slide of bulleted lists. You may see a chart here or there and an occasional bit of clip art thrown in for comic effect, but the bread and butter of presentations is the bulleted list. It sounds boring, but it's the best way to make sure that your message gets through.

For this reason, presentations lend themselves especially well to outlining. Presentations are light on prose but heavy in the point and subpoint department — and that's precisely where outlines excel. PowerPoint's Outline view enables you to focus on your presentation's main points and subpoints. In other words, it enables you to focus on *content* without worrying about *appearance*. You can always switch back to Slide view to make sure that your slides look good. But when you want to make sure that your slides make sense, Outline view is the way to go.

Switching to Outline View

PowerPoint normally runs in Slide view, which displays slides one at a time in a *what-you-see-is-what-you-get* (WYSIWYG) manner. Outline view shows the same information, but in the form of an outline. You can switch to Outline view in two ways:

✔ Choose the View⇨Outline menu command.

✔ Click the Outline view button on the status bar near the bottom-left corner of the PowerPoint window.

Figure 3-1 shows an example of a presentation in Outline view.

Understanding Outline View

The key to understanding PowerPoint's Outline view is realizing that Outline view is just another way of looking at your presentation. The outline is not a separate entity from the presentation. Instead, switching to Outline view takes

Figure 3-1:
A
presentation
in Outline
view.

the data from your slides and redisplays it in the form of an outline. Any changes you make to the presentation while in Outline view are automatically reflected in the presentation when you return to Slide view, and any changes you make while in Slide view automatically appear when you switch to Outline view. The reason is that Slide view and Outline view are merely two ways of displaying the content of your presentation.

The following list highlights a few important things to notice about Outline view:

✔ The outline is made up of the titles and body text of each slide. Any other objects you have added to a slide — such as pictures, charts, and so on — are not included in the outline. Also, if you add any text objects to the slide in addition to the basic title and body text objects that are automatically included when you create a new slide, the additional text objects are not included in the outline.

✔ Each slide is represented by a high-level heading in the outline. The text of this heading is drawn from the slide's title, and a button that represents the entire slide appears next to the heading. Also, the slide number appears to the left of the slide button.

✔ Each text line from a slide's body text appears as an indented heading, subordinate to the slide's main title heading.

✔ As Figure 3-1 shows, an outline can contain subpoints that are subordinate to the main points on each slide. PowerPoint enables you to create as many as five heading levels on each slide, but your slides probably will get too complicated if you go beyond two headings. You can find more about working with heading levels in the section "Promoting and Demoting Paragraphs," later in this chapter.

✔ When you switch to Outline view, the Drawing toolbar on the left side of the PowerPoint window changes to the Outline toolbar. Each button on this toolbar is explained in this chapter.

✔ Figure 3-1 shows several complete slides in Outline view. In Slide view, you can see only one slide at a time. By presenting your content more concisely, Outline view enables you to focus on your presentation's structure and content. Of course, only the smallest of presentations fits entirely on-screen even in Outline view, so you still have to use the scroll bars to view the entire presentation.

Selecting and Editing an Entire Slide

When you work in Outline view, you often have to select an entire slide. PowerPoint provides three ways to do that:

✔ Click the slide's slide icon.

✔ Click the slide's number.

✔ Triple-click anywhere in the slide's title text.

When you select an entire slide, the slide title and all its body text are highlighted. In addition, any extra objects such as graphics that are on the slide are selected as well.

To delete an entire slide, select it and then press the Delete key.

To cut or copy an entire slide to the Clipboard, select it and then press Ctrl+X (Cut) or Ctrl+C (Copy). You can then move the cursor to any location in the outline and press Ctrl+V to paste the slide from the Clipboard.

To duplicate a slide, select it and then invoke the Edit⇨Duplicate command or press Ctrl+D. This step places a copy of the selected slide immediately in front of the selection.

Selecting and Editing One Paragraph

You can select and edit an entire paragraph along with all its subordinate paragraphs. Just click the bullet next to the paragraph you want to select or triple-click anywhere in the text. To delete an entire paragraph along with its subordinate paragraphs, select it and then press the Delete key.

To cut or copy an entire paragraph to the Clipboard along with its subordinates, select it and then press Ctrl+X (Cut) or Ctrl+C (Copy). You can then press Ctrl+V to paste the paragraph anywhere in the presentation. To duplicate a paragraph, select it and then invoke the Edit⇨Duplicate command or press Ctrl+D.

Promoting and Demoting Paragraphs

To *promote* a paragraph means to move it up one level in the outline. If you promote the "Relies on polymers" line in Figure 3-1, for example, that line becomes a separate main point under "The Secret of Transparent Aluminum" slide rather than a subpoint under "Ordinary Plexiglass." If you promote it again, it becomes a separate slide.

To *demote* a paragraph is just the opposite: The paragraph moves down one level in the outline. If you demote the "Dr. Nichols hired 1984" paragraph in Figure 3-1, it becomes a subpoint under "Founded in 1965 . . ." rather than a separate main point.

Promoting paragraphs

To promote a paragraph, place the cursor anywhere in the paragraph and then perform any of the following techniques:

- ✔ Click the Promote button (shown in the margin) on the Outline toolbar (this button also appears on the right side of the Formatting toolbar).
- ✔ Press the Shift+Tab key.
- ✔ Use the keyboard shortcut Alt+Shift+←.

The paragraph moves up one level in the outline pecking order.

You cannot promote a slide title. Slide title is the highest rank in the outline hierarchy.

If you want to promote a paragraph and all its subordinate paragraphs, click the point's bullet or triple-click anywhere in the paragraph. Then promote it. You can also promote text by dragging it with the mouse. See the section "Dragging paragraphs to new levels," later in this chapter.

Demoting paragraphs

To demote a paragraph, place the cursor anywhere in the paragraph and then do one of the following:

- ✔ Click the Demote button (shown in the margin) on the Outline toolbar (this button also appears at the right side of the Formatting toolbar).
- ✔ Press the Tab key.
- ✔ Use the keyboard shortcut Alt+Shift+→.

The paragraph moves down one level in the outline pecking order.

If you demote a slide title, the entire slide is subsumed into the preceding slide. In other words, the slide title becomes a main point in the preceding slide.

To demote a paragraph and all its subparagraphs, click the paragraph's bullet or triple-click anywhere in the paragraph text. Then demote it. You can also demote text by dragging it with the mouse. See the following section, "Dragging paragraphs to new levels."

Be sensitive when you demote paragraphs. Being demoted can be an emotionally devastating experience.

Dragging paragraphs to new levels

When you move the mouse pointer over a bullet (or the slide button), the pointer changes from a single arrow to a four-cornered arrow. This arrow is your signal that you can click the mouse to select the entire paragraph (and any subordinate paragraphs). Also, you can use the mouse to promote or demote a paragraph along with all its subordinates.

To promote or demote with the mouse, follow these steps:

1. Point to the bullet you want to demote or promote.

The mouse pointer changes to a four-cornered arrow. To demote a slide, point to the slide button. (Remember that you cannot promote a slide. It's already at the highest level.)

2. Click and hold the mouse button down.

3. Drag the mouse to the right or left.

The mouse pointer changes to a double-pointed arrow, and a vertical line appears that shows the indentation level of the selection. Release the button when the selection is indented the way you want. The text is automatically reformatted for the new indentation level.

If you mess up, press Ctrl+Z to <u>U</u>ndo the promotion or demotion. Then try again.

Adding a New Paragraph

To add a new paragraph to a slide, move the cursor to the end of the paragraph you want the new paragraph to follow and then press the Enter key. PowerPoint creates a new paragraph at the same outline level as the preceding paragraph.

If you position the cursor at the beginning of a paragraph and press the Enter key, the new paragraph is inserted *to the left of* the cursor position. If you position the cursor in the middle of a paragraph and press the Enter key, the paragraph is split in two.

After you add a new paragraph, you may want to change its level in the outline. To do that, you must promote or demote the new paragraph. To create a subpoint for a main point, for example, position the cursor at the end of the main point and press the Enter key. Then demote the new paragraph. For details about how to promote or demote a paragraph, see the section "Promoting and Demoting Paragraphs," earlier in this chapter.

Adding a New Slide

You can add a new slide in many ways when you're working in Outline view. This list shows the most popular methods:

- ✔ Promote an existing paragraph to the highest level. This method splits a slide into two slides. In Figure 3-1, for example, you can create a new slide by promoting the "Transparent Aluminum" paragraph. That step splits "The Secret of Transparent Aluminum" slide into two slides.

- ✔ Add a new paragraph and then promote it to the highest level.

- ✔ Place the cursor in a slide's title text and press the Enter key. This method creates a new slide before the current slide. Whether the title text stays with the current slide, goes with the new slide, or is split between the slides depends on the location of the cursor within the title when you press Enter.

- ✔ Place the cursor anywhere in a slide's body text and press Ctrl+Enter. This method creates a new slide immediately following the current slide. The position of the cursor within the existing slide doesn't matter; the new slide is always created after the current slide. (The cursor must be in the slide's body text for this method to work, though. If you put the cursor in a slide title and press Ctrl+Enter, the cursor jumps to the slide's body text without creating a new slide.)

- ✔ Place the cursor anywhere in a slide and click the New Slide button (shown in the margin) in the status bar at the bottom of the screen.

- ✔ Place the cursor anywhere in a slide and click the Insert New Slide button (shown in the margin) in the Standard toolbar.

- ✔ Place the cursor anywhere in the slide and invoke the Insert⇨New Slide command or its keyboard shortcut, Ctrl+M.

- ✔ Select an existing slide by clicking the slide button or triple-clicking the title and then duplicate it by using the Edit⇨Duplicate command or its keyboard shortcut, Ctrl+D.

(My, aren't there a number of ways to create a new slide in Outline view?)

Because Outline view focuses on slide content rather than on layout, new slides are always given the basic Bulleted List layout, which includes title text and body text formatted with bullets. If you want to change the layout of a new slide, you must return to Slide view and click the Layout button to select a new slide layout.

Moving Text Up and Down

Outline view is also handy for rearranging your presentation. You easily can change the order of individual points on a slide, or you can rearrange the order of the slides.

Moving text up or down by using the keyboard

To move text up or down, first select the text you want to move. To move just one paragraph (along with any subordinate paragraphs), click its bullet. To move an entire slide, click its slide button.

To move the selected text up, use either of the following techniques:

- Click the Move Up button (shown in the margin) on the Outline toolbar on the left side of the screen.
- Press Alt+Shift+↑.

To move the selected text down, use either of the following techniques:

- Click the Move Down button (shown in the margin) on the Outline toolbar on the left side of the screen.
- Press Alt+Shift+↓.

Dragging text up or down

To move text up or down by using the mouse, follow these steps:

1. Point to the bullet next to the paragraph you want to move.

The mouse pointer changes to a four-cornered arrow. To move a slide, point to the slide button.

2. Click and hold the mouse button down.

3. Drag the mouse up or down.

The mouse pointer changes again to a double-pointed arrow, and a horizontal line appears, showing the horizontal position of the selection. Release the mouse when the selection is positioned where you want it.

Be careful when you're moving text in a slide that has more than one level of body text paragraphs. Notice the position of the horizontal line as you drag the selection; the entire selection is inserted at that location, which may split up subpoints. If you don't like the result of a move, you can always Undo it by pressing Ctrl+Z.

Expanding and Collapsing the Outline

If your presentation has many slides, you may find it difficult to grasp its overall structure even in Outline view. Fortunately, PowerPoint enables you to *collapse* the outline so that only the slide titles are shown. Collapsing an outline does not delete the body text; it merely hides it so that you can focus on the order of the slides in your presentation.

Expanding a presentation restores the collapsed body text to the outline so that you can once again focus on details. You can collapse and expand an entire presentation, or you can collapse and expand one slide at a time.

Collapsing an entire presentation

To collapse an entire presentation, you have two options:

> ✔ Click the Show Titles button (shown in the margin) on the Outline toolbar on the left side of the screen.
>
> ✔ Press Alt+Shift+1.

Expanding an entire presentation

To expand an entire presentation, try one of these methods:

> ✔ Click the Show All button (shown in the margin) on the Outline toolbar on the left side of the screen.
>
> ✔ Press Alt+Shift+A.

Collapsing a single slide

To collapse a single slide, position the cursor anywhere in the slide you want to collapse. Then do one of the following:

✔ Click the Collapse Selection button (shown in the margin) on the Outline toolbar, on the left side of the screen.

✔ Press Alt+Shift+– (the minus sign).

Expanding a single slide

To expand a single slide, position the cursor anywhere in the title of the slide you want to expand. Then perform one of the following techniques:

 ✔ Click the Expand Selection button (shown in the margin) on the Outline toolbar on the left side of the screen.

✔ Press Alt+Shift++ (the plus sign).

Showing and Hiding Formats

The idea behind Outline view is to shield you from the appearance of your presentation so that you can concentrate on its content. With PowerPoint, you can take this idea one step further by removing the text formatting from your outline. The outline shown in Figure 3-1 includes text formatting. As you can see, the text for slide titles appears larger than the body text, and the bullet character varies depending on its level in the outline hierarchy.

Figure 3-2 shows the same outline with text formatting hidden. All text is displayed in the same vanilla font, and fancy bullet characters are replaced by simple bullets. The advantage of this layout is that you can see more of the outline on-screen. Notice that part of slide 5 is now visible; in Figure 3-1, you can see only the first four slides.

To hide character formatting in Outline view, do one of the following:

 ✔ Click the Show Formatting button (shown in the margin) on the Outline toolbar on the left side of the screen.

✔ Press the slash key (/), the one on the numeric keypad, just above the number 8.

To restore formatting, just click the Show Formatting button or press the slash key again.

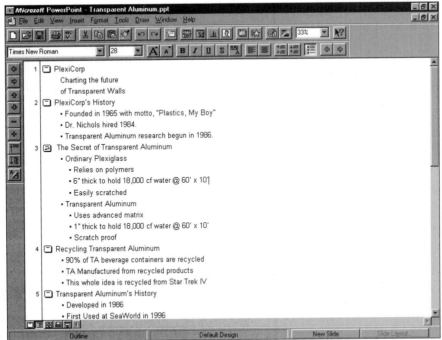

Figure 3-2:
The text
formatting is
hidden here.

Hiding character formatting does not remove the formatting attributes from your presentation. It simply hides them while you're in Outline view so that you can concentrate on your presentation's content rather than on its appearance. Hiding character formatting removes not only character fonts and fancy bullets but also basic character styles, such as italics, bold, and underlining. Too bad. Hiding formats would be more useful if it still showed these basic character styles.

Chapter 4

Doing It with Style

- -

In This Chapter

▶ Checking your presentation for embarrassing stylistic mistakes

▶ Checking your spelling

▶ Capitalizing correctly

▶ Placing periods consistently

- -

Spelling errors in a word processing document are bad, but at least they're small. In a PowerPoint presentation, spelling errors are small only until you put the transparency or the 35mm slide in the projector. Then they get all blown out of proportion. Nothing is more embarrassing than a 2-foot-tall spelling error.

Fortunately, PowerPoint has a pretty decent spell checker. It also has two other nifty features to help catch innocent typographical errors before you show your presentation to a board of directors: a capitalization whirligig that fixes your capitalization (capital idea, eh?) and a period flinger that ensures that each line either does or does not end with a period. You can perform all three checks automatically using a new PowerPoint 95 feature called the *Style Checker*.

Checking Your Spelling

I was voted Worst Speller in the Sixth Grade. Not that that qualifies me to run for vice president or anything, but it shows how much I appreciate computer spell checkers. Spelling makes no sense to me. I felt a little better after watching *The Story of English* on public television. Now at least I know who to blame for all the peculiarities of English spelling — the Angles, the Norms (including the guy from *Cheers*), and the Saxophones.

Thank goodness for PowerPoint's spell checker. It works its way through your presentation, looking up every word in its massive list of correctly spelled words and bringing any misspelled words to your attention. It performs this task without giggling or snickering. The spell checker gives you the opportunity, in fact, to tell it that *you* are right and *it* is wrong and that it should learn how to spell words the way you do.

The following steps show you how to check a presentation's spelling:

1. **If the presentation you want to spell check is not already open, open it.**

   It doesn't matter which view you're in. You can spell check from any of these views: Slide, Outline, Notes Pages, or Slide Sorter.

2. **Fire up the spell checker.**

   Click the Spelling button on the Standard toolbar, press F7, or choose the Tools⇨Spelling command.

3. **Tap your fingers on your desk.**

   PowerPoint is searching your presentation for embarrassing spelling errors. Be patient.

4. **Don't be startled if PowerPoint finds a spelling error.**

   If PowerPoint finds a spelling error in your presentation, it switches to the slide that contains the error, highlights the offensive word, and displays the misspelled word along with a suggested correction, as shown in Figure 4-1.

5. **Choose the correct spelling or laugh in PowerPoint's face.**

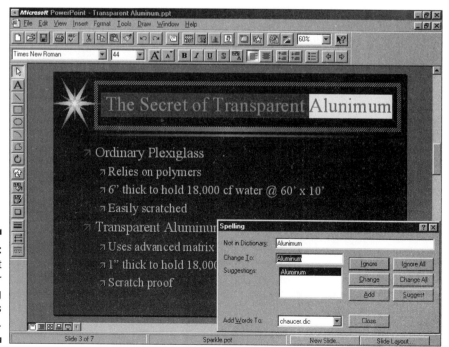

Figure 4-1: PowerPoint gloats over a spelling error it has found.

If you agree that the word is misspelled, scan the list of corrections that PowerPoint offers and click the one you like. Then click the Change button. If you like the way you spelled the word in the first place (maybe it's an unusual word that isn't in PowerPoint's spelling dictionary, or maybe you like to spell like Chaucer did), click the Ignore button. Watch as PowerPoint turns red in the face.

6. **Repeat Steps 4 and 5 until PowerPoint gives up.**

   When you see the following message:

   ```
   Finished spell checking entire presentation
   ```

   you're finished.

PowerPoint always spell checks your entire presentation from start to finish. Unlike Microsoft Word's spell checker, you cannot check the spelling for a single word or a selected range. Too bad. On the other hand, you don't have to worry about returning to the top of the document before running the spell checker. PowerPoint always checks spelling for the entire presentation, beginning with the first slide.

PowerPoint checks the spelling of titles, body text, notes, and text objects added to slides. It doesn't check the spelling for embedded objects, however, such as charts or graphs.

If PowerPoint cannot come up with a suggestion or if none of its suggestions is correct, you can type your own correction and click the Change button. If the word you type isn't in the dictionary, PowerPoint asks you whether you're sure that you know what you're doing. Double-check and click OK if you really mean it.

If you want PowerPoint to ignore all occurrences of a particular misspelling, click the Ignore All button. Likewise, if you want PowerPoint to correct all occurrences of a particular misspelling, click the Change All button.

If you get tired of PowerPoint always complaining about a word that's not in its standard dictionary (such as PlexiCorp), click Add to add the word to the custom dictionary. If you cannot sleep at night until you know more about the custom dictionary, read the following sidebar entitled "Don't make me tell you about the custom dictionary."

The speller cannot tell the difference between *your* and *you're, ours* and *hours, angel* and *angle,* and so on. In other words, if the word is in the dictionary, PowerPoint passes it by regardless of whether you used the word correctly. PowerPoint's spell checker is no substitute for good, old-fashioned proofing. Print your presentation, sit down with a cup of cappuccino, and *read* it.

Don't make me tell you about the custom dictionary

PowerPoint's spell checker uses two spelling dictionaries: a standard dictionary, which contains untold thousands of words all reviewed for correctness by George Bernard Shaw himself (just kidding!), and a *custom dictionary*, which contains words you have added by clicking the Add button when the spell checker found a spelling error.

The custom dictionary lives in a file named CUSTOM.DIC, which makes its residence in the \WINDOWS\MSAPPS\PROOF folder. Other Microsoft programs that use spell checkers — most notably Microsoft Word — share the same custom dictionary with PowerPoint. So if you

add a word to the custom dictionary in Word, PowerPoint's spell checker knows about the word, too.

What if you accidentally add a word to the dictionary? Then you have a serious problem. You have two alternatives. You can petition Noah Webster to have your variant spelling officially added to the English language, or you can edit the CUSTOM.DIC file, search through the file until you find the bogus word, and delete it. CUSTOM.DIC is a standard text file that you can edit with just about any text editor, including Notepad, the jiffy editor that comes free with Windows.

Capitalizing Correctly

PowerPoint's Change Case command enables you to capitalize the text in your slides properly. These steps show you how to use it:

1. **Select the text you want to capitalize.**

2. **Invoke the Format⇨Change Case command.**

    The Change Case dialog box appears, as shown in Figure 4-2.

Figure 4-2:
The Change
Case dialog
box.

3. **Study the options for a moment and then click the one you want.**

    The case options follow:

- **Sentence case:** The first letter of the first word in each sentence is capitalized. Everything else is changed to lowercase.

- **lowercase:** Everything is changed to lowercase.

- **UPPERCASE:** Everything is changed to capital letters.

- **Title Case:** The first letter of each word is capitalized. PowerPoint is smart enough to leave certain words, such as *a* and *the* lowercase, but you should double-check to ensure that it worked properly.

- **tOGGLE cASE:** This option turns capitals into lowercase and turns lowercase into capitals, for a ransom-note look.

4. Click OK or press Enter and check the results.

Always double-check your text after using the Change Case command to make sure that the result is what you intended.

Slide titles almost always should use title case. The first level of bullets on a slide can use either title or sentence case. Lower levels usually should use sentence case.

Avoid uppercase, if you can. It's harder to read and looks like you're shouting.

To Period or Not to Period. Period.

One dead giveaway of poor proofing is a slide in which some lines end with periods and others don't. Fortunately, PowerPoint has a Periods command that enables you to add or remove periods from the end of each line in a selection of text. These steps show you how to use it:

1. Select the text you want to periodicalize.

Periodicolate? Emperiod? I never pass up an opportunity to coin a new word!

2. Invoke the Format⇨Periods command.

The Periods dialog box pops up, as shown in Figure 4-3.

Figure 4-3:
The Periods
dialog box.

3. To add periods, check Add Periods. To remove them, check Remove Periods.

4. Click OK or press the Enter key.

Double-check your text to make sure that PowerPoint added or removed the periods satisfactorily.

If your bullets consist of full sentences, they should end with periods. If they are sentence fragments, leave the periods off. (If your bullets are a mixture of complete sentences and sentence fragments, rewrite them so that they are all either one or the other.)

When in doubt, no one is going to sue you if you leave the periods off when you should include them or include them when you should leave them off, as long as you're consistent. Use periods on every bullet in the slide or on none of them.

Using the Style Checker

PowerPoint 95's new Style Checker feature automatically checks your presentation's spelling, verifies the consistency of punctuation and capitalization, and also warns you about slides that may be difficult to read because they contain too many bullets or text that is too small. It's a great feature, one that I recommend you use before printing the final copy of your presentation.

To use the Style Checker, follow these simple steps:

1. Choose the Tools⇨Style Checker command.

The dialog box shown in Figure 4-4 appears.

Figure 4-4:
The Style
Checker
dialog box.

Style Checker	? X
Check For	Start
☑ Spelling	Cancel
☑ Visual Clarity	Options...
☑ Case and End Punctuation	

2. Choose the style checks that you would like the Style Checker to perform.

The Style Checker performs three basic types of checks:

- **Spelling:** Select this option if you want the Style Checker to run the spell checker to check your presentation's spelling.

- **Visual Clarity:** Select this option if you want the Style Checker to check for visual clarity. If you choose this option, the Style Checker warns you about slides that have too many different fonts, titles or body text that are too small to read or are too long, slides that have too many bullets, or slides that have text that runs off the page.

- **Case and End Punctuation:** Select this option if you want the Style Checker to make sure that your capitalization and punctuation are consistent.

3. **Click Start.**

4. **If you requested a spell check, use the Spelling dialog box to correct any spelling errors that are detected.**

   Refer to the "Checking Your Spelling" section if you're not sure how to use the spell checker.

5. **Correct any capitalization and punctuation errors found by the Style Checker.**

   These errors are displayed in a dialog box similar to the one shown in Figure 4-5. This dialog box works just like the Spelling dialog box, with buttons that allow you to ignore the error (Ignore); ignore all errors of the same type (Ignore All); correct the error (Change); or correct all errors of this type (Change All).

Figure 4-5:
The Style
Checker
discovers a
punctuation
error.

6. **Correct any visual clarity errors that appear.**

   If any visual clarity errors are discovered, they are displayed in a dialog box such as the one shown in Figure 4-6. Be sure to correct these errors — or at least carefully consider each one.

If you wish, you can change the rules the Style Checker uses as it searches for style errors. When the Style Checker dialog box appears, click the Options button. Clicking this button brings up a dialog box that has two tabbed sections — one for setting Case and End Punctuation options, the other for setting Visual Clarity options.

Figure 4-6:
The Style
Checker
thinks that
one of my
slides is too
verbose.

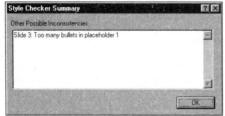

Figure 4-7 shows the Case and End Punctuation options. This dialog box lets you set the capitalization (case) style for title text and body text and lets you Remove, Add, or Ignore the end punctuation marks on slide titles and body text paragraphs. You can use other punctuation, but periods are most common.

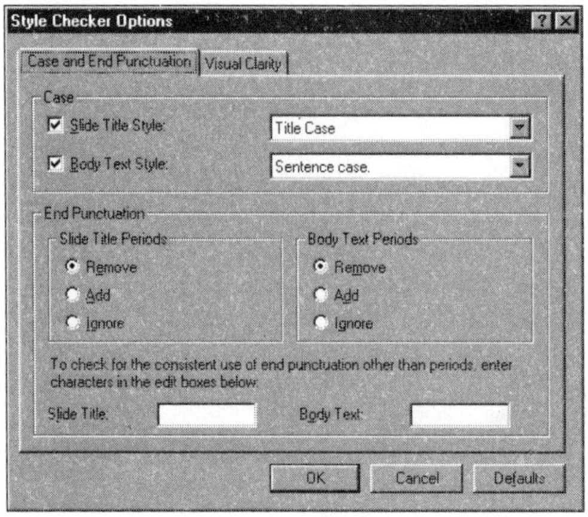

Figure 4-7:
Case and
End
Punctuation
options for
the Style
Checker.

Figure 4-8 shows the Style Checker's Visual Clarity options. These options let you indicate the number of different fonts that are to be tolerated for each slide, the minimum acceptable point size for title text and body text, the maximum number of bullets per slide, the maximum number of lines to allow for titles and body text, and whether to check for title and body text that extends beyond the slide margins. (If you mess around with these options, you can reset them to their factory default values by clicking the Defaults button.)

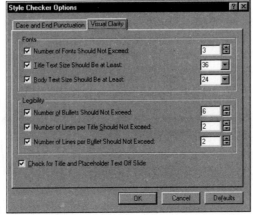

Figure 4-8:
Visual
Clarity
options for
the Style
Checker.

The 5th Wave By Rich Tennant

THE NEW DESKTOP PRESENTATION SOFTWARE NOT ONLY LETS RAGS PRODUCE A PROFESSIONAL LOOKING SLIDE PRESENTATION QUICKLY AND INEXPENSIVELY, BUT IT ALSO LETS HIM SAY IT HIS WAY.

Chapter 5

Printing Your Presentation

. . . .

In This Chapter

▶ Printing slides

▶ Printing handouts

▶ Printing speaker notes

▶ Printing an outline

▶ Whoa! Why doesn't it print?

. . . .

The Print command. The Printmeister. Big presentation comin' up. Printin' some slides. The Printorama. The Mentor of de Printor. Captain Toner of the Good Ship Laseroo.

Don't worry — no one's waiting to ambush you with annoying one-liners like that guy who used to be on *Saturday Night Live* when you print a PowerPoint presentation. Just a handful of boring dialog boxes with boring check boxes. Point-point, click-click, print-print. (Hey, humor me, okay? The French think that I'm a comic genius!)

The Quick Way to Print

 The fastest way to print your presentation is to click the Print button found in the Standard toolbar. Clicking this button prints your presentation without further ado, using the current settings for the Print dialog box, which I explain in the remaining sections of this chapter. Usually, this results in printing a single copy of all the slides in your presentation. But if you have altered the Print dialog box settings, clicking the Print button uses the altered settings automatically.

Using the Print Dialog Box

For precise control over how you want your presentation printed, you must conjure up the Print dialog box. You can do so in more ways than the government can raise revenue without calling it a tax, but the three most common are shown in this list:

- ✔ Choose the File⇨Print command.
- ✔ Press Ctrl+P.
- ✔ Press Ctrl+Shift+F12.

Any of these actions summons the Print dialog box, shown in Figure 5-1. Like the Genie in Disney's movie *Aladdin,* this box grants you three wishes, but with two limitations: It cannot kill anyone ("ix-nay on the illing-kay"), and it cannot make anyone fall in love with you.

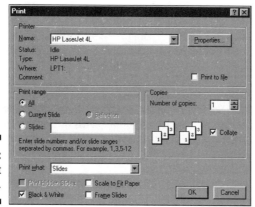

Figure 5-1:
The Print
dialog box.

After you unleash the Print dialog box, click OK or press Enter to print all the slides in your presentation. Or fiddle around with the settings to print a select group of slides, print more than one copy, or print handouts, speaker notes, or an outline. This chapter shows you the treasures that lie hidden in this dialog box.

Printing can be *es-el-oh-double-ewe*. PowerPoint politely displays a status box to keep you informed of its progress, so at least you know that the darn program hasn't gone AWOL on you.

Don't panic if your printer doesn't start spewing forth pages immediately after the Print dialog box goes away. PowerPoint printouts tend to demand a great deal from the printer, so sometimes the printer has to work for a while before it can produce a finished page. Be patient. The Printer wizard has every intention of granting your request.

Oh, by the way, if you see a vague error message that says something like this

Put paper in the printer, dummy!

try putting paper in the printer.

Changing printers

If you are lucky enough to have two or more printers at your disposal, you can use the <u>N</u>ame field to pick which printer you want to use. Each printer must first be successfully installed in Windows 95 — a topic that is beyond the reach of this humble book, but that you will find plenty of information about in Andy Rathbone's *Windows 95 For Dummies* (IDG Books Worldwide, Inc.).

Even if your computer doesn't have two printers physically attached to it, your computer may be connected to a computer network that does have two or more printers. In that case, you can use the <u>N</u>ame field to select one of these networked printers to print your presentation.

The <u>P</u>roperties button calls forth the Windows 95 Printer Properties dialog box, which lets you futz with various printer settings. Avoid it if you can.

See that innocent-looking Print to fi<u>l</u>e checkbox floating aimlessly beneath the <u>P</u>roperties button? It can come in handy if you have a friend lucky enough to have that new $20,000 Binford color LaserBlaster 32-MegaDot 200-page-per-minute printer. Print to file asks you for a filename and then sends your print output to the file you indicate. You then can copy that file to a floppy disk, pack it over to your friend's computer, and print it on his or her printer by issuing a command similar to this one:

```
copy cheap.prt lpt1: /b
```

In this grisly example, CHEAP.PRT is the name of the print file that was created by way of the Print to fi<u>l</u>e option. Don't forget the /b doohickey; the command doesn't work without it.

Note that you must get to a DOS command prompt before you can type the Copy command. In Windows 95, you do that by clicking the Start button, choosing Programs, and then choosing MS-DOS Prompt.

This command works even if your friend doesn't have Windows 95. Just get to an MS-DOS prompt on your friend's computer and type the copy command shown previously.

Of course, if your buddy has a new $20,000 Binford color LaserBlaster 32-MegaDot printer, she or he can probably afford a copy of PowerPoint. If the computer that has the printer you want to use also has a copy of PowerPoint, don't bother with the Print to file option. Just save your PowerPoint presentation file to a floppy disk, airmail it to your friend's computer, and print it from there directly from PowerPoint.

Printing part of a presentation

When you first use the Print command, the All option is checked so that your entire presentation prints. The other options in the Print Range portion of the Print dialog box enable you to tell PowerPoint to print just part of your presentation. In addition to All, you have three options:

- ✔ **Current Slide:** Prints just the current slide. Before you invoke the Print command, you should move to the slide you want to print. Then check this option in the Print dialog box and click OK. This option is handy when you make a change to one slide and don't want to reprint the entire presentation.

- ✔ **Selection:** Prints just the portion of the presentation you selected before invoking the Print command. This option is easiest to use in Outline or Slide Sorter view. First, select the slides you want to print by dragging the mouse to highlight them. Then invoke the Print command, click the Selection box, and click OK. (Note that if you don't select anything before you call up the Print dialog box, this field is grayed out, as shown in Figure 5-1.)

- ✔ **Slides:** Enables you to select specific slides for printing. You can print a range of slides by typing the beginning and ending slide numbers, separated by a hyphen, as in **5-8** to print slides 5, 6, 7, and 8. Or you can list individual slides, separated by commas, as in **4,8,11** to print slides 4, 8, and 11. And you can combine ranges and individual slides, as in **4,9-11,13** to print slides 4, 9, 10, 11, and 13.

To print a portion of a presentation, first call up the Print dialog box. Next, select the Slide Range option you want. Then click OK or press Enter.

Printing more than one copy

The Number of copies field in the Print dialog box enables you to tell PowerPoint to print more than one copy of your presentation. You can click one of the arrows next to this field to increase or decrease the number of copies, or you can type directly in the field to set the number of copies.

Below the Number of copies field is a check box labeled Collate. If this box is checked, PowerPoint prints each copy of your presentation one at a time. In other words, if your presentation consists of ten slides and you select three copies and check the Collate box, PowerPoint first prints all ten slides of the first copy of the presentation, and then all ten slides of the second copy, and then all ten slides of the third copy. If you do not check the Collate box, PowerPoint prints three copies of the first slide, followed by three copies of the second slide, followed by three copies of the third slide, and so on.

The Collate option saves you from the chore of manually sorting your copies. If your presentation takes forever to print because it's loaded down with heavy-duty graphics, however, you probably can save time in the long run by unchecking the Collate box. Why? Because many printers are fast when it comes to printing a second or third copy of a page. The printer may spend ten minutes figuring out how to print a particularly complicated page, but after it figures it out, the printer can chug out umpteen copies of that page without hesitation. If you print collated copies, the printer must labor over each page separately for each copy of the presentation it prints.

What do you want to print?

The Print what field in the Print dialog box enables you to select which type of output you want to print. The following choices are available:

- ✔ **Slides:** Prints slides. Note that if you have used build effects in the presentation, this option doesn't appear. Instead, it is replaced with two similar options: *Slides (with Builds)* and *Slides (without Builds)*. If you don't know what builds are — and there's no reason you should, unless you've been reading ahead — just ignore the next two options.

- ✔ **Slides (with Builds):** Prints slides. If you use the Build command with a slide, a separate page is printed for each bulleted item on the slide. The first page has just the first bulleted item; the second page shows the first and second bullets; and so on. Builds are covered in Chapter 18.

- ✔ **Slides (without Builds):** Prints slides but ignores builds. One page is printed for each slide, whether or not you used the Build command for the slide.

- ✔ **Notes pages:** Prints speaker notes pages, which are covered in Chapter 18.

- ✔ **Handouts (2 Slides per Page):** Prints audience handout pages. Each handout page shows two slides.

- ✔ **Handouts (3 Slides per Page):** Prints audience handout pages. Each handout page shows three slides.

    ✓ **Handouts (6 Slides per Page):** Prints audience handout pages. Each
      handout page shows six slides.

    ✓ **Outline view:** Prints an outline of your presentation.

Select the type of output you want to print and then click OK or press Enter. Off
you go!

When you're printing slides to be used as overhead transparencies, print a
proof copy of the slides on plain paper before committing the output to transparencies. Transparencies are too expensive to print on until you're sure that
your output is just right.

To change the orientation of your printed output from Landscape to Portrait
mode (or vice versa), use the File⇨Slide Setup command.

To print handouts with two, three, or six slides per page, PowerPoint naturally
must shrink the slides to make them fit. Because slides usually have outra-
geously large type, the handout slides are normally still readable, even at their
reduced size.

What are all those other check boxes?

The Print command has four additional check boxes, which hide out near the
bottom of the dialog box, hoping to slip by unnoticed. This list shows you what
they do:

    ✓ **Print Hidden Slides:** You can *hide* individual slides by way of the
      Tools⇨Hide Slide command. After a slide is hidden, it does not print unless
      you check the Print Hidden Slides option in the Print dialog box.

      In Figure 5-1, this option is shaded, which indicates that it is not available.
      That happens when the presentation being printed doesn't have any
      hidden slides. The Print Hidden Slides option is available only when the
      presentation has hidden slides. Chapter 28 has more information about
      hidden slides, if you're curious.

    ✓ **Scale to Fit Paper:** Adjusts the size of the printed output to fit the paper in
      the printer. Leave this option unchecked to avoid bizarre printing
      problems.

    ✓ **Black & White:** Check this option if you have a black-and-white printer; it
      improves the appearance of color slides when printed in black and white.

    ✓ **Frame Slides:** Draws a thin border around the slides.

Note: Microsoft considered licensing TurnerVision technology to colorize slides printed with the Black & White option, but decided against it when it was discovered that most audiences dream in black and white when they fall asleep during a boring presentation.

Printing Boo-Boos

On the surface, printing seems as though it should be one of the easiest parts of using PowerPoint. After all, all you have to do to print a presentation is click the Print button, right? Well, usually. Unfortunately, all kinds of things can go wrong between the time you click the Print button and the time gorgeous output bursts forth from your printer. If you run into printer trouble, check out the things discussed in this section.

Your printer must be ready and raring to go before it can spew out printed pages. If you suspect that your printer is not ready for action, this list presents some things to check:

- Make sure that the printer's power cord is plugged in and that the printer is turned on.

- The printer cable must be connected to both the printer and the computer's printer port. If the cable has come loose, turn off both the computer and the printer, reattach the cable, and then restart the computer and the printer. (You know better, of course, than to turn off your computer without first saving any work in progress, exiting from any active application programs, and shutting down Windows. So I won't say anything about it. Not even one little word.)

- If your printer has a switch labeled *On-line* or *Select,* press it until the corresponding On-line or Select light comes on.

- Make sure that the printer has plenty of paper. (I have always wanted to write a musical about a printer that ate people rather than paper. I think that I'll call it *Little DOS of Horrors.* Try typing this command at the DOS command prompt: **Prompt: Feed Me:**)

- If you're using a dot-matrix printer, make sure that the ribbon is okay. For a laser printer, make sure that the toner cartridge has plenty of life left in it.

Chapter 6

Help!

In This Chapter

▶ Accessing Help

▶ Finding help that holds your hand

▶ Searching for specific Help topics

▶ Using the Answer Wizard

▶ Getting help online

*T*he ideal way to use PowerPoint would be to have a PowerPoint expert sitting patiently at your side, answering your every question with a straight-forward answer, gently correcting you when you make silly mistakes, and otherwise minding his or her own business. All you'd have to do is occasionally toss the expert a Twinkie and let him or her outside once a day.

Short of that, the next best thing is to find out how to use PowerPoint's built-in help system. No matter how deeply you're lost in the PowerPoint jungle, help is never more than a few keystrokes or mouse clicks away.

 PowerPoint's Help system is similar to the Help system found in other Windows programs, so if you know how to use another program's Help, you'll have no trouble figuring out PowerPoint's.

Several Ways to Get Help

As with everything else in Windows, more than one method is available for calling up help when you need it. The easiest thing to do would be to simply yell, "Skipper!!!!!!" in your best Gilligan voice. Otherwise, you have the following options:

✔ Press F1 at any time and help is on its way. If you press F1 when you're in the middle of something, odds are PowerPoint will come through with help on doing just the task you are trying to accomplish. This slick little bit of wizardry is called *context-sensitive help.*

✔ If you click <u>H</u>elp on the menu bar, you get a whole menu of help stuff, most of which is only moderately helpful. <u>H</u>elp⟹Microsoft PowerPoint <u>H</u>elp Topics is the option you'll use most. Details on finding your way around the <u>H</u>elp commands are found in later sections of this chapter.

✔ Whenever a dialog box is displayed, you can click the question mark in the upper-right corner of the dialog box. The mouse pointer changes to a question mark; you can then click any dialog box control (such as a text box, button, or check box) to see a brief explanation of what that dialog box control does.

✔ If you're baffled by an icon on the icon bar, try pointing at it and allowing the mouse pointer to hover over the button for a moment. A brief explanation of the button's function will appear shortly.

✔ With a sound card, a microphone, and the right voice-recognition software, you probably can teach your computer to call up Help when you yell, "Skipper!" That would be kind of silly, though, don't you think?

Finding Your Way Around in Help

If you click <u>H</u>elp in the PowerPoint menu bar or press Alt+H, you see the menu shown in Figure 6-1. The <u>H</u>elp menu is similar to the Help menus found in most other Windows 95 programs, except that it contains a few commands that are specific to PowerPoint, just to complicate your life. If you know how to use Help in any other Windows 95 program, you already have a head start.

Note, however, that Help works a bit differently in Windows 95 than it did in Windows 3.1. If you're used to Windows 3.1 Help, you may be aggravated at first by the differences in Windows 95 Help. After a while, however, you'll probably be pleasantly surprised to see that the new Windows 95 Help system is actually easier to use and more powerful than the old Windows 3.1 Help.

To get started with Help, choose the <u>H</u>elp⟹Microsoft PowerPoint <u>H</u>elp Topics command. You are greeted with the dialog box shown in Figure 6-2, which lists the table of contents for all of PowerPoint's help topics.

Figure 6-1:
The <u>H</u>elp
menu.

Help

Microsoft PowerPoint <u>H</u>elp Topics
Answer <u>W</u>izard

The Microsoft <u>N</u>etwork...
Ti<u>p</u> of the Day...

<u>A</u>bout Microsoft PowerPoint

Figure 6-2:
PowerPoint's
Help
Contents.

To display help on one of these subjects, just double-click it. Doing so expands
the Help Contents to show the help that is available for a specific topic. For
example, Figure 6-3 shows the expanded help contents for "Working With
Slides."

Figure 6-3:
Expanded
help
contents for
"Working
With
Slides."

To display a particular Help topic, double-click the topic title in the contents
list. For example, Figure 6-4 shows the Help topic for "Go to a specific slide."

Figure 6-4:
The Help
topic for "Go
to a specific
slide."

After you get yourself this deep into the Help system, you need to heed the following advice to find your way around and get out when you find out what you want to know:

✔ Click the Help Topics button to return directly to the contents screen.

✔ If you find a Help topic that you consider uncommonly useful, click the Options button and then choose the Print Topic command from the menu that appears.

✔ If you see an underlined word or phrase, you can click it to zip to a Help page that describes that word or phrase. By following these underlined words, you can bounce your way around from Help page to Help page until you eventually find the help you need.

✔ Sometimes, Help offers several choices under a heading such as "What do you want to do?" Each choice is preceded by a little button; click the button to display step-by-step help for that choice.

✔ You can retrace your steps by clicking the Help window's Back button. You can use Back over and over again, retracing all your steps if necessary.

✔ Help operates as a separate program, so you can work within PowerPoint while the Help window remains on-screen. The Help window has a stay-on-top feature, which causes the Help window to remain visible even when you are working in the PowerPoint window. If the Help window gets in the way, you can move it out of the way by dragging it by the title bar. Or you can minimize it by clicking the minimize button in the top-right corner of the window.

✔ When you've had enough of Help, you can dismiss it by pressing Esc, choosing File⇨Exit, or double-clicking Help's control box in the upper-left corner of the Help window.

Take-You-by-the-Hand Help

Some PowerPoint help screens do more than just tell you what to do; they actually show you by using animation. For example, if you choose "Delete a slide" from "Working With Slides," the mouse pointer slowly moves to the Edit menu and then highlights the Edit⇨Delete Slide command. Then a text box explaining how to delete a slide appears, as shown in Figure 6-5.

Searching for Lost Help Topics

If you can't find help for a nasty problem by browsing through the Help Contents, try using the Help Index. It lets you browse through an alphabetical listing of all the Help topics that are available. With luck, you can quickly find the help you're looking for.

When you click the Index tab in the Help dialog box, the screen shown in Figure 6-6 is displayed. Here, you can type the text that you want to search for to zip quickly through the list to the words you want to find.

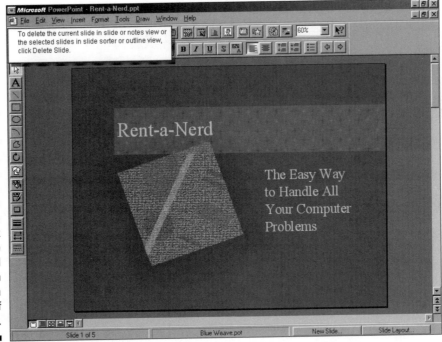

Figure 6-5: Some of PowerPoint's Help topics use animation to demonstrate how a task should be performed and then display a summary of the steps.

Figure 6-6:
Using the
Index.

If you see a match that looks as if it may be helpful, double-click it. Doing so either takes you directly to help for that topic or displays a list of related topics, as shown in Figure 6-7. Double-click the topic you want to display.

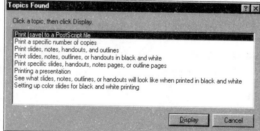

Figure 6-7:
PowerPoint
displays a
list of
related Help
topics.

If the index doesn't turn up what you're looking for, try clicking the Find tab in the Help Topics dialog box. The first time you do so, Help offers to build a *find index* — a file that contains every word that appears anywhere within all of PowerPoint's help. Click Next, then click Finish, and wait a moment while the find index is created.

After you've created a find index, you can use it to locate help on any topic imaginable. Using Find is a three-step process, as shown in Figure 6-8. First, you type the word you're looking for. Then you select one of several alternative words Help offers to narrow the search. Then you double-click the specific help topic you want to display.

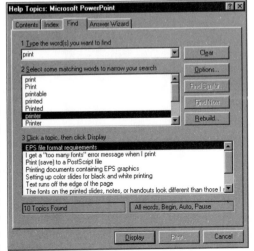

Figure 6-8:
Using the
Find
command to
locate help
on an
obscure
topic.

Using the Answer Wizard

PowerPoint's *Answer Wizard* is supposed to make help easier to find for novice users, and sometimes it actually works. Rather than search for individual words, the Answer Wizard lets you type in what you want to do in normal English. Then the Answer Wizard attempts to locate help topics that relate to your request.

For example, Figure 6-9 shows the Answer Wizard's response to a request for help on how to "Print more than one copy at a time." As you can see, the Answer Wizard found several help topics that it thinks may contain the answer to your question. The first topic — "Print a specific number of copies" — is right on the money. Some of the other topics in the list seem unrelated, such as "Copy or duplicate objects" or "Control what happens when you start Microsoft PowerPoint." Although the Answer Wizard is apt to come up with more unrelated topics as relevant ones, it usually comes up with one or two topics that fit the bill.

There are two ways to conjure up the Answer Wizard:

✔ Choose the Help⇨Answer Wizard command.

✔ Choose the Help⇨Microsoft PowerPoint Help Topics command and then click the Answer Wizard tab.

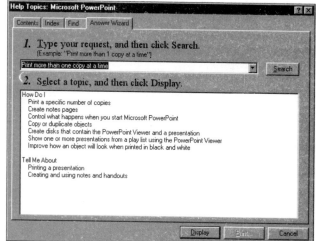

Figure 6-9:
Using the
Answer
Wizard.

Getting Help on The Microsoft Network

Microsoft's new online service, called *The Microsoft Network,* or *MSN* for short, is yet another way to get help with PowerPoint or any other Microsoft program. All you need to use MSN is a modem and a credit card.

To make MSN easy to use, Microsoft added a <u>H</u>elp⇨The Microsoft <u>N</u>etwork to PowerPoint and to other Microsoft Office programs. When you choose this command, a dialog box listing the various support forums within MSN appears. Double-click MICROSOFT POWERPOINT 95 FORUM.MCC, and you are automatically connected to MSN's PowerPoint support forum. Once there, you can compose a detailed message explaining your problem or question. Then you can check back in a day or two to see if another MSN user or a Microsoft representative has posted an answer to your question.

The only drawback to using The Microsoft Network is the cost. Before you can use MSN, you must sign up for the service — a process that includes handing over a credit card number. Microsoft bills you $4.95 each month for the privilege of using MSN for three hours each month. If you use MSN more than three hours, additional hours are billed at $2.95 per hour. If you're not careful, you can easily wind up spending $50 or more each month on MSN charges.

For more information about MSN, check out my book, *The Microsoft Network For Dummies* (IDG Books Worldwide, Inc.).

Part II
Looking Mahvelous

The 5th Wave — By Rich Tennant

"Remember, Charles and Di can be pasted next to anyone but each other, and your Elvis should appear bald and slightly hunched- nice Big Foot, Brad- keep your two-headed animals in the shadows and your alien spacecrafts crisp and defined."

In this part...

1 read recently that Roseanne Arnold had a slew of cosmetic surgeries as part of a take-control-of-your-life binge. The chapters in this part are all about cosmetic surgery for your presentations. You'll learn how to perform such procedures as typosuction, ClipArt-lifts, and color tucks.

The good news is that if health care reform ever goes through, the government might even pick up the tab!

Chapter 7
Fabulous Text Formats

- -

In This Chapter

▶ Using bold, italics, underlining, and other character effects

▶ Changing the text font and size

▶ Using bullets and colors

▶ Lining things up

▶ Tabbing and indenting

▶ Spacing things out

- -

A good presentation should be like a fireworks show: At every new slide, the audience gasps, "O-o-o-h. A-a-a-h." The audience is so stunned by the spectacular appearance of your slides that no one really bothers to read them.

This chapter gets you on the road toward ooohs and aaahs by showing you how to format text. If you use the AutoContent Wizard or base your new presentations on a template, your text is already formatted acceptably. But to really pull out the pyrotechnic stops, you have to know a few basic formatting tricks.

Many of PowerPoint's text-formatting capabilities work the same as Microsoft Word's do. If you want to format text a certain way and you know how to do it in Word, try formatting the same way in PowerPoint. Odds are that it works.

Changing the Look of Your Characters

PowerPoint enables you to change the look of individual characters in subtle or drastic ways. You can control all character attributes by way of the Font dialog box, which you summon by using the Format⇨Font command (see Figure 7-1).

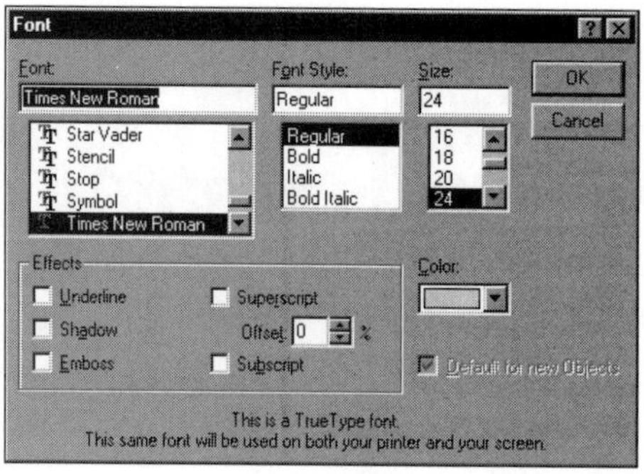

Figure 7-1:
The
cumbersome
Font dialog
box.

The Font dialog box is a bit cumbersome to use, but fortunately PowerPoint provides an assortment of shortcuts for your formatting pleasure. These shortcuts are listed in Table 7-1; the procedures for using them are described in this section.

Table 7-1	**Character-Formatting Shortcuts**	
Button	*Keyboard Shortcut*	*Format*
 **B**	Ctrl+B	**Bold**
 *I*	Ctrl+I	*Italic*
 U	Ctrl+U	Underline
(none)	Ctrl+spacebar	Normal
 Times New Roman	Ctrl+Shift+F	Font
 24	Ctrl+Shift+P	Change point size
 A	Ctrl+Shift+>	Increase point size
 A	Ctrl+Shift+<	Decrease point size
 A	(none)	Text color
 S	(none)	Text shadow

It's true — PowerPoint has many keyboard shortcuts for character formatting. You don't have to learn them all, though. The only ones I know and use routinely are for bold, italic, underline, and normal. Learn those and you'll be in good shape. You get the added bonus that these keyboard shortcuts are the same as the shortcuts many other Windows programs use, including Microsoft Word 6.

If you want, you can instruct these formats to gang-tackle some text. In other words, text can be bold, italic, and underlined for extra, extra emphasis. You can gang-tackle text with any combination of formats you want.

You also can remove all text formats in one swell foop by highlighting the text and pressing Ctrl+spacebar.

Most of the formatting options covered in this chapter are available only in Slide or Notes Pages view. If you try to apply a format and nothing happens, switch to Slide or Notes Pages view and try again.

Another way to summon the Font dialog box is to highlight the text you want to format and right-click the mouse. A menu appears. Choose the Font option from the menu and voilà! — the Font dialog box appears.

To boldly go . . .

Want to emphasize a point? Make it bold. Remember: Martin Luther said that if you must sin, sin boldly.

To make existing text bold, follow these steps:

1. Highlight the text that you want to make bold.

 2. Press Ctrl+B or click the Bold button (shown in the margin) on the Formatting toolbar.

To type new text in boldface, follow these steps:

 1. Press Ctrl+B or click the Bold button on the Formatting toolbar.

2. Type some text.

Make a bold effort.

3. Press Ctrl+B or click the Bold button to return to typing normal text.

You can use the Format⇨Font command to make text bold, but who wants to mess with a cumbersome dialog box when you can click the Bold button or press Ctrl+B instead? The rule is to use whatever is easiest for you.

You can remove the bold attribute also by highlighting the bold text and pressing Ctrl+spacebar. This technique removes not only the bold attribute but also other character attributes, such as italics and underlining. In other words, Ctrl+spacebar returns the text to normal.

Italics

Another way to emphasize a word is to italicize it. To italicize existing text, follow these steps:

1. **Highlight the text you want to italicize.**

2. **Press Ctrl+I or click the Italic button (shown in the margin) on the Formatting toolbar.**

To type new text in italics, follow these steps:

1. **Press Ctrl+I or click the Italic button on the Formatting toolbar.**

2. **Type some text.**

   Don't be afraid, Luke.

3. **Press Ctrl+I or click the Italic button to return to typing normal text.**

The cumbersome Format⇨Font command has an italic option, but why bother? Ctrl+I and the Italic button are too easy to ignore.

Pressing Ctrl+spacebar removes italics along with any other character formatting you applied. Use this key combination to return text to normal or, as NASA would say, to "reestablish nominal text."

Underlines

Back in the days of typewriters, underlining was the only way to add emphasis to text. You can underline text in PowerPoint, but you may as well use a typewriter. Underlining usually looks out of place in today's jazzy presentations, unless you're shooting for a nostalgic effect.

To underline existing text, follow these steps:

1. **Highlight the text you want to underline.**

2. **Press Ctrl+U or click the Underline button (shown in the margin) on the Formatting toolbar.**

To type new text and have it automatically underlined, follow these steps:

1. **Press Ctrl+U or click the Underline button on the Formatting toolbar.**

2. **Type some text.**

3. **Press Ctrl+U or click the Underline button to return to typing normal text.**

The Format⇨Font command enables you to underline text, but Ctrl+U or the Underline button is easier to use.

You can remove the underlines and all other character formats by highlighting the text and pressing Ctrl+spacebar.

Big and little characters

If text is hard to read or you simply want to draw attention to it, you can make part of the text bigger than the surrounding text.

To increase or decrease the font size for existing text, follow these steps:

1. **Highlight the text whose size you want to change.**

2. **To increase the font size, press Ctrl+Shift+> or click the Increase Font Size button (shown in the margin) on the Formatting toolbar.**

   To decrease the font size, press Ctrl+Shift+< or click the Decrease Font Size text box (shown in the margin) on the Formatting toolbar.

   To set the font to a specific size, press Ctrl+Shift+P or click the Font Size button (shown in the margin) on the Formatting toolbar and type the point size you want.

To type new text in a different font size, change the font size by using a method from Step 2. Then type away. Change back to the original font size when you are finished.

Again, you can use the Format⇨Font command to change the point size, but why bother when the controls are right there on the Formatting toolbar? Only a masochist would mess with the Format⇨Font command.

Ctrl+spacebar clears font attributes, such as bold and italic, but it cannot reset the font size.

Text fonts

If you don't like the looks of a text font, you can easily switch to a different font. To change the font for existing text, follow these steps:

1. **Highlight the text whose font you can't stand.**

2. **Click the arrow next to the Font control on the Formatting toolbar. A list of available fonts appears. Click the one you want to use.**

   Or press Ctrl+Shift+F and then press the down-arrow key to display the font choices.

To type new text in a different font, change the font as described in Step 2 and begin typing. Change back to the original font when you are finished.

Yes, yes, yes — with the Format⇨Font command, you can change the font. But with the Font control sitting right there on the Formatting toolbar for the whole world to see, why waste time navigating your way through menus and dialog boxes?

Pressing Ctrl+spacebar does not reset the font.

If you want to change the font for all the slides in your presentation, you should switch to Slide Master view and then change the font. Details on how to do so are covered in the next chapter.

PowerPoint automatically moves the fonts you use the most to the head of the font list. This feature makes it even easier to pick your favorite font.

Don't overdo it with fonts! Just because you have 37 different typefaces doesn't mean that you should try to use them all on the same slide. Don't mix more than two or three typefaces on a slide, and use fonts consistently throughout the presentation. PowerPoint's Style Checker, which I cover back in Chapter 4, reminds you if you use too many fonts.

The color purple

Color is an excellent way to draw attention to text in a slide if, of course, your slides print in color or you can display them on a color monitor. Follow this procedure for changing text color:

1. **Highlight the text whose color you want to change.**

2. **Click the Text Color button (shown in the margin) on the Formatting toolbar.**

   A little box with color choices appears. Click the color you want to use.

To type new text in a different color, change the color and then begin typing. When you have had enough, change back to the original color and continue.

If you don't like any color that the Text Color button offers, click where it reads *Other Color*. A bigger dialog box with more color choices appears. If you still cannot find the right shade of teal, click the Custom tab and have at it. Check out Chapter 9 if you need still more color help.

If you want to change the text color for your entire presentation, do so on the Slide Master (see Chapter 8 for details).

The shadow knows

Adding a shadow behind your text can make the text stand out against its background, which makes the entire slide easier to read. For that reason, many of the templates supplied with PowerPoint use shadows. These steps show you how to apply a text shadow:

1. **Highlight the text you want to shadow.**

2. **Click the Shadow button (shown in the margin).**

Sorry — PowerPoint has no keyboard shortcut for this one. Oh, well. It's about time you finally learn how to use the mouse. You can set the shadow format by using the Format⇨Font command if you just can't master the mouse (or you don't have one).

Embossed text

When you choose to emboss text, PowerPoint adds a dark shadow below the text and a light shadow above it to produce an embossed effect, as shown in Figure 7-2. Try it. It's very cool.

To create embossed text, follow these simple steps:

1. **Highlight the text you want to emboss.**

2. **Use the Format⇨Font command to pop up the Font dialog box.**

   Sorry — PowerPoint has no keyboard shortcut or toolbar button for embossing. You have to do it the hard way.

3. **Check the Emboss option.**

4. **Click the OK button.**

When you emboss text, PowerPoint changes the text color to the background color to enhance the embossed effect.

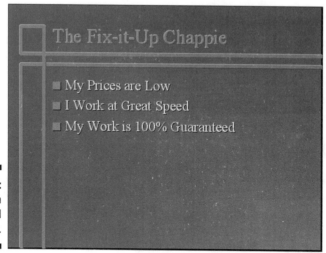

Figure 7-2:
A slide with embossed text.

Embossed text is hard to read in smaller point sizes. This effect is best reserved for large titles.

Biting the Bullet

Most presentations have at least some slides that include a bulleted list — a series of paragraphs accented by special characters lovingly known as *bullets*. In the old days, you had to add bullets one at a time. Nowadays, PowerPoint comes with a semiautomatic bullet shooter that is illegal in 27 states.

To add bullets to a paragraph or series of paragraphs:

1. **Highlight the paragraphs to which you want to add bullets.**

   To add a bullet to just one paragraph, you don't have to highlight the entire paragraph. Just place the cursor anywhere in the paragraph.

 2. **Click the Bullet button (shown in the margin).**

   PowerPoint adds a bullet to each paragraph you select.

The Bullet button works like a toggle: Press it once to add bullets and press it again to remove bullets. To remove bullets from previously bulleted text, therefore, you select the text and click the Bullet button again.

If you don't like the appearance of the bullets PowerPoint uses, you can choose a different bullet character by using the Format⇨Bullet command. This command displays the Bullet dialog box, shown in Figure 7-3. From this dialog box, you can choose a different bullet character, change the bullet's color, or change its size relative to the text size.

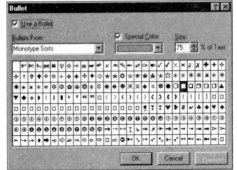

Figure 7-3:
The Bullet
dialog box.

This list shows you some pointers for using the Bullet dialog box:

✔ Notice the Use a Bullet check box in the upper-left corner of the Bullet dialog box. Check this box to add a bullet to your text; uncheck it to remove the bullet.

✔ Several collections of characters are available for choosing bullet characters. If you don't like any of the bullet characters displayed on-screen, change the option in the Bullets From drop-down list box. The Wingdings collection contains such useful bullets as pointing fingers, a skull and crossbones, and a time bomb. You may see other collections in the Bullets From list box as well.

✔ If the bullet characters don't seem large enough, increase the Size value in the Bullet dialog box. The size is specified as a percentage of the text size.

✔ To change the bullet color, check the Special Color check box and choose the color you want to use. When you click Special Color, a menu of eight color choices appears. If the color you're looking for isn't there, you can click Other Color to call forth a dialog box offering 128 color choices. If you still cannot find a color you like, click the Other Color dialog box's Custom tab and pick from among 64 million colors. For more information about using colors, see Chapter 9.

You can use certain bullet characters for good comic effect in your presentations. Be creative, but also be careful. A thumbs-down bullet next to the name of your boss may get a laugh, but it may also get you fired.

Lining Things Up

PowerPoint enables you to control the way your text lines up on the slide. You can center text, line it up flush left or flush right, or justify it. You can change these alignments by using the Format➪Alignment command, or you can use the convenient toolbar buttons and keyboard shortcuts.

Centering text

Centered text lines up right down the middle of the slide. (Actually, down the middle of the text object that contains the text; A text line appears centered on the slide only if the text object is centered on the slide.)

To center existing text, follow this procedure:

1. **Select the line or lines you want to center.**

2. **Click the Center button (shown in the margin) on the Formatting toolbar or press Ctrl+E.**

   It's true that E doesn't stand for center. Ctrl+C was already taken (for Copy, remember?), so the Microsoft jocks decided to use Ctrl+E. They consider it to be some sort of demented practical joke.

3. **Admire your newly centered text.**

To type new centered text, skip Step 1; just click the Center button or press Ctrl+E and begin typing.

Flush to the left

Centered text is sometimes hard to read. Align the text *flush left,* and the text lines up neatly along the left edge of the text object. All the bullets line up too. These steps show you how to make text flush left:

1. **Select the line or lines you want to scoot to the left.**

2. **Click the Align Left button (shown in the margin) on the Formatting toolbar or press Ctrl+L.**

   Hallelujah! The L in Ctrl+L stands for — you guessed it — *left.*

3. **Toast yourself for your cleverness.**

If you want to type new flush-left text, just click the Align Left button or press Ctrl+L and begin typing.

Other terms for flush left are *left justified* and *ragged right.* Just thought you may want to know.

Flush to the right

Yes, you can align text against the right edge too. I don't know why you want to, but you can.

1. **Select the line or lines you want to shove to the right.**

2. **Press Ctrl+R.**

   Sorry, PowerPoint has no button for aligning text on the right. Mercifully, the keyboard shortcut is easy to remember. R equals right — get it?

3. **Have a drink on me.**

If you want to type new flush-right text, just press Ctrl+R and continue.

Other terms for flush right are *right justified* and *ragged left.* With this extra cocktail party verbiage to add to your vocabulary, you'll be the hit at any nerd party.

 Actually, I lied about there being no toolbar button for right-justifying text. Although no such button appears in the Formatting toolbar as supplied by Microsoft, PowerPoint does come with a hidden Align Right button that you can access via the Tools⇨Customize command.

Stand up, sit down, justify!

You also can tell PowerPoint to *justify* text: to line up both the left and right edges. The keyboard shortcut is Ctrl+J (J is for *justified*). And although there is no Justify button in the Formatting toolbar, you can add such a button via the Tools⇨Customize command.

Messing with Tabs and Indents

PowerPoint enables you to set tab stops to control the placement of text within a text object. For most presentations, you don't have to fuss with tabs. Each paragraph is indented according to its level in the outline, and the amount of indentation for each outline level is preset by the template you use to create the presentation.

Although there's little need to, you can mess with the indent settings and tab stops if you're adventurous and have no real work to do today. Here's how you do it:

1. **Click the Slide button to switch to Slide view.**

   You cannot mess with tabs or indents in Outline view. You can make changes in Notes Pages view, but Slide view is more convenient.

2. **Activate the ruler by using the View⇨Ruler command.**

   Rulers appear above and to the left of the presentation window and show the current tab and indentation settings. You must activate the ruler if you want to change tab stops or text indents.

   Figure 7-4 shows a PowerPoint presentation with the ruler activated.

3. **Select the text object whose tabs or indents you want to change.**

   Each text object has its own tabs and indents setting. After you click a text object, the ruler shows that object's tabs and indents.

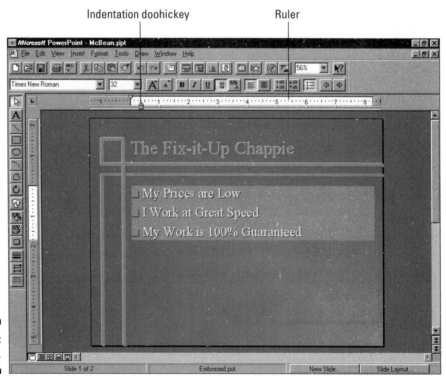

Figure 7-4:
The ruler.

4. Click the ruler to add a tab stop.

Move the mouse pointer to the ruler location where you want to add a tab stop and then click. A tab stop appears.

5. Grab the indentation doohickey and drag it to change the indentation.

Try dragging the different parts of the indentation doohickey to see what happens. Have fun. Good luck.

Tabs and indents can be pretty testy, but fortunately you don't have to mess with them for most presentations. If you're one of the unlucky ones, keep these pointers in mind:

✔ Each text object has its own tab settings. The tab settings for an object apply to all the paragraphs within the object, so you can't change tab settings for individual paragraphs within a text object.

✔ The ruler shows as many as five different indentation levels, one for each outline level. Only those levels used in the text object are shown, so if the object has only one outline level, only one indent is shown. To see additional indents, demote text within the object by pressing the Tab key.

If all this stuff about outline levels and demotions upsets you, refer to Chapter 3, where you can find a comforting explanation of PowerPoint outlines.

Each text object is set up initially with default tab stops set at every inch. When you add a tab stop, any default tab stops to the left of the new tab stop disappear.

To remove a tab stop, use the mouse to drag the stop off the ruler (click the tab stop, drag it off the ruler, and then release the mouse button).

Spacing Things Out

Feeling a little spaced out? Try tightening the space between text lines. Feeling cramped? Space out the lines a little. These steps show you how to do it all:

1. Switch to Slide view.

You can change line spacing in Slide view or Notes Pages view only. Slide view is more convenient.

2. Highlight the paragraph or paragraphs whose line spacing you want to change.

Don't even bother with this stuff about tab types

PowerPoint isn't limited to just boring left-aligned tabs. In all, it has four distinct types of tabs: left, right, center, and decimal. The square button at the far left side of the ruler tells you which type of tab is added when you click the ruler. Click this button to cycle through the four types of tabs:

L Standard left-aligned tab. Press Tab to advance the text to the tab stop.

⌐ Right-aligned tab. Text is aligned flush right with the tab stop.

⊥ Centered tab. Text lines up centered over the tab stop.

⊥· Decimal tab. Numbers line up with the decimal point centered over the tab stop.

3. Use the Format⇨Line Spacing command.

Sorry, PowerPoint has no keyboard shortcut for this step. The Line Spacing dialog box, shown in Figure 7-5, suddenly appears.

4. Change the dialog box settings to adjust the line spacing.

Figure 7-5:
The Line
Spacing
dialog box.

Line Spacing refers to the space between the lines within a paragraph. Before Paragraph adds extra space before the paragraph, and After Paragraph adds extra space after the paragraph.

You can specify spacing in terms of lines or points. The size of a line varies depending on the size of the text font. If you specify spacing in terms of points, PowerPoint uses the exact spacing you specify, regardless of the size of the text font.

5. Click the OK button or press Enter.

 You can also increase or decrease the spacing between paragraphs by clicking the Increase Paragraph Spacing or Decrease Paragraph Spacing buttons (shown in the margin) found in the Formatting toolbar.

Chapter 8

Masters of the Universe Meet the Templates of Doom

• •

In This Chapter

▶ Finding out stuff about Masters you have to know

▶ Changing Masters

▶ Using Masters

▶ Working with headers and footers

▶ Using templates

• •

*W*ant to add a bit of text to every slide in your presentation? Or maybe add your name and phone number at the bottom of your audience handouts? Or place a picture of Rush Limbaugh at the extreme right side of each page of your speaker notes?

Masters are the surefire way to add something to every slide. No need to toil separately at each slide. Add something to the Master and it automatically shows up on every slide. Remove it from the Master and — poof! — it disappears from every slide. Very convenient.

Masters govern all aspects of a slide's appearance: its background color, objects that appear on every slide, text that appears on all slides, and more.

Although tinkering with the Masters lets you fine-tune the appearance of a presentation, changing the presentation's template allows you to make drastic changes to a presentation's appearance. A *template* is a special type of presentation file that holds Masters. When you apply a template to an existing presentation, the presentation's existing Masters are replaced with the Masters from the template, thus completely changing the appearance of the presentation without changing its content.

With templates, you can easily try on different looks for your presentation before settling on a final design.

Working with Masters

In PowerPoint, a Master governs the appearance of all the slides or pages in a presentation. Each presentation has four Masters:

- ✓ **Slide Master:** Dictates the format of your slides. You work with this Master most often as you tweak your slides to cosmetic perfection.

- ✓ **Title Master:** Prescribes the layout of the presentation's title slide. This Master allows you to give your title slides a different look from the other slides in your presentation.

- ✓ **Handout Master:** Controls the look of printed handouts.

- ✓ **Notes Master:** Determines the characteristics of printed speaker notes.

Each Master specifies the appearance of text (font, size, and color, for example), the slide's background color, and text or other objects you want to appear on each slide or page.

Each presentation has just one of each type of Master. The Master governs the appearance of all slides or pages in the presentation.

Masters are not optional. Every presentation has them. You can, however, override the formatting of objects contained in the Master for a particular slide. This capability enables you to vary the appearance of slides when it's necessary.

The quick way to call up a Master is to hold down the Shift key while you click one of the view buttons at the left side of the status bar at the bottom of the screen.

Changing the Slide Master

If you don't like the layout of your slides, call up the Slide Master and do something about it, as shown in these steps:

 1. **Choose the** **View⇨Master⇨Slide Master** **command or hold down the Shift key while clicking the Slide View button.**

If you use the View⇨Master command, a submenu pops up with a listing of the four Masters. Choose Slide Master to call up the Slide Master.

2. **Behold the Slide Master in all its splendor.**

Figure 8-1 shows a typical Slide Master. You can see the placeholders for the slide title and body text in addition to other background objects. Note also that the Slide Master includes placeholders for three objects that appear at the bottom of each slide: the Date Area, Footer Area, and Number Area. These special areas are used by the View⊃Header and Footer command and are described later in this chapter, under the heading "Using Headers and Footers."

3. Make any formatting changes you want.

Select the text you want to apply a new style to and make your formatting changes. If you want all the slide titles to be in italics, for example, select the title text and press Ctrl+I or click the Italic button on the Formatting toolbar.

If you're not sure how to change text formats, consult Chapter 7.

 4. Click the Slide View button to return to Slide view.

The effect of your Slide Master changes should be apparent immediately.

PowerPoint applies character formats such as bold, italics, point size, and font to entire paragraphs when you work in Slide Master view. You don't have to select the entire paragraph before you apply a format; just click anywhere in the paragraph.

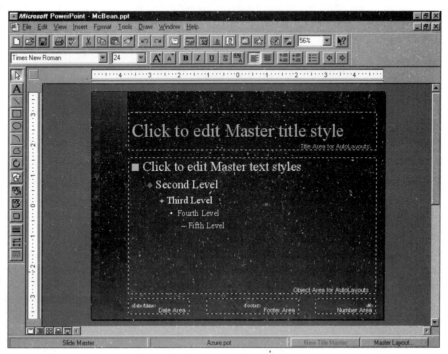

Figure 8-1:
A Slide
Master.

Notice that the body object contains paragraphs for five outline levels formatted with different point sizes, indentations, and bullet styles. If you want to change the way an outline level is formatted, this is the place.

You can type all you want in the title or object area placeholders, but the text you type doesn't appear on the slides. The text that appears in these placeholders is provided only so that you can see the effect of the formatting changes you apply. (To insert text that appears on each slide, see the next section, "Adding recurring text.")

You can edit any of the other objects on the Master by clicking them. Unlike the title and object area placeholders, any text you type in other Slide Master objects appears exactly as you type it on each slide.

Adding recurring text

To add recurring text to each slide, follow this procedure:

1. **Call up the Slide Master if it's not displayed already.**

   The menu command is View➪Master➪Slide Master. Or you can Shift+click the Slide View button.

    2. **Click the Text Tool button (shown in the margin) on the Drawing toolbar.**

   This step highlights the text button. The mouse cursor turns into an upside-down cross.

3. **Click where you want to add text.**

   PowerPoint places a text object at that location.

4. **Type the text that you want to appear on each slide.**

   For example: **Call 1-800-555-NERD today! Don't delay! Operators standing by!**

5. **Format the text however you want (bold, for example — Ctrl+B).**

    6. **Click the Slide View button (shown in the margin) to return to Slide view.**

   Now's the time to gloat over your work. Lasso some coworkers and show 'em how proud you are.

You can add other types of objects to the Slide Master, too. You can click the Clip Art button (shown in the margin) on the Standard toolbar, for example, to insert any of the clip art pictures supplied with PowerPoint. Or you can use the Insert➪Sound command to insert a sound bite. (Clip art is described in detail in Chapter 10; sound bites in Chapter 15. Other types of objects are covered in the other chapters in Part III.)

After you place an object on the Slide Master, you can grab it with the mouse and move it around or resize it any way you want. The object appears in the same location and size on each slide.

To delete an object from the Slide Master, click it and press the Delete key. To delete a text object, you must first click the object and then click again on the object frame. Then press Delete.

If you can't highlight the object no matter how many times you click it, you probably have returned to Slide view. Shift+click the Slide View button or choose the View⇨Master⇨Slide Master command again to call up the Slide Master.

Changing the Master color scheme

You can use the Slide Master to change the color scheme used for all slides in a presentation. To do that, follow these steps:

1. **Choose the View⇨Master⇨Slide Master command or Shift+click the Slide button to summon the Slide Master.**

2. **Choose the Format⇨Slide Color Scheme command to change the color scheme.**

   Treat yourself to a bag of Doritos if it works the first time.

PowerPoint color schemes are hefty enough that I have devoted an entire chapter to them. Skip to Chapter 9 now if you can't wait.

If you don't have a color printer, don't waste your time messing with the color scheme unless you're going to make your presentation on-screen. Mauve, teal, azure, and cerulean all look like gray when they're printed on a noncolor laser printer.

PowerPoint's color schemes were chosen by professionals who are color-blind in no more than one eye. Stick to these schemes to avoid embarrassing color combinations! (I wish that my sock drawer came with a similar color-scheme feature.)

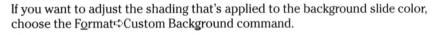

If you want to adjust the shading that's applied to the background slide color, choose the Format⇨Custom Background command.

Changing the Title Master

PowerPoint keeps a separate Master layout for title slides. That way, you can give your title slides a different layout than the other slides in your presentation.

There are two ways to call up the Title Master:

- ✔ Display the title slide and then Shift+click the Slide button.
- ✔ Choose the <u>V</u>iew⇨<u>M</u>aster⇨<u>T</u>itle Master command.

Figure 8-2 shows a Title Master. As you can see, it contains the same layout elements as the Slide Master, except that the "Object Area for AutoLayouts" is replaced with "Subtitle Area for AutoLayouts," and the title area is centered on the slide.

Changing the Handout and Notes Masters

Like the Slide Master, the Handout and Notes Masters contain formatting information that's automatically applied to your presentation. This section tells you how you can modify these Masters.

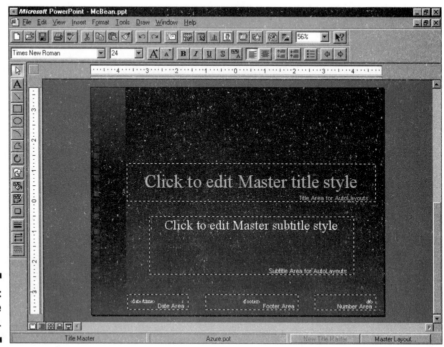

Figure 8-2:
A Title
Master.

Changing the Handout Master

Follow these simple steps to change the Handout Master:

1. **Choose the <u>V</u>iew⇨<u>M</u>aster⇨Han<u>d</u>out Master command or hold down the Shift key and click the Slide Sorter View button.**

   The Handout Master rears its ugly head, as shown in Figure 8-3.

2. **Mess around with it.**

   The Handout Master contains immovable placeholders for slides printed two, three, and six per page. You cannot move these, resize them, or delete them. Sniff. But you can add or change elements that you want to appear on each handout page, such as your name and phone number, a page number, or maybe a good lawyer joke.

3. **Go back.**

   Click the Slide View button, for example, to return to Slide view.

4. **Print a handout to see whether your changes take effect.**

   Handout Master elements are invisible until you print them, so you should print at least one handout page to check your work.

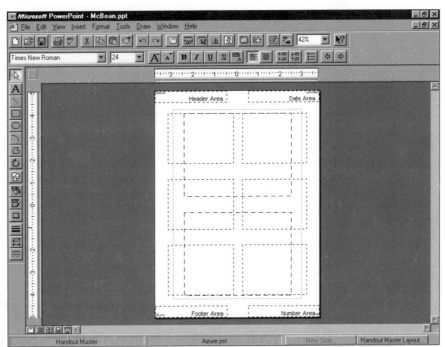

Figure 8-3:
A Handout
Master.

When you print handout pages, the slides themselves are formatted according to the Slide Master. You cannot change the appearance of the slides from the Handout Master.

Changing the Notes Master

Notes pages consist of a reduced image of the slide, plus notes you type to go along with the slide. For more information about creating and using notes pages, see Chapter 18.

When printed, notes pages are formatted according to the Notes Master. To change the Notes Master, follow these steps:

1. **Choose the <u>V</u>iew⇨<u>M</u>aster⇨<u>N</u>otes Master command or hold down the Shift key and click the Notes View button.**

   The Notes Master comes to life.

2. **Indulge yourself.**

   The Notes Master contains two placeholders: one for your notes text and the other for the slide. You can move or change the size of either of these objects, and you can change the format of the text in the notes place-holder. You also can add or change elements that you want to appear on each handout page.

3. **Click the Notes button to return to Notes Pages view.**

   Admire your handiwork. Unlike you do when using the Outline Master and Handout Master, you don't have to print anything to check the results of changes you make to the Notes Master. You can see them clearly when you switch to Notes Pages view.

At the least, you should add page numbers to your speaker notes. If you drop a stack of notes pages without page numbers, you will be up a creek without a paddle!

If public speaking gives you severe stomach cramps, add the text *Just picture them naked* to the Notes Master. It works every time for me.

Using Masters

You don't have to do anything special to apply the formats from a Master to your slide; all slides automatically pick up the Master format unless you specify otherwise. So this section really should be titled "Not Using Masters" because it talks about how to *not* use the formats provided by Masters.

Overriding the Master text style

To override the text style specified by a Slide Master or Notes Master, simply format the text however you want while you're working in Slide, Outline, or Notes Pages view. The formatting changes you make apply only to the selected text. The Slide Master and Notes Master aren't affected.

The only way to change one of the Masters is to do it directly by switching to the appropriate Master view. Thus, any formatting changes you make while in Slide view affect only that slide.

If you change the slide text style and then decide that you liked it better the way it was, you can quickly reapply the text style from the Slide Master by switching to Slide view and using the Format⇨Slide Layout command. A Slide Layout dialog box appears; click the Reapply button to restore text formatting to the format specified in the Slide Master.

If you change the notes text style and want to revert to the text style specified in the Notes Master, switch to Notes Pages view and use the Format⇨Notes Layout command. When the Notes Layout dialog box appears, check the Reapply Master check box and click OK.

The Ctrl+spacebar key combination clears all text attributes, including those specified in the Slide Master or Notes Master. This key combination can wreak havoc on your formatting efforts. Suppose that the Slide Master specifies shadowed text. If you italicize a word and then decide to remove the italics by pressing Ctrl+spacebar, the shadow is removed as well.

Changing the background for just one slide

Both Slide Masters and Notes Masters enable you to add background objects that appear on every slide or notes page in your presentation. You can, however, hide the background objects for selected slides or notes pages. You can also change the background color or effect used for an individual slide or notes page. These steps show you how:

1. **Display the slide or notes page you want to show with a plain background.**

2. **Summon either the Custom Background or Notes Background dialog box.**

   To change the background for a slide, use the Format⇨Custom Background command. The Custom Background dialog box appears, as shown in Figure 8-4. For notes, use Format⇨Notes Background. (The Notes Background dialog box looks much like the Custom Background dialog box; the only difference is their titles.)

Figure 8-4:
The Custom
Background
dialog box.

3. Check the Omit Background Graphics from Master check box.

Check this box if you want to hide the Master background objects.

4. Change the Background Fill if you wish.

You can change to a different background color, or you can add an effect such as a pattern fill or a texture. These details are covered in Chapter 9.

5. Click the Apply button or press Enter.

If you checked the Omit Background Graphics from Master check box (Step 3), the background objects from the Slide Master or Notes Master vanish from the slide or page, respectively. If you changed the background color or effect, you see that change, too.

Hiding background objects or changing the background color or effect applies only to the current slide or notes page. Other slides or notes pages are unaffected.

If you want to remove some but not all the background objects from a single slide, try this trick:

1. Follow the preceding procedure to hide background objects for the slide.

2. Call up the Slide Master (View⇨Master⇨Slide Master).

3. Hold down the Shift key and click each object that you want to appear on the slide.

4. Press Ctrl+C to copy these objects to the Clipboard.

5. Return to Slide view.

6. Press Ctrl+V to paste the objects from the Clipboard.

7. Choose the Draw⇨Send to Back command if the background objects obscure other slide objects or text.

Using Headers and Footers

Headers and footers provide a convenient way to place repeating text at the top or bottom of each slide, handout, or notes page. You can add the time and date, slide number or page number, or any other information that you want to appear on each slide or page, such as your name or the title of your presentation.

PowerPoint's Slide and Title Masters include three placeholders for such information:

✔ The *date area* can be used to display a date and time.

✔ The *number area* can be used to display the slide number.

✔ The *footer area* can be used to display any text that you want to see on each slide.

In addition, Handout and Notes Masters include a fourth placeholder:

✔ The *header area* provides an additional area for text that you want to see on each page.

Although the date, number, and footer areas normally appear at the bottom of the slide in the Slide and Title Masters, you can move them to the top by switching to Slide or Title Master view and then dragging the placeholders to the top of the slide.

Adding a date, number, or footer to slides

To add a date, a slide number, or a footer to your slides, follow these steps:

1. **Choose the View⇨Header and Footer command.**

   The Header and Footer dialog box appears, as shown in Figure 8-5. (If necessary, click the Slide tab so that you see the slide header and footer options as shown in the figure.)

2. **To display the date, check the Date and Time check box. Then select the date format you want in the list box beneath the Update Automatically option button.**

   Alternatively, you can type any text you wish in the Fixed text box. The text you type appears in the Date Area of the Slide or Title Master.

3. **To display slide numbers, check the Slide Number check box.**

4. **To display a footer on each slide, check the Footer check box and then type the text that you want to appear on each slide in the Footer text box.**

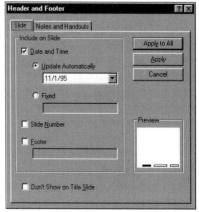

Figure 8-5:
The Header
and Footer
dialog box
for Slides.

For example, you might type your name, your company name, or the name of your presentation.

5. **If you want the date, number, and footer to appear on every slide except the title slide, check the Don't Show on Title Slide check box.**

6. **Click Apply to All.**

If you are going to be giving a presentation on a certain date in the future (for example, at a sales conference or a trade show), type the date that you will be giving the presentation on directly into the Fixed text box.

If you want to change the footer areas for just one slide, click Apply instead of Apply to All. This option comes in handy for those occasional slides that contain a graphic or a block of text that crowds up against the footer areas. You can easily suppress the footer information for that slide to make room for the large graphic or text.

Adding a header or footer to notes or handout pages

To add header and footer information to Notes or Handouts pages, follow the steps described in the preceding section, "Adding a date, number, or footer to slides," except click the Notes and Handouts tab when the Header and Footer dialog box appears. Clicking this tab displays the dialog box shown in Figure 8-6.

This dialog box is similar to the Header and Footer dialog box for Slides, except that it gives you an additional option to add a header that appears at the top of each page. After you indicate how you want to print the date, header, number, and footer areas, click the Apply to All button.

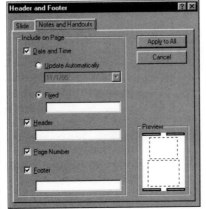

Figure 8-6:
The Header
and Footer
dialog box
for Notes
and
Handouts.

Editing the header and footer placeholders directly

If you wish, you can edit the text that appears in the header and footer place-holders directly. First, display the appropriate Master — Slide, Title, Handout, or Notes. Then click on the date, number, footer, or header placeholder and start typing.

You may notice that the placeholders include special codes for the options you indicated in the Header and Footer dialog box. For example, the Date place-holder may contain the text *<date,time>* if you indicated that the date should be displayed. You can type text before or after these codes, but you should leave the codes themselves alone.

Thank Heavens for Templates

If you had to create Slide Masters from scratch every time you built a new presentation, you probably would put PowerPoint back in its box and use it as a bookend. Creating a Slide Master is easy. Creating one that looks good is a different story. Making a good-looking Master is tough even for the artistically inclined. For right-brain, nonartistic types like me, it's next to impossible.

Thank heavens for templates. When you create a presentation, PowerPoint gives you the option of stealing Masters from an existing template presentation. Any PowerPoint presentation can serve as a template, including presentations you create yourself. But PowerPoint comes with more than 100 template presentations designed by professional artists who understand color combina-tions and balance and all that artsy stuff. Have a croissant and celebrate.

Because the templates that come with PowerPoint look good, any presentation you create by using one of them will look good, too. It's as simple as that. When you pick one of PowerPoint's templates, you can rest assured that you won't get laughed out of the auditorium because your slides look like they were designed by Dan Quayle. Better still, most of your audience will assume that you designed the slides yourself. "Geez," they'll say, "I didn't realize that you were so artistic. I don't remember a word you said, but the slides were absolutely stunning!"

In addition to Masters, the template also supplies the color scheme for your presentation. You can override it, of course, but you do so at your own risk. The color police are everywhere, you know. You don't want to be taken in for Felony Color Clash.

A *template* is simply a PowerPoint presentation file with predefined formatting settings. Templates use the special file extension POT, but you can also use ordinary PowerPoint presentation files (PPT) as templates. You can therefore use any of your own presentations as a template. If you make extensive changes to a presentation's Masters, you can use that presentation as a template for other presentations you create. Or you can save the presentation as a template by using the POT file extension.

Because a template is a presentation, you can open it and change it if you want.

Applying a different template

You're halfway through creating a new presentation when you realize that you can't stand the look of the slides. Oops — you picked the wrong template when you started the new presentation! Don't panic. PowerPoint enables you to assign a new presentation template at any time. These steps show you how:

1. **Choose the Format⇨Apply Design Template command.**

   The Apply Design Template dialog box appears, as shown in Figure 8-7.

2. **Rummage around for a template you like better.**

   Templates are stored in two folders that are found in the \MSOFFICE\TEMPLATES folder:

   - **PRESENTATIONS:** Contains 20 templates that include suggested content. These templates are used by the AutoContent Wizard to create skeleton presentations when you tell the Wizard the type of presentation you want to create.

   - **PRESENTATION DESIGNS:** Contains 28 designer templates. These templates do not contain sample content, but they look better than the templates found in PRESENTATIONS.

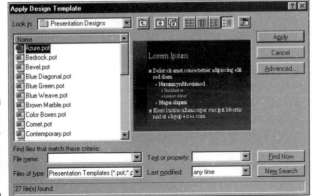

Figure 8-7:
The Apply
Design
Template
dialog box.

If you have a CD-ROM drive and purchased MS-Office or PowerPoint on CD-ROM, you'll find an additional 58 designer templates on the CD-ROM in the folder \VALUEPACK\PPTMPL.

When you click a presentation name, PowerPoint displays a preview of the template's appearance in the Apply Design Template dialog box.

3. **Click the Apply button or double-click the template filename to apply the template.**

Make sure that you like the new template better than the first one!

You may still want to make minor adjustments to the Slide Master to make the slides look just right.

When you apply a new template, PowerPoint copies the Masters and the color scheme into your presentation. As a result, any changes you made to the presentation's Masters or color scheme are lost. Too bad. If you added background objects to the Slide Master, you have to add them again.

You don't have to worry about the new template undoing any formatting changes that you have made to individual slides. PowerPoint remembers these deviations from the Master format when it applies a new template.

Another way to bring up the Apply Design Template dialog box is to double-click the name of the template in the status bar at the bottom of the PowerPoint window.

Creating a new template

If none of the templates that come with PowerPoint appeals to you, you can easily create your own. All you have to do is create a presentation with the Masters and the color scheme set up just the way you want and then save it as a template. Here are a few points to remember about templates:

- ✔ The design templates that come with PowerPoint have no slides in them. To create a template without any slides, choose the New button, and then click the Cancel button when the Add New Slide dialog box appears. Then choose the View➪Masters command to switch to the Slide, Title, Notes, or Handout Master.

- ✔ If you want to make minor modifications to one of the supplied templates, open the template by using the File➪Open command and then immediately save it under a new name by using the File➪Save As command. Then change the Masters and the color scheme. Don't forget to save the file again when you're finished!

- ✔ Your templates are easily accessible if you store them in the \MSOFFICE\TEMPLATES\PRESENTATION DESIGNS folder along with the templates supplied with PowerPoint.

- ✔ You can also create your own presentation templates complete with skeleton slides. Just create the template as a normal presentation and add however many slides you want to include. Then save the presentation as a template in the folder, \MSOFFICE\TEMPLATES\PRESENTATIONS.

Creating a new default template

When you create a new presentation, PowerPoint asks whether you want to base the presentation on an existing template or to create a blank presentation. This question is a little misleading because it suggests that the blank presentation doesn't use a template. It does — it uses a default template named BLANK PRESENTATION.POT to obtain bare-bones Masters and a black-on-white color scheme.

If you want to create your own default template, all you have to do is save your template file by using the filename BLANK PRESENTATION.POT in the \MSOFFICE\TEMPLATES folder. Then, whenever you create a blank presentation, the Masters and the color scheme are copied from your new default template rather than from the bland default template that comes with PowerPoint.

Make a copy of the original BLANK PRESENTATION.POT file before you overwrite it with your own changes. You may someday want to revert to PowerPoint's standard default template. To make a copy of the default template, open it and choose the File➪Save As command to save it with a new name (for example, OLD BLANK PRESENTATION.POT).

These steps show you how to create a new default template:

1. **Open the default template.**

   It's named BLANK PRESENTATION.POT and lives in the \MSOFFICE\TEMPLATES folder.

2. **Make any changes you want.**

   For example, add your name to the Slide Master and add the page number and date to the Notes Master, Title Master, and Handout Master.

3. **Save your changes.**

Chapter 9

When I Am Old, I Shall Make My Slides Purple

In This Chapter

▶ Using color schemes

▶ Changing the colors in a color scheme

▶ Creating new colors

▶ Shading the slide background

▶ Coloring objects and text

▶ Copying colors from other objects

*W*elcome to the Wonderful World of Color. Here is your opportunity to unleash the repressed artist hidden deep within you. Take up your palette, grasp your brush firmly, and prepare to attack the empty canvas of your barren slides.

PowerPoint enables you to use more than 16 million colors, but you shouldn't feel obligated to use them all right away. Pace yourself. Now would be a good time to grow a goatee or to cut off your ear. (Just kidding.)

Using Color Schemes

PowerPoint's templates come with built-in *color schemes*, which are coordinated sets of colors chosen by color professionals. Microsoft paid these people enormous sums of money to debate the merits of using mauve text on a teal background. You can use these professionally designed color schemes, or you can create your own if you think that you have a better eye than Microsoft's hired color guns.

As far as I'm concerned, PowerPoint's color schemes are the best thing to come along since Peanut M&Ms. Without color schemes, people like me are free to pick and choose from among the 16 million or so colors that PowerPoint lets you incorporate into your slides. The resulting slides can easily appear next to Cher and Roseanne in *People* magazine's annual "Worst Dressed of the Year" issue.

Each color scheme has eight colors, with each color designated for a particular use, as shown in this list:

- **Background color:** Used for the slide background.

- **Text-and-lines color:** Used for any text or drawn lines that appear on the slide, with the exception of the title text (described in this list). It is usually a color that contrasts with the background color. If the background color is dark, the text-and-lines color is generally light, and vice versa.

- **Shadows color:** Used to produce shadow effects for objects drawn on the slide. It is usually a darker version of the background color.

- **Title text color:** Used for the slide's title text. Like the text-and-lines color, the title text color contrasts with the background color so that the text is readable. The title text usually complements the text-and-lines color to provide an evenly balanced effect. (That sounds like something an artist would say, doesn't it?)

- **Fills color:** When you create an object, such as a rectangle or an ellipse, this color is the default fill color to color the object.

- **Accent colors:** The last three colors in the color scheme. They are used for odds and ends that you add to your slide. They may be used to color the bars in a bar chart, for example, or the slices in a pie chart.

Each slide in your presentation can have its own color scheme. The Slide Master also has a color scheme, used for all slides that don't specify their own deviant color scheme. To ensure that your slides have a uniform look, simply allow them to pick up the color scheme from the Slide Master. If you want one slide to stand out from the other slides in your presentation, assign it a different color scheme.

PowerPoint picks up the initial color scheme for a presentation from the template on which the presentation is based as a part of the template's Slide Master. But each template also includes several alternate color schemes, which are designed to complement the main color scheme for the template. You can change the Master scheme later, but if you apply a new template, the new template's scheme overrides any change you made to the original template's color scheme.

If you find a template you like but aren't happy with any of its color schemes, you can create your own. The easiest way is to choose a scheme that's close to the colors you want and then modify the scheme's colors. The procedure to do so is presented later in this chapter.

You can override the Master color scheme for an individual slide. You also can change the color for any object to any color in the scheme, or to any other color known to science. You can find step-by-step instructions later in this chapter.

Don't get all in a tizzy about color schemes if you plan to print overhead slides on a black-and-white laser printer. The slides look dazzling on-screen, but all those stunning colors are printed in boring shades of gray.

Using a different color scheme

If you don't like your presentation's color scheme, change it! Here's a simple way:

1. **Switch to Slide view so you can see what you're doing.**

   Shift+click the Slide View button or use the View⇨Master⇨Slide Master command to do so.

2. **Choose the Format⇨Slide Color Scheme command.**

   The Color Scheme dialog box appears, as shown in Figure 9-1.

Metaphor alert!

If you want, you can think of the color scheme as a magic artist's palette. The artist squeezes out eight little dabs of paint to use for various elements of a painting: one for the sky, another for the mountains, and still another for the trees. Then the artist paints the picture. So far, nothing special. But here's what makes this palette magic: If the artist sets it down and picks up a different palette (with eight different little dabs of color squeezed out), the entire painting is instantly transformed to the new colors, as though the artist used the second palette all along.

This magic palette enables the artist to make subtle changes to the painting's appearance with little effort. The artist can change the painting from midday to dusk, for example, simply by switching to a palette that has a darker blue for the sky color. Or the artist can change the scene from spring to fall by switching to a palette that has yellow or orange paint rather than green paint for the trees. Or maybe switch to a winter scene by changing the mountain color to white.

PowerPoint color schemes work just like this magic palette. The color scheme gives you eight colors to work with, with each color assigned to a different slide element. If you change the color scheme, the entire presentation changes as well.

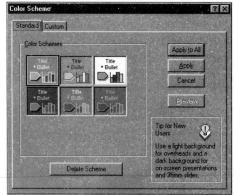

Figure 9-1:
The Color
Scheme
dialog box
(Standard
tab).

3. **Click the color scheme you want to use.**

   The color schemes that appear in the Color Scheme dialog box vary
   depending on the template that's being used, but most templates have at
   least three alternate color schemes to choose from.

4. **Click Apply to All.**

   The color scheme is applied to all slides in the presentation. In addition,
   the color scheme for the Slide and Title Masters is changed so that any
   new slides added to the presentation assume the new color scheme.

   You're done!

Overriding the color scheme

If you want a few slides to use a different color scheme from the rest of the
presentation, you can override the color scheme for just those slides. Follow
the steps outlined in the preceding section, with one important exception: Click
Apply rather than Apply to All. With this choice, the color scheme you select is
applied only to the current slide, not to the entire presentation.

You may want to use this technique to color-code your slides so that your
audience has an immediate visual clue to your slide's contents. If a market-
analysis presentation frequently shifts back and forth between current data and
last year's data, for example, consider using a different color scheme for the
slides that depict last year's data. That way, the audience is less likely to
become confused.

You can override a slide's color scheme from Slide Sorter view also. This feature
is handy if you want to change the color scheme for several slides at one time.
Hold down the Shift key and click each slide you want to change. Then choose
the Format⇨Slide Color Scheme command, pick a new color scheme, and then
click the Apply button.

When you change the color scheme for the entire presentation by clicking Apply to All, any slides to which you have applied a custom color scheme are changed as well. For example, suppose you create a presentation using a color scheme that has a deep blue background, and you highlight certain slides by applying an alternate (light blue) color scheme for those slides. You then decide that you'd rather use a maroon background for the bulk of the slides, so you call up the Format⇨Slide Color Scheme command, select the new color scheme, and click Apply to All. After you do so, you discover that *all* slides are changed to the maroon background — even the ones that you had highlighted with the light blue color scheme.

Changing colors in a color scheme

To change one or more of the colors in the current color scheme, follow these steps:

1. Select the slide whose color scheme you want to change.

If you are going to change the color scheme for all slides, you can skip this step. But if you want to change the applied color scheme for just one slide, switch to Slide view and display the slide whose color scheme you want to change.

To change the color scheme for several slides, switch to Slide Sorter view and hold down the Shift key while you click the slides you want to change.

2. Choose the Format⇨Slide Color Scheme command.

The Slide Color Scheme dialog box appears. Refer to Figure 9-1 if you have forgotten what it looks like.

3. Click the Custom tab to display the color scheme's colors.

As you can see in Figure 9-2, choosing the Custom tab displays the eight colors that make up the color scheme.

Figure 9-2: The Color Scheme dialog box (Custom tab).

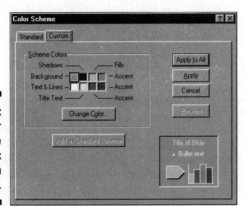

4. Click the color box you want to change.

To change the background color, for example, click the Background color box.

5. Click the Change Color button.

A dialog box similar to the one in Figure 9-3 appears. As you can see, PowerPoint displays what looks like a tie-dyed version of Chinese checkers.

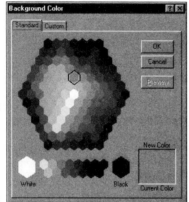

Figure 9-3:
Changing a color-scheme color.

6. Click the color you want and click OK.

If you want white or black or a shade of gray, click one of the color hexagons at the bottom of the dialog box. Otherwise, click one of the colored hexagons. After you click OK, you zip back to the Color Scheme dialog box (see Figure 9-2).

7. Choose Apply or Apply to All.

To apply the change to just the slide or slides you chose, click Apply. To apply the change to all the slides in the presentation, click Apply to All.

Be warned that after you deviate from the preselected color scheme combinations, you better have some color sense. If you can't tell chartreuse from lime, you better leave this stuff to the pros.

The color choice dialog box in Figure 9-3 shows 127 popular colors, plus white, black, and shades of gray. If you want to use a color that doesn't appear in the dialog box, click the Custom tab. This step draws forth the custom color controls, shown in Figure 9-4. From this dialog box, you can construct any of the 16 million colors that are theoretically possible with PowerPoint. You need a Ph.D. in physics to figure out how to adjust the Huey, Dewey, and Louie controls, though. Mess around with this stuff if you want, but you're on your own.

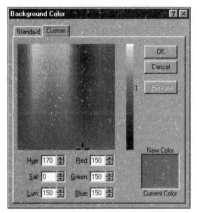

Figure 9-4:
Creating a
new color.

Shading the slide background

You may have noticed that the slide background used in many of the
PowerPoint templates is not a solid color. Instead, the color is gradually shaded
from top to bottom. This shading creates an interesting visual effect. For
example, look at the slide in Figure 9-5. This slide was based on the templates
supplied with PowerPoint, but I modified the color scheme and the background
shading to achieve the effect that I wanted.

Shading for the slide background works much like the color scheme. If you
apply it to all slides, the Slide Master is affected as well so that any new slides
pick up the new shading. Alternatively, you can apply it to an individual slide.

Figure 9-5:
A slide that
uses
background
shading
for an
interesting
effect.

These steps show you how to shade the slide background:

1. **Choose the slide you want to shade.**

   This step isn't necessary if you want to apply the shading to all slides in the presentation. To shade several slides, switch to Slide Sorter view and hold down the Shift key while you click the slides you want to shade.

2. **Summon the Format⇨Custom Background command.**

   The Custom Background dialog box appears. This dialog box includes a drop-down list under the Background Fill, as shown in Figure 9-6.

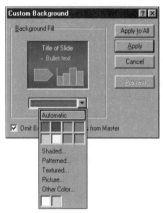

Figure 9-6:
The Custom Background dialog box with the Background Fill drop-down list activated.

3. **Select Shaded from the drop-down list.**

   The Shaded Fill dialog box appears, as shown in Figure 9-7.

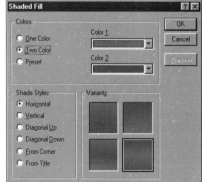

Figure 9-7:
The Shaded Fill dialog box.

4. Choose the shade style you want.

Start by selecting a one-color shade, in which a single color fades to white or black, or a two-color shade, in which one color fades into another. Then select the Shade Style — Horizontal, Vertical, Diagonal Up, and so on. Finally, select one of the variants that appears in the Variants area.

Alternatively, you can select one of several preset shadings by picking the Preset option. The preset shading options include Early Sunset, Nightfall, Rainbow, and several other interesting effects.

5. Click Apply or Apply to All.

Clicking the Apply button applies the shading to just the slide or slides you chose (in Step 1). Clicking Apply to All applies the shading to all slides.

You're done! Admire your work. Play with it some more if you don't like it.

When you apply a template, any background shading specified for the template's Masters is applied along with the color scheme.

Using other background effects

Besides shading, the Format⇨Custom Background command provides several other types of interesting background effects. All these effects are accessible via the drop-down list in the Custom Background dialog box, as shown back in Figure 9-6. The following paragraphs describe each effect.

Patterned: If you select Patterned from the drop-down list in the Custom Background dialog box, you see the dialog box shown in Figure 9-8. Here, you can choose from any of 36 different patterns using your choice of foreground and background colors. After you select the pattern you want to use, click OK to return to the Custom Background dialog box.

Figure 9-8:
The Pattern
Fill dialog
box.

Textured: If you select Textured, the dialog box shown in Figure 9-9 appears. Here, you can choose one of several textures to give your presentation that polished Formica look.

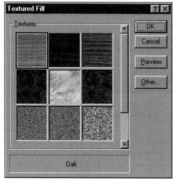

Figure 9-9:
The Formica
dialog box
(just
kidding).

Picture: Choose this option to call forth the dialog box (shown in Figure 9-10), which lets you select a bitmap picture image to use as a slide background. You can find several dozen useful pictures on the PowerPoint or Microsoft Office CD-ROM, in the VALUPACK\PPPHOTOS folder.

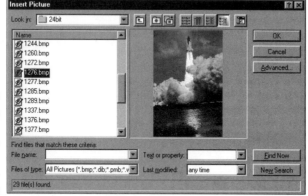

Figure 9-10:
Choosing a
picture to
use as a
background.

Coloring Text and Objects

Normally, the color scheme you choose for a slide determines the color of the various objects on the slide. If the text color is yellow, for example, all text on the slide is yellow (except the title text, which is controlled by the color scheme's Title Text color). Similarly, if the fill color is orange, any filled objects on the slide are orange.

If you change the colors in the color scheme, all the objects on the slide that follow the scheme are affected. But what if you want to change the color of just one object without changing the scheme or affecting other similar objects on the slide? No problemo. PowerPoint enables you to override the scheme color for any object on a slide. The following sections explain how.

Applying color to text

To change the color of a text object, follow these steps:

1. **Highlight the text whose color you want to change.**

2. **Summon the Format⇨Font command.**

   The Font dialog box appears. Click the Color control, and a cute little Color menu appears (see Figure 9-11).

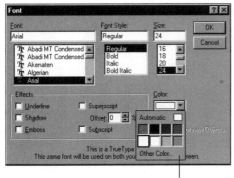

Figure 9-11:
The cute little Color menu in the Font dialog box.

Cute little color menu

   Alternatively, click the Text Color button on the Formatting toolbar. The same cute little Color menu appears directly under the button.

3. **Click the color you like from the cute little Color menu.**

   The eight colors in the Color menu are the colors from the slide's color scheme. Choose one of these colors if you want to be sure that the colors coordinate. If you're bold and trust your color sense, continue to Step 4.

4. **Click Other Color and choose a color you like.**

   The same dialog box you used to handpick colors for the color scheme appears (refer to Figure 9-3). You can choose one of the many sensible colors displayed therein, or you can toss caution to the wind, put on your painting clothes, and click the Custom tab to build your own color by setting the Huey, Louie, and Dewey buttons (see Figure 9-4).

5. OK yourself back home.

You may have to click OK several times to fully unwind yourself.

Good news! If you use the Other Color option to assign a color, PowerPoint automatically adds to the Color menu the color you choose. Figure 9-12 shows how the Color menu may look after you have added some of your colors to it. You can distinguish your colors from the color scheme colors because your custom colors are underneath the Other Color option.

Figure 9-12:
The cute little Color menu with some cute little custom colors added to it.

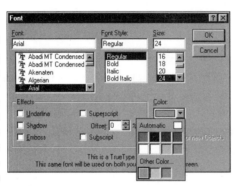

Changing an object's fill color

When you draw an object such as a rectangle or an ellipse, PowerPoint fills in the object with the color scheme's fill color. If you want to change the color used for that object, or if you want the object to be transparent, follow these steps:

1. Choose the object whose fill color you want to change.

 2. Click the Fill Color button (shown in the margin) on the Drawing toolbar.

The menu shown in Figure 9-13 appears.

Figure 9-13:
The menu that appears after you click the Fill Color button.

3. Choose the fill color that you want to use.

   To remove the fill, choose No Fill. To use the fill color from the color scheme, select Automatic.

   That's all!

Notice that the Fill Color button's menu includes the same options as the Background Color drop-down list that appeared in the Custom Background dialog box (refer to Figure 9-6). Thus, you can fill any object with shading, a pattern, or a texture.

Creating a semi-transparent object

You can create a ghostly semi-transparent fill by following these steps:

1. Choose the object that you want to give a ghostly appearance.

2. Choose the Format⇨Colors and Lines command.

   The Colors and Lines dialog box appears, as shown in Figure 9-14.

Figure 9-14:
The Colors and Lines dialog box.

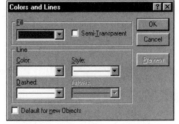

3. Click the Semi-Transparent check box.

4. Click OK.

Note that this dialog box also lets you control the fill options for the object, plus it lets you set the line style for the border that's drawn around the object (if any).

Copying color from an existing object

If you want to force one object to adopt the color of another object, you can use a fancy tool called the *Format Painter*. It sucks up the formatting of one object and then spits it out onto another object at your command. It's a bit messy, but it gets the job done. (You should see it eat.)

To use the Format Painter, follow these steps:

1. **Choose the object whose color you like.**

   You can select a bit of text or an entire object.

2. **Click the Format Painter button (shown in the margin) on the Standard toolbar.**

   This step sucks up the good color so that you can spit it out onto other objects.

3. **Click the object whose color you don't like.**

   This step spits out the desirable color onto the object.

If you prefer the stodgy menus, choose the object whose color you want to copy and use the Format⇨Pick Up Style command. Then choose the object and use the Format⇨Apply Object Style command.

In addition to the fill color, the Format Painter also picks up other object attributes, such as shading, textures, optional trim package, and aluminum alloy hubcaps.

If you want to apply one object's format to several objects, select the object whose color you like and then double-click the Format Painter. Now you can click as many objects as you want to apply the first object's format to. When you're done, press the Esc key.

Don't be spooked by the Pick Up and Apply commands on the Format menu, which seem to change themselves at random. The wording in these commands is adjusted to reflect the selected object. When you select text, the commands read *Pick Up Text Style* and *Apply To Text Style*. When you choose an object, the commands read *Pick Up Object Style* and *Apply To Object Style*. When you don't select anything, the Pick Up command is unavailable, and the Apply command changes to *Apply to Object Defaults*.

If you want to pick up an object's style and apply it as the default for all new objects you create, choose the object and use the Format⇨Pick Up Style command. Then click away from any object so that no object is selected and choose the Format⇨Apply to Object Defaults command.

Chapter 10

Using Clip Art

In This Chapter

▶ Using free pictures

▶ Finding a picture you like

▶ Moving, sizing, and stretching pictures

▶ Adding a box, shaded background, or shadow to a picture

▶ Editing a clip art picture

▶ Adding your own pictures to the ClipArt Gallery

▶ Letting PowerPoint pick the clip art for you

*F*ace it: Most of us are not born with even an ounce of artistic ability. Someday, hopefully soon, those genetic researchers combing through the billions and billions of genes strung out on those twisty DNA helixes will discover *The Artist Gene.* Then, in spite of protests from the DaVincis and Monets among us (who fear that their NEA grants will be threatened), doctors will splice the little bugger into our own DNA strands so that we all can be artists. Of course, this procedure will not be without its side effects: Some will develop an insatiable craving for croissants, and others will inexplicably develop French accents. But artists we shall be.

Until then, we have to rely on clip art.

Free Pictures!

PowerPoint comes with almost 200 clip art pictures that you can pop directly into your presentations. These pictures were drawn by high-tech sidewalk artists who work at Microsoft and include subjects ranging from cartoons to pickaxes to stop signs. In addition, PowerPoint includes hundreds of additional clip art images on the CD-ROM in the VALUPACK\CLIPART folder.

PowerPoint's clip art pictures are managed by a program called the *ClipArt Gallery*. This nifty little program keeps track of clip art files spread out all over your hard disk and spares you the unpleasant chore of rummaging through your directories to look for that picture of Elvis you know that you have somewhere. ClipArt Gallery also takes the guesswork out of using clip art: Rather than choose a filename like ELVISFAT.PCX and hope that it's the one you remembered, you can see the clip art before you add it to your presentation.

ClipArt Gallery organizes your clip art files into categories, such as Architecture, Flags, and Gestures. This organization makes it easy to search through the clip art images that come with PowerPoint and find just the right one. (Wouldn't it be great if the Metropolitan Museum of Art used similar categories?)

ClipArt Gallery works with several other Microsoft applications, most notably Microsoft Publisher. The clip art that comes with those programs is tossed in with the PowerPoint clip art so that you can easily get to it.

You also can add your own pictures to ClipArt Gallery. You may whip out a detailed replica of the *Mona Lisa* in Windows Paintbrush, for example, and then toss it into ClipArt Gallery.

Don't overdo the clip art. One surefire way to guarantee an amateurish look to your presentation is to load it down with three clip art pictures on every slide. Judicious use of clip art is much more effective.

Dropping In Some Clip Art

These steps show you how to drop clip art into your presentation:

1. Move to the slide on which you want to plaster the clip art.

If you want the same clip art picture to appear on every slide, move to Slide Master view by using the View⇨Master⇨Slide Master command (or Shift+click the Slide View button).

2. Choose the Insert⇨Clip Art command.

Sorry, PowerPoint offers no shortcut key for this command. If you like the mouse, though, you can click the Insert Clip Art button instead (shown in the margin).

Where you place the cursor before you choose the Insert⇨Clip Art command doesn't matter. PowerPoint sticks the clip art picture right smack dab in the middle of the slide anyway. The picture is probably way too big, so you have to move and shrink it.

3. Behold the ClipArt Gallery in all its splendor.

After a brief moment's hesitation, the ClipArt Gallery pops up. Figure 10-1 shows what the gallery looks like.

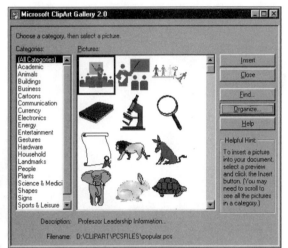

Figure 10-1:
The ClipArt
Gallery.

4. Choose the clip art picture you want.

To find the picture you want, first choose the clip art category that contains the picture (if you're not sure, make your best guess). When you first pop up the ClipArt Gallery, All Categories is the default; this category shows all the clip art pictures in your collection. To narrow your search, scroll through the Categories list until you find the category you want and then click it.

Next, find the specific picture you want. ClipArt Gallery shows 12 pictures at a time, but you can display other pictures from the same category by scrolling through the pictures. When the picture you want comes into view, click it.

Notice the text at the bottom of the ClipArt Gallery dialog box. This text tells you the description and filename of the picture that's selected.

5. Click Insert to insert the picture.

Or simply double-click the picture. You're done!

Bammo! PowerPoint inserts the clip art picture as an object on the slide, as shown in Figure 10-2.

You can see that PowerPoint sticks the picture right in the middle of the slide, which is probably not where you want it. And it's probably too big. You have to wrestle with the picture to get it just the way you want it. See the section "Moving, Sizing, and Stretching Pictures" later in this chapter for instructions for forcing the picture into compliance.

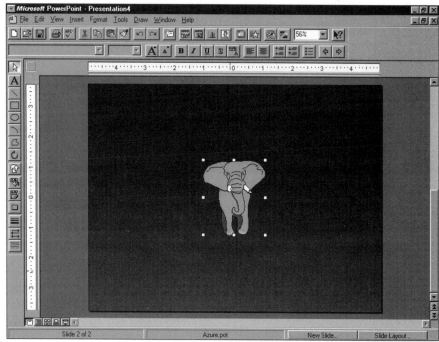

Figure 10-2:
A clip art
picture
inserted in a
presentation
slide.

The first time you use ClipArt Gallery after installing PowerPoint, ClipArt Gallery realizes that it hasn't added PowerPoint's clip art to the gallery. So off it goes, politely updating itself so that it can handle PowerPoint's clip art. Well, ClipArt Gallery isn't really all that polite because the updating takes about three days (at least it seemed to take that long the first time I did it). This is a good time to get caught up on your reading or take your family to Disneyland. Mercifully, this updating happens only the first time you power up the ClipArt Gallery.

If you can't find the clip art picture you're looking for, click the Find button in the ClipArt Gallery dialog box. This step enables you to search for clip art based on the category, description, or filename. For example, you can look for all pictures that have the word *world* in their description.

Moving, Sizing, and Stretching Pictures

Because PowerPoint inserts clip art right in the middle of the slide, you undoubtedly want to move the clip art to a more convenient location. You probably also want to change its size if it is too big.

Follow these steps to force your inserted clip art into full compliance:

1. Click the picture and drag it wherever you want.

You don't have to worry about clicking exactly the edge of the picture or one of its lines; just click anywhere in the picture and drag it around.

2. Notice the eight handles. Drag one of them to resize the picture.

Flip back to Figure 10-2 and notice the eight handles that surround the clip art. You can click and drag any of these handles to adjust the size of the picture. When you click one of the corner handles, the proportion of the picture stays the same as you change its size. When you drag one of the edge handles (top, bottom, left, or right) to change the size of the picture in just one dimension, you distort the picture's outlook as you go.

When you resize a picture, the picture changes its position on the slide. As a result, you can count on moving it after you resize it. If you hold down the Ctrl key while dragging a handle, however, the picture becomes anchored at its center point as you resize it. Therefore, its position is unchanged, and you probably don't have to move it.

Stretching a clip art picture by dragging one of the edge handles can dramatically change the picture's appearance. To illustrate, Figure 10-3 shows how the same clip art picture can resemble both Arnold Schwarzenegger *and* Danny DeVito. I just stretched one copy of the picture vertically to make it tall and stretched the other copy horizontally to make it, er, stout.

Figure 10-3:
Twins.

Boxing, Shading, and Shadowing a Picture

PowerPoint enables you to draw attention to a clip art picture by drawing a box around it, shading its background, or adding a shadow. Figure 10-4 shows what these embellishments can look like.

The following steps show you how to use these features:

1. **Click the picture you want to entomb.**

2. **Use the Format➪Colors and Lines command to draw a box around the picture or to shade its background.**

   Figure 10-5 shows the Colors and Lines dialog box. Choose a color from the Fill drop-down list box to give the picture a background color. Then choose a color from the Color drop-down list box to draw a line around the picture. You also can choose the line style and set up dashed lines. Click OK to draw the box.

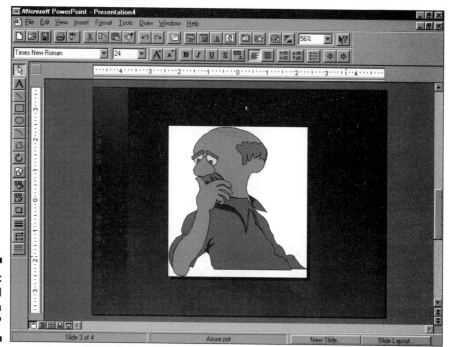

Figure 10-4:
Ever feel trapped in a box?

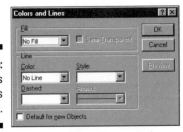

Figure 10-5:
The Colors
and Lines
dialog box.

 3. **Use the Format⇨Shadow command or click the Shadow On/Off button (shown in the margin) to give the picture a shadow.**

Figure 10-6 shows the Shadow dialog box, summoned by the Format⇨Shadow command. To add a shadow, pick a color from the Color drop-down list box. This creates a shadow below and to the right of the clip art picture. The default offset for the shadow is 6 points, but you can change the offset if you wish. (A *point* is one-twelfth of an inch.)

Figure 10-6:
The Shadow
dialog box.

If you click the Shadow On/Off button, PowerPoint uses the shadow color from the slide's color scheme to create a shadow.

Editing a Clip Art Picture

Sometimes one of the clip art pictures supplied with PowerPoint is close but not exactly what you want. In that case, you can insert the picture and then edit it to make whatever changes are needed. For example, Figure 10-7 shows the same clip art picture shown in Figure 10-2, but this time it has been edited to give the lowly elephant the ability to fly.

Figure 10-7:
I'll be — I've
done seen
about
everything.

You can't directly edit a clip art picture. Instead, you must first convert the picture to an equivalent bunch of PowerPoint shape objects. Then you can individually select and edit the objects using the shape editing tools described in Chapter 11.

These steps tell how to edit a clip art picture:

1. **Choose the picture you want to edit.**

2. **Use the Draw⊅Ungroup command to convert the picture to PowerPoint shapes that you can edit.**

   When you do the ungrouping, PowerPoint displays the warning message shown in Figure 10-8. If you do indeed want to convert the picture to PowerPoint shape objects that you can edit, click OK.

Figure 10-8:
Pay no
attention to
this silly
warning
message.

3. **Now edit the picture.**

   The clip art picture has been converted to an equivalent group of PowerPoint shape objects, so you can use PowerPoint's shape editing tools to change their appearance. You can drag any of the control handles to reshape an object, or you can change colors or add new stuff to the picture. See Chapter 11 for the details on editing PowerPoint shape objects.

If you double-click a clip art picture that hasn't been converted to a PowerPoint object, the ClipArt Gallery is summoned so that you can choose a different clip art picture. To edit the picture, you must first convert it to PowerPoint objects. You do that by using the Draw⇨Ungroup command. (I know, I know: They should have added a Draw⇨Convert command or something like that to convert a clip art picture to PowerPoint objects. Don't blame me; I'm just the messenger.)

Don't read this groupie stuff

What is all this talk of *grouping* and *ungrouping*? These common drawing terms are explained in more detail in Chapter 11. For now, consider how you can draw a simple picture of a face. You may start with a circle for the head and then add ellipses for the eyes, nose, and mouth. By the time you finish, you have five ellipse objects.

The only problem is, suppose that you want to move the face you just drew to the other side of the slide. If you just clicked and dragged it, odds are you would move only the nose or one of the eyes. To move the whole thing, you have to select all five ellipses.

Wouldn't it be great if you could treat all five ellipses as a single object? That's what *grouping* is all about. When you group objects, they are treated as if they were a single object. When you click any one of the grouped objects, you click them all. Move one, and they all move. Delete one, and they all vanish.

What happens if after grouping the five face ellipses you discover that you made the nose too big? You have to *ungroup* them so that they become five separate objects again. Then you can select and resize just the nose.

Most complex drawings use grouping. PowerPoint clip art pictures are no exception. That's why you have to ungroup them before you can edit them. Clip art pictures have the added characteristic that when you ungroup a clip art picture, you sever its connection to the ClipArt Gallery. The picture is no longer a ClipArt Picture Object but is now merely a bunch of PowerPoint rectangles, ellipses, and free-form shapes.

Oops, this is way too much stuff about grouping for the clip art chapter. Maybe you should skip ahead to Chapter 11 if you're really this interested.

Most PowerPoint clip art pictures are constructed from groups of groups of groups of maybe more groups. To tweak the shape of an object, you must keep ungrouping it until the Ungroup command is no longer available from the Draw menu.

After you have ungrouped and edited a picture, you may want to regroup it. You're much less likely to pull the nose off someone's face if the face is a group rather than a bunch of ungrouped ellipse objects.

When you convert a picture to PowerPoint objects, you're actually placing a copy of the ClipArt Gallery picture in your presentation. Any changes you make to the picture are reflected only in your presentation; the original version of the clip art picture is unaffected.

Colorizing a Clip Art Picture

After inserting a clip art picture into your presentation, you might find that the colors used in the clip art clash with the colors you've chosen for the presentation's color scheme. Never fear! PowerPoint allows you to selectively change the colors used in a clip art picture. Just follow these steps:

1. Click the clip art picture with the right mouse button, and then choose the Recolor command.

The Recolor Picture dialog box appears, as shown in Figure 10-9.

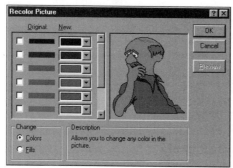

Figure 10-9:
The Recolor
Picture
dialog box.

2. Click the original color you want to change in the Original list of colors.

For example, to change the color of the man's shirt, click the blue that matches his shirt.

3. **Select a new color to replace the chosen color from the drop-down list adjacent to the original color you chose.**

   The drop-down list displays a standard color menu, with the colors from the color scheme and an Other Color command that brings up a dialog box that allows you to choose a custom color.

4. **Repeat Steps 2 and 3 for any other colors you want to change.**

5. **Click OK when you're done.**

Adding Your Own Pictures to the ClipArt Gallery

If you're artistic and like to draw your own pictures, or if you've purchased a set of clip art pictures that you use frequently, you can easily add them to the ClipArt Gallery. After you add them, you can insert them in your presentations by using the same steps that you use to insert the clip art that comes with PowerPoint.

If you click the Organize button in the ClipArt Gallery (review Figure 10-1), the Organize ClipArt dialog box appears, as shown in Figure 10-10.

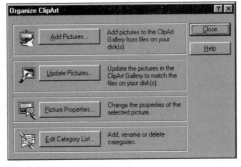

Figure 10-10:
The
Organize
ClipArt
dialog box.

From this dialog box, you can choose four options:

  ✓ **Add Pictures:** Enables you to add your own clip art to the ClipArt Gallery. When you click the Add button, a dialog box pops up that lets you thrash around on your disk drive until you find a picture that you want to add. Note that if you have added Microsoft Publisher to your computer, this button lets you add Publisher's clip art to ClipArt Gallery.

✔ **Update Pictures:** Scans your entire hard disk and looks for picture files that are out of sync with the thumbnail pictures in ClipArt Gallery or pictures that ClipArt Gallery doesn't yet know about. The update scan also removes any ClipArt Gallery thumbnail sketches that belong to pictures you've deleted. (If you don't know what thumbnail pictures are — and there's no reason you should — check out the sidebar "Don't bite your thumbnails!")

The <u>U</u>pdate option takes a long time to run, so don't run it if you're in a hurry.

✔ **Picture Properties:** Where to go if you think that the written description of a picture isn't precise.

✔ **Edit Category List:** Who knows — maybe you just don't like the category names that PowerPoint assigns to its clip art. You can change them with this option. Or you can delete categories you've added but would now like to drop.

Don't bite your thumbnails!

What's all this talk about "updating the thumbnail pictures" or "adding thumbnail pictures" in the gallery's Organize ClipArt dialog box? Does PowerPoint come with a bunch of pictures of people's thumbs?

Nope. The term *thumbnail picture* refers to how the ClipArt Gallery is capable of efficiently displaying those little pictures of all those clip art pictures. If ClipArt Gallery really opened each clip art file just to display those little pictures, you would never use ClipArt Gallery because it would be too danged slow.

To achieve acceptable performance, ClipArt Gallery stores all those little pictures together in one file. Whenever you add a clip art picture to the Gallery, a thumbnail picture for the clip art is created for the picture. Then whenever you call up ClipArt Gallery, it retrieves the thumbnail pictures from the file and displays them. As a result, ClipArt Gallery doesn't have to read the clip art picture files every time you use it.

The drawback to this technique is that it's possible for ClipArt Gallery to become out of sync with the clip art files on your disk. If you modify a clip art file (perhaps by editing it with Paintbrush), for example, you have to tell ClipArt Gallery to refresh its thumbnail picture. You refresh the clip art by clicking the <u>U</u>pdate Pictures button in the Organize ClipArt dialog box. If you don't, the thumbnail picture may not accurately represent the clip art picture that is inserted. Similarly, if you delete a clip art file, you should update ClipArt Gallery's thumbnail pictures.

Adding Pictures from the PowerPoint CD-ROM

The CD-ROM that PowerPoint comes on (whether you purchase PowerPoint by itself or in combination with Microsoft Office) includes hundreds of additional clip art images that you can incorporate into ClipArt Gallery. Follow these steps:

1. **Click the Insert Clip Art button to call up the ClipArt Gallery.**

   ClipArt Gallery appears (see Figure 10-1).

2. **Click the Organize button.**

   The Organize ClipArt dialog box appears (see Figure 10-10).

3. **Click the Add Pictures button.**

   The Add Pictures to Gallery dialog box appears, which resembles a standard File Open dialog box.

4. **Navigate your way to the VALUPACK\CLIPART folder on the CD-ROM drive.**

5. **Press Ctrl+A to select all the files in the VALUPACK\CLIPART folder.**

6. **Click Open.**

7. **Take a nap.**

   It takes a few minutes for ClipArt gallery to add all the files from the CD-ROM.

Inserting Pictures without Using the ClipArt Gallery

PowerPoint also enables you to insert pictures directly into your document without using the ClipArt Gallery. Use this technique to insert clip art that you haven't added to the ClipArt Gallery. These steps show you how:

1. **Move to the slide on which you want to splash the clip art.**

   If you want the clip art to show up on every slide, conjure up Slide Master view with the View⇨Master⇨Slide Master command (or Shift+click the Slide View button).

2. Choose the Insert⇨Picture command.

Greet the Insert Picture dialog box, shown in Figure 10-11, with a smile.

Figure 10-11:
The Insert
Picture
dialog box.

3. Dig through the bottom of your disk drive until you find the file you want.

The picture you want can be anywhere. Fortunately, the Insert Picture dialog box has all the controls you need to search high and low until you find the file.

4. Click the file and then click OK.

You're done!

You also can paste a picture directly into PowerPoint by way of the Clipboard. Anything you can copy to the Clipboard you can paste into PowerPoint. For example, you can doodle a sketch in Paintbrush, copy it, and then zap over to PowerPoint and paste it. Voilà — instant picture!

If you want to narrow your search to files of a particular type, use the Files of type drop-down list box. PowerPoint comes with *filters* that can convert as many as 20 different types of picture files to PowerPoint. Table 12-1 lists the formats you're most likely to use.

If the file type you want doesn't show up in the Files of type drop-down list box, you may not have installed all the graphics filters when you installed PowerPoint. Run the PowerPoint Setup program and see whether the graphics filter you want is available. Better yet, bribe your local computer guru to do this for you. This is definitely Guru Stuff.

Table 10-1	Formats for Picture Files
Format	**What It Is**
BMP	Garden variety Windows bitmap file, used by Paintbrush and many other programs
CDR	CorelDRAW!, a popular, upper-crust drawing program
CGM	Computer Graphics Metafiles
DIB	Device Independent Bitmap files, a special format used by some Windows programs
DRW	Micrografx Designer or Micrografx Draw, two popular ooh-aah drawing programs
DXF	AutoCAD, a popular drafting program
EMF	Yet another type of Windows MetaFile format
EPS	Encapsulated PostScript, a format used by some high-end drawing programs
GIF	Graphics Interchange Format, commonly found on CompuServe
HGL	HP Graphics Language files
JPG	JPEG files, a popular format for exchanging images on the Internet
PCD	Kodak's Photo CD format
PCT	Macintosh PICT files
PCX	A variant type of bitmap file, also used by Paintbrush and other programs
TGA	Targa files
TIF	Tagged Image Format file; another bitmap file format, used by highbrow drawing programs
WMF	Windows MetaFile, a format that many programs recognize
WPG	DrawPerfect, WordPerfect's artistic sibling

If you insert a picture by using the Insert⇨Picture command and then double-click the picture, PowerPoint throws you into the program that was used to create the file, where you can edit it any way you want. You also can ungroup the picture by using the Draw⇨Ungroup command to convert the picture to PowerPoint objects, which you can edit directly in PowerPoint.

Chapter 11

Drawing on Your Slides

• •

In This Chapter

▶ Drawing lines and fancy shapes

▶ Adding text to an object

▶ Changing colors and line types

▶ Changing shapes

▶ Understanding layers and groups

▶ Lining things up

• •

*C*him-chiminey, chim-chiminey, chim-chim cheroo,
I draws what I likes and I likes what I drew. . . .

Art time! Everybody get your crayons and glue and don an old paint shirt. You're going to cut out some simple shapes and paste them on your PowerPoint slides so that people will either think that you are a wonderful artist or scoff at you for not using clip art.

This chapter covers PowerPoint's drawing features. PowerPoint isn't a full-featured drawing program, but it gives you some rudimentary drawing tools to spice up your charts with a bit of something here and a bit of something there.

Some General Drawing Tips

PowerPoint's drawing tools aren't as powerful as the tools provided with a full-featured drawing program such as CorelDRAW! or Illustrator, but they are powerful enough to create some pretty fancy pictures. Before getting into the specifics of using each tool, this section describes a handful of general tips for drawing pictures.

Zoom in

When you work with PowerPoint's drawing tools, increase the zoom factor so that you can draw more accurately. I often work at 200, 300, or even 400 percent when I'm drawing. To change the zoom factor, click the down arrow next to the Zoom Control button (near the right side of the Standard toolbar) and choose a zoom factor from the list. Or you can click the zoom factor, type a new zoom percentage, and press Enter.

Before you change the zoom factor to edit an object, choose the object you want to edit. That way, PowerPoint zooms in on that area of the slide. If you don't choose an object before you zoom in, you may need to scroll around to find the right location.

Activate the Drawing+ toolbar

PowerPoint has two toolbars that provide buttons for drawing objects on slides. The basic Drawing toolbar is normally visible, but the advanced Drawing+ toolbar is hidden. To reveal it, choose the View➪Toolbars command and click the Drawing+ option. Then click OK.

Figure 11-1 shows what the PowerPoint window looks like with the Drawing+ toolbar revealed. The drawing functions provided by each button on both toolbars are explained later in this chapter.

I used PowerPoint's drawing buttons to draw the face shown in Figure 11-1. The sidebar "Don't let me tell you how I drew that funny face!" later in this chapter shows you, step by step, how I drew this face.

All the Drawing+ toolbar's functions are available from the Draw menu, so you can draw pictures without calling up the Drawing+ toolbar. If you plan to do extensive work with drawn objects, however, having these commands available at the click of a button is convenient.

Display the ruler

If you want to be precise about lining up objects on the slide, consider activating the ruler. If you can't see the ruler on-screen already, choose View➪Ruler to display it.

When you work with drawing objects, PowerPoint formats the ruler so that zero is at the middle of the slide. When you edit a text object, the ruler changes to a text ruler that measures from the margins and indicates tab positions.

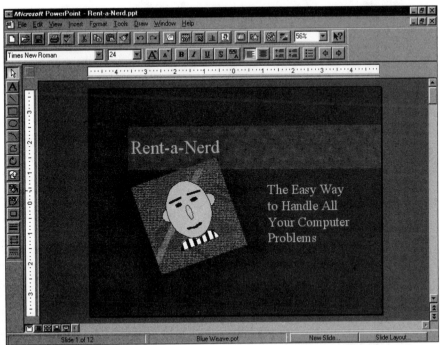

Figure 11-1:
PowerPoint
with both
Drawing
toolbars.

Stick to the color scheme

You can assign individual colors to each object you draw, but the point of
PowerPoint's color schemes is to talk you out of doing that. If possible, let solid
objects default to the color scheme's fill color. If you must assign a separate
color to an object, choose one of the eight colors that's a part of the color
scheme. (If you decide to arbitrarily choose one of PowerPoint's 64 million
colors for an object, a good lawyer may be able to get you off by using the
"irresistible urge" defense.)

Save frequently

Drawing is tedious work. You don't want to spend two hours working on a
particularly important drawing only to lose it all just because a comet strikes
your building or an errant Scud lands in your backyard. You can prevent
catastrophic loss from incidents such as these by pressing Ctrl+S frequently as
you work. And always wear protective eyewear.

Don't forget Ctrl+Z

Don't forget that you're never more than one keystroke away from erasing a boo-boo. If you do something silly — like forgetting to group a complex picture before trying to move it — you can always press Ctrl+Z to undo your last action. Ctrl+Z is my favorite and most frequently used PowerPoint key combination. (For left-handed mouse users, Alt+Backspace does the same thing.)

Drawing Simple Lines and Shapes

PowerPoint provides a whole row of drawing tools, located on the basic Drawing toolbar. Table 11-1 shows you what each drawing tool does.

Table 11-1	Basic Drawing Tools	
Drawing Tool	*What It's Called*	*What It Does*
	Selection button	Not really a drawing tool, but rather the generic mouse pointer used to choose objects.
	Text button	Adds a text object.
	Line button	Adds a line. You can later change the attributes of the line to create thick lines, dashed lines, or lines with arrowheads.
	Rectangle button	Used to draw rectangles. To make a perfect square, hold down the Shift key while you draw.
	Ellipse button	Draws circles and ovals. To create a perfect circle, hold down the Shift key while you draw.
	Arc button	Not Noah's arc, but a curved line. To create a perfect quarter-circle arc, hold down the Shift key while you draw.
	Freeform button	Draws polygons (remember that from ninth-grade geometry?) or irregular shapes.
	Free Rotate button	When you click here, the Rotate button leaps from the water to make its escape into the open sea while Michael Jackson sings an inspiring song.
	AutoShapes button	Activates the AutoShapes toolbar, which contains a bevy of shapes you can draw, such as arrows and crosses.

To draw an object on a slide, you just click the button that represents the object you want to draw and then use the mouse to draw the object on the slide. Well, it's not always as simple as that. You'll find detailed instructions for drawing with the more important tools in the following sections.

If the Drawing toolbar has disappeared, you can make it appear again by choosing View⇨Toolbars and checking the Drawing check box.

Before you draw an object, move to the slide on which you want to draw the object. If you want the object to appear on every slide in the presentation, display the Slide Master by choosing View⇨Master⇨Slide Master or Shift+clicking the Slide View button on the status bar.

PowerPoint has two types of objects: shapes, such as circles, rectangles, and crosses; and lines and arcs. PowerPoint enables you to add text to any shape object, but you can't add text to a line or arc object.

Made a mistake? You can delete the object you just drew by pressing the Delete key; then try drawing the object again. Or you can change its size or stretch it by clicking it and dragging its love handles.

Table 11-2 summarizes some handy shortcuts that you can use while drawing. The last shortcut needs a bit of explanation. If you click a drawing tool button once (such as the rectangle or ellipse button), the mouse cursor reverts to an arrow after you draw an object. To draw another object, you must click a drawing tool button again. If you know in advance that you want to draw more than one object of the same type, double-click the drawing tool button. Then you can keep drawing objects of the selected type till who laid the rails. To stop drawing, click the Selection Tool button (the arrow at the top of the Drawing toolbar).

I have no idea what the expression "till who laid the rails" means. One of the residents of River City (the mayor, I believe) used it in *The Music Man,* and I've liked it ever since.

Table 11-2	Drawing Shortcuts
Shortcut	*What It Does*
Shift	Hold down the Shift key to force lines to be horizontal or vertical, to force arcs and ellipses to be true circles, to force rectangles to be squares, or to draw other regular shapes.
Ctrl	Hold down the Ctrl key to draw objects from the center rather than from end to end.
Ctrl+Shift	Hold down these two keys to draw from the center and to enforce squareness.
Double-click	Double-click any drawing button on the Drawing toolbar if you want to draw several objects of the same type.

Drawing straight and curved lines

To draw a straight line, follow these steps:

1. Click the Line button (shown in the margin).

2. Point to where you want the line to start.

3. Click and drag the mouse cursor to where you want the line to end.

4. Release the mouse button when you reach your destination.

The steps for drawing an arc are the same except that you click the Arc button (shown in the margin) rather than the Line button.

You can use the Format⇨Colors and Lines command to change the line color and other features (thickness, dashes, and arrowheads) for a line or arc object. Or you can use buttons on the Drawing toolbars to change these attributes.

The ends of an arc are always 90 degrees apart. In other words, an arc is always one-quarter of a circle or ellipse.

After you have drawn a line or arc, you can adjust it by clicking it and then dragging either love handle that appears.

Remember, you can force a line to be perfectly horizontal or vertical by holding down the Shift key while you draw.

Sorry, PowerPoint doesn't include powerful tools for drawing precise curves. If you need better curves than the Arc button can provide, get yourself a more powerful drawing program.

Drawing rectangles, squares, and circles

To draw a rectangle, follow these steps:

1. Click the Rectangle button (shown in the margin).

2. Point to where you want one corner of the rectangle to be positioned.

3. Click the mouse button and drag to where you want the opposite corner of the rectangle to be positioned.

4. Release the mouse button.

The steps for drawing a circle or ellipse are the same except that you click the Ellipse button (shown in the margin) rather than the Rectangle button.

You can use the Format⇨Colors and Lines command to change the fill color or the line style for a rectangle or ellipse object. You also can use the buttons on the Drawing toolbars to change the color and line style.

To apply a shadow, use the Format⇨Shadow command or click the Shadow On/Off button.

Hold down the Shift key while you draw to create an even square or a perfectly round circle. Also, you can adjust the size or shape of a rectangle or circle by clicking it and dragging any of its love handles.

Drawing a polygon or freeform shape

Mr. Arnold, my seventh-grade math teacher, taught me that a *polygon* is a shape that has many sides and has nothing to do with having more than one spouse (one is certainly enough for most of us). Triangles, squares, and rectangles are polygons, but so are hexagons and pentagons, as are any unusual shapes whose sides all consist of straight lines. Politicians are continually inventing new polygons when they revise the boundaries of congressional districts.

PowerPoint's Freeform button is designed to create polygons, with a twist: Not all the sides have to be straight lines. The Freeform button enables you to build a shape whose sides are a mixture of straight lines and freeform curves. Figure 11-2 shows three examples of shapes that I created with the Freeform button.

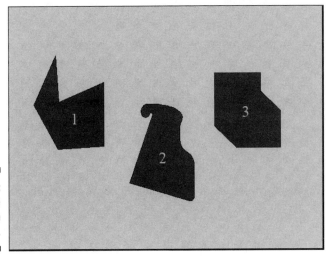

Figure 11-2:
Three
freeform
shapes.

Follow these steps to create a polygon or freeform shape:

1. **Click the Freeform button (shown in the margin).**

2. **Click where you want to position the first corner of the object.**

3. **Click where you want to position the second corner of the object.**

4. **Keep clicking wherever you want to position a corner.**

5. **To finish the shape, click near the first corner, the one you created in Step 2.**

   You don't have to be exact; if you click anywhere near the first corner you put down, PowerPoint assumes that the shape is finished.

You're finished! The object assumes the line and fill color from the slide's color scheme.

To draw a freeform side on the shape, hold down the mouse button when you click a corner and then draw the freeform shape with the mouse. When you get to the end of the freeform side, release the mouse button. Then you can click again to add more corners. Shape 2 in Figure 11-2 has one freeform side.

If you look at a freeform side closely, you see that it isn't freeform at all. Instead, it consists of a series of small, straight line segments that approximates the curvy line you tried to draw with the mouse. The line segments are small enough that when you view them at normal size, they appear to be a smooth curve, just as you drew it. Figure 11-3 shows a portion of shape 2 from Figure 11-2 with the zoom factor set to 300 percent so that you can see what I mean.

You can reshape a polygon or freeform shape by double-clicking it and then dragging any of the love handles that appear on the corners.

If you hold down the Shift key while you draw a polygon, the sides are constrained to 45-degree angles. Shape 3 in Figure 11-2 was drawn in this manner. How about a constitutional amendment requiring Congress to use the Shift key when it redraws congressional boundaries?

You also can use the Freeform button to draw a multisegmented line, called an *open shape.* To draw an open shape, you can follow the steps in this section, except that you skip Step 5. Instead, double-click or press the Esc key when the line is done.

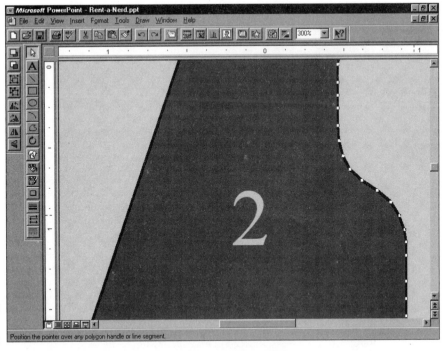

Figure 11-3:
A freeform
line is
nothing
more than a
conflation
of small,
straight
lines.

Using the AutoShapes button

Rectangles and circles aren't the only two shapes PowerPoint can draw automatically. When you click the AutoShapes button on the Drawing toolbar, a complete toolbar list of 24 *AutoShapes* appears. These AutoShape buttons make it easy to draw common shapes.

These steps show you how to draw an AutoShape:

 1. Click the AutoShapes button on the Drawing toolbar.

The AutoShapes toolbar appears, as shown in Figure 11-4.

2. Click the AutoShape you want to draw.

3. Click the slide where you want the shape to appear and then drag the shape to the desired size.

When you release the mouse button, the AutoShape object takes on the current fill color and line style.

4. Start typing if you want the shape to contain text.

Figure 11-4:
The
AutoShapes
toolbar.

Hold down the Shift key while drawing the AutoShape to create an undistorted shape.

To dismiss the AutoShapes toolbar, double-click its close button in the upper-right corner. If your AutoShapes toolbar is sitting right on top of where you want to draw the shape, move it by dragging its title bar. If you move it to the edge of the presentation window, it sticks there like the other toolbars do.

Some AutoShape buttons — such as the Seal and Balloon buttons — cry out for text. Figure 11-5 shows how you can use the Seal shape to add a jazzy burst to a slide.

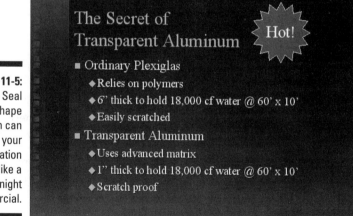

Figure 11-5:
The Seal
AutoShape
button can
make your
presentation
look like a
late-night
infomercial.

You can change an object's AutoShape at any time by selecting the object and then choosing the Draw⇨Change AutoShape command.

Some AutoShape buttons have an extra love handle that enables you to adjust some aspect of the object's shape. For example, the arrows have a love handle that enables you to increase or decrease the size of the arrowhead. Figure 11-6 shows how you can use these extra love handles to vary the shapes produced by several AutoShape buttons. For each of the six buttons, the first object shows how the AutoShape is initially drawn; the other two objects drawn with each AutoShape button show how you can change the shape by dragging the extra handle.

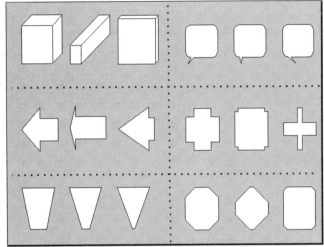

Figure 11-6:
Interesting variations are possible by grabbing these AutoShapes' extra love handle.

Setting the Fill Color, Line Style, and Shadow

PowerPoint objects have various attributes that you can change. These attributes are defined as follows:

 ✔ **Fill color:** The interior color of an object. One of the eight colors from the color scheme is designated as the fill color, but you can override the color scheme's fill color and use any color you want. If the object has no fill color, the background color shows through.

 ✔ **Line color:** The color of the lines that outline the object (or in the case of a line or arc, the color of the actual line or arc). The default line color comes from the color scheme, but you can set the line color to any color you want. If the object has no line color, the lines are not visible.

 ✔ **Shadow:** The presence or absence of a shadow on the object. If a shadow is used, the color for the shadow is taken from the color scheme, but you can override it via the Format⇨Shadow command.

 ✔ **Line style:** The thickness of the lines that outline the object.

✔ **Arrowheads:** Lines can have an arrowhead at either or both ends. Arrowheads are used mostly on line and arc objects.

✔ **Dashed lines:** The dashing pattern used for the lines that outline the object. The default uses a solid line, but different patterns are available to create dashed lines.

To change any of these object attributes, simply select the object or objects you want to change, and then click the appropriate button to change the color or style.

If you have a dialog box fetish, you can use the Format⇨Colors and Lines command and the Format⇨Shadow command to change colors, line styles, and shadows. These commands pop up dialog boxes like those shown in Figure 11-7 and Figure 11-8. Fiddle with them if you want, but I prefer the buttons.

Figure 11-7:
The Colors and Lines dialog box.

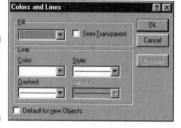

Figure 11-8:
The Shadow knows.

When you experiment with shadows, be sure to try out the Embossed shadow type. It adds a dark shadow below the object and a light shadow above it to create the illusion that the object is carved out of the background. Very cool.

Flipping and Rotating Objects

To *flip* an object means to create a mirror image of it. To *rotate* an object means to turn it about its center. PowerPoint enables you to flip objects horizontally or vertically, rotate objects in 90-degree increments, or freely rotate an object to any angle.

Flipping an object

PowerPoint enables you to flip an object vertically or horizontally to create a mirror image of the object. To flip an object, follow these steps:

1. **Choose the object that you want to flip.**

 2. **Click the Flip Horizontal or Flip Vertical button on the Drawing+ toolbar (shown in the margin).**

Rotating an object 90 degrees

You can rotate an object in 90-degree increments by following these steps:

1. **Choose the object you want to rotate.**

 2. **Click the Rotate Left or Rotate Right button on the Drawing+ toolbar.**

3. **To rotate the object 180 degrees, click the appropriate Rotate button again.**

Using the Free Rotate button

Rotating an object in 90-degree increments is useful sometimes, but if you want to give just a bit of slant to an object, 90-degree rotation won't do. That's when the Free Rotate button comes in handy. It enables you to rotate an object to any arbitrary angle just by dragging it with the mouse. Figure 11-9 shows an example of a slide with a rotated object. I rotated the face to give it just the right inquisitive slant.

The following steps show you how to use the Free Rotate button:

1. **Choose the object you want to rotate.**

 2. **Click the Free Rotate button on the Drawing toolbar (shown in the margin).**

3. Drag one of the corner love handles around the object.

As you drag, an outline of the object rotates around. When you get the object's outline to the angle you want, release the mouse button, and the object is redrawn at the new angle.

To restrict the rotation angle to 45-degree increments, hold the Shift key while dragging around the corner handle.

When you hold down the Ctrl key while dragging a corner handle, the object rotates about the opposite corner handle rather than the center. This feature is very strange, but it's occasionally useful.

Remember how all the bad guys' hideouts were slanted in the old *Batman* TV show? Wasn't that cool?

Drawing a Complicated Picture

When you add more than one object to a slide, several problems come up. What happens when the objects overlap? How do you line up objects so that they don't look like they were thrown at the slide from a moving car? And how do you keep together objects that belong together?

This section shows you how to use PowerPoint features to handle overlapped objects, align objects, and group objects. If you're interested in a description of how these PowerPoint features are used together to draw a picture, check out the sidebar titled "Don't let me tell you how I drew that funny face!"

Don't let me tell you how I drew that funny face!

In case you're interested, you can follow the bouncing ball to see how I created the face that keeps popping up in the figures in this chapter. By studying this creature, you can get an idea of how you use layers, groups, and alignment to create complicated pictures, as shown in these steps:

1. I drew this basic shape by using the Ellipse button. Then I filled it with gray.

(In this color scheme, the fill color for this slide wasn't gray, so I used the Fill Color button to do this step.)

2. To draw the eyes, I started by using the Ellipse button to draw an ellipse for the left eye, which I filled with black.

Next, I pressed Ctrl+D to make a duplicate of the ellipse. Then I dragged the duplicate eye to the right side of the face. Finally, I used the Line button to draw the two lines that make the eyebrows and the line that represents the mouth.

3. I drew the nose and ears by using the Ellipse tool.

The only trick with the ears was using the Send Backward button over and over again until each ear finally dropped behind the face where it belonged.

4. To add the body, I used the Freehand button. Then I used the Line button to make the stripes. Finally, I filled the stripes with black by using the Fill Color button.

Oh, I almost forgot. The last step is to choose all the objects that make up the face and group them by using the Group button or the Draw⇨Group command. That way, I don't have to worry about accidentally dismembering the face.

Changing layers

Whenever you have more than one object on a slide, the potential exists for objects to overlap one another. Like most drawing programs, PowerPoint handles this problem by layering objects like a stack of plates. The first object you draw is at the bottom of the stack; the second object is on top of the first; the third is atop the second; and so on. If two objects overlap, the one that's at the highest layer wins; objects below it are partially covered.

So far, so good — but what if you don't remember to draw the objects in the correct order? What if you draw a shape that you want to tuck behind a shape you've already drawn, or what if you want to bring an existing shape to the top of the pecking order? No problem. PowerPoint enables you to change the stack order by moving objects toward the front or back so that they overlap just the way you want.

PowerPoint provides four commands for changing the stacking order:

- ✔ **Draw⇨Bring to Front:** Brings the chosen object to the top of the stack.

- ✔ **Draw⇨Send to Back:** Sends the chosen object to the back of the stack.

- ✔ **Draw⇨Bring Forward:** Brings the chosen object one step closer to the front of the stack (the button is shown in the margin).

- ✔ **Draw⇨Send Backward:** Sends the object one rung down the ladder (the button is shown in the margin).

Layering problems are most obvious when objects have a fill color. If an object has no fill color, objects behind it are allowed to show through. In this case, the layering doesn't matter much.

To bring an object to the top of another, you may have to use the Bring Forward command several times. The reason is that even though the two objects appear to be adjacent, other objects may occupy the layers between them.

Line 'em up

Nothing looks more amateurish than objects dropped randomly on a slide with no apparent concern for how they line up with one another. PowerPoint provides several features that enable you to line up objects as you draw them:

- ✔ **Snap to Grid:** When Snap to Grid is on, an invisible grid to which objects are aligned overlays the entire slide. Whenever you create a new object or move an existing object, it automatically sticks to the nearest grid line. To turn Snap to Grid mode on or off, use the Draw⇨Snap to Grid command.

In case you're interested, the grid spacing is 12 lines per inch.

You can't see the grid, but trust me; it's there. When you increase the zoom setting enough, you see the effects of objects snapping to it.

✔ **Guides:** If you activate PowerPoint's guides, two lines — one horizontal, the other vertical — appear on-screen. These lines do not show up in printed output, but any object that comes within a pixel's breath of one of these guidelines snaps to it. Guides are a great way to line up objects in a neat row.

To display the guides, use the View➪Guides command (use the same command again to hide them). The guides initially pop up like cross hairs centered on the slide, but you can move them to any location you want simply by dragging them with the mouse.

The keyboard shortcut to display or hide the guides is Ctrl+G.

When you move the guides, PowerPoint shows the ruler measurement for the guide as you move it. Very interesting. The whiz kids at Microsoft love to add features like that, but do you get a truly good Align command? Read on.

✔ **Align command:** The Draw➪Align command enables you to choose several objects and then line them up. You can align the objects horizontally to the top, bottom, or middle of the objects, or vertically to the left edges, right edges, or center.

Figure 11-10 and Figure 11-11 show how these Align commands work. Figure 11-10 shows three objects as they were originally drawn. Figure 11-11 shows the result of choosing all three objects and using the various Draw➪Align commands.

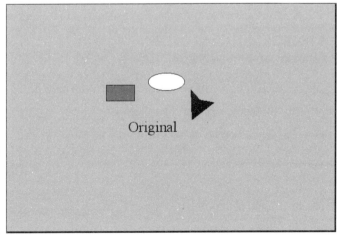

Figure 11-10:
Three
unaligned
objects.

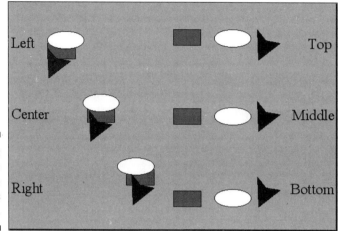

Figure 11-11:
Putting the
Align
commands
to work.

To center two or more objects, choose the objects and then use the Draw⇨Align⇨Middles command followed by the Draw⇨Align⇨Centers command.

Unfortunately, PowerPoint offers no keyboard shortcuts or toolbar buttons for the Align commands.

Group therapy

A *group* is a collection of objects that PowerPoint treats as though it were one object. Using groups properly is one key to putting simple shapes together to make complex pictures without becoming so frustrated that you have to join a therapy group. ("Hello, my name is Doug, and PowerPoint drives me crazy.")

To create a group, follow these steps:

1. **Choose all objects that you want to include in the group.**

2. **Conjure up the Draw⇨Group command.**

 Or click the Group button on the Drawing+ toolbar (shown in the margin).

To take a group apart so that PowerPoint treats the objects as individuals again, follow these steps:

1. **Choose the object group that you want to break up.**

2. **Invoke the Draw⇨Ungroup command.**

 Or click the Ungroup button on the Drawing+ toolbar (again, in the margin).

If you create a group and then ungroup it so that you can work on its elements individually, you can easily regroup the objects. These steps show you how:

1. **Select at least one object that was in the original group.**

2. **Choose the Draw⇨Regroup command.**

   PowerPoint remembers which objects were in the group and automatically includes them.

PowerPoint enables you to create groups of groups. This capability is useful for complex pictures because it enables you to work on one part of the picture, group it, and then work on the next part of the picture without worrying about accidentally disturbing the part you've already grouped. After you have several such groups, select them and group them. You can create groups of groups of groups, and so on, ad nauseam.

Part III

Neat Things You Can Add to Your Slides

The 5th Wave   By Rich Tennant

"NO, THAT'S NOT A PIE CHART, IT'S JUST A HUNK OF 'CHEEZ-WHIZ' THAT GOT SCANNED INTO THE SLIDE."

In this part...

You'll hear nothing but yawns from the back row if your presentation consists of slide after slide of text and bulleted lists. Mercifully, PowerPoint is well equipped to add all sorts of embellishments to your slides — drawings, graphs, organizational charts, equations, and more. You can even make your presentations belch on command.

Not that any of this is easy. That's why I devote an entire part to wrestling with these ornaments.

Chapter 12

Graphs

● ●

In This Chapter

▶ Creating a graph with Microsoft Graph

▶ Moving and resizing a graph

▶ Embellishing a graph with titles, legends, and other stuff

▶ Importing graph data from a spreadsheet

● ●

*O*ne of the best ways to prove a point is with numbers ("numbers don't lie"), and one of the best ways to present numbers is in a graph. Just ask Ross Perot. With PowerPoint, adding a graph to your presentation is easy. And it's usually easy to get the graph to look the way you want. It takes a great deal of pointing and clicking, but it works.

Wouldn't it have been great if I could have talked Ross Perot into writing this chapter for me? I imagine something like this:

> "Now. Do you want to just sit around and talk about making graphs, or do you want to get in there and do it? Ya understand what I'm sayin'? If all you want to do is form a committee to study these graphs and whatnot, I'm not your man. And don't bother me if all you want to do is import cheap graphs from Mexico."

PowerPoint graphs are drawn by Microsoft's latest and greatest graphing program, Microsoft Graph 5. Microsoft Graph works so well with PowerPoint that you probably wouldn't know that it was a separate program if I hadn't just told you.

> "Do you mind? No, I didn't interrupt you. That was just downright rude. Now. Here's the thing. Microsoft spent something like $50 billion so that PowerPoint can make world-class graphs. It took tens of thousands of talented American programmers to do it, too. Do you think that Canadian programmers could have done this? Not in a million years. This is world-class, American-made software. So stop talking about it — let's get to work."

Okay, okay.

Understanding Microsoft Graph

If you've never worked with a graphing program, Microsoft Graph can be a little confusing. It takes a series of numbers and renders it as a graph. You can supply the numbers yourself, or you can copy them from an Excel or Lotus 1-2-3 worksheet. Microsoft Graph can create all kinds of different graphs that range from simple bar graphs and pie charts to exotic doughnut charts and radar graphs. Very cool, but a little confusing to the uninitiated.

This list shows some of the jargon you have to contend with when you're working with graphs:

- **Graph or chart:** Same thing. These terms are used interchangeably. A graph or chart is nothing more than a bunch of numbers turned into a picture. After all, a picture is worth a thousand numbers.

- **Graph object:** A graph inserted on a slide. Microsoft Graph draws the graph, so whenever you try to modify the chart's appearance, PowerPoint summons Microsoft Graph.

- **Graph type:** Microsoft Graph supports several graph types: bar graphs, column graphs, pie graphs, line graphs, scatter graphs, area graphs, radar graphs, Dunkin' Donut graphs, and others (see Figures 12-5 and 12-6). Different types of graphs are better suited to displaying different types of data.

- **3-D graph:** Some graph types have a 3-D effect that gives them a jazzier look. Nothing special here; the effect is mostly cosmetic.

- **Datasheet:** Supplies the underlying data for a graph. After all, a graph is nothing more than a bunch of numbers made into a picture. The numbers come from the datasheet. It works just like a spreadsheet program, so if you know how to use Excel or Lotus 1-2-3, learning how to use the datasheet should take you about 30 seconds. The datasheet is part of the graph object, but it doesn't appear on the slide. Instead, the datasheet appears only when you edit the graph object.

- **Series:** A collection of related numbers. For example, a graph of quarterly sales by region may have a series for each region. Each series has four sales totals, one for each quarter. Each series is usually represented by a row on the datasheet, but you can change the datasheet so that each column represents a series. Most graph types can plot more than one series. Pie graphs can graph only one series at a time, however.

- **Axes:** The lines on the edges of a graph. The X-axis is the line along the bottom of the graph; the Y-axis is the line along the left edge of the graph. The X-axis is usually used to indicate categories. Actual data values are plotted along the Y-axis. Microsoft Graph automatically provides labels for the X and Y axes, but you can change them.

- **Legend:** A box used to identify the various series plotted on the graph. Microsoft Graph can create a legend automatically if you want one.

COMPUTER BOOK SERIES FROM IDG

PowerPoint For Windows® 95 For Dummies®

Cheat Sheet

Standard Toolbar

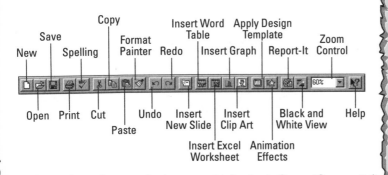

New · Save · Spelling · Copy · Format Painter · Redo · Insert Word Table · Insert Graph · Apply Design Template · Report-It · Zoom Control

Open · Print · Cut · Paste · Undo · Insert New Slide · Insert Clip Art · Insert Excel Worksheet · Animation Effects · Black and White View · Help

Formatting Toolbar

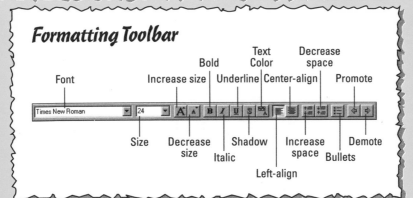

Font · Increase size · Bold · Underline · Text Color · Center-align · Decrease space · Promote

Size · Decrease size · Italic · Shadow · Left-align · Increase space · Bullets · Demote

Drawing Toolbar

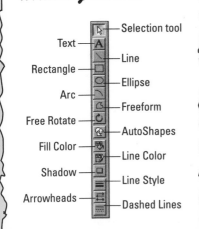

Selection tool · Text · Line · Rectangle · Ellipse · Arc · Freeform · Free Rotate · AutoShapes · Fill Color · Line Color · Shadow · Line Style · Arrowheads · Dashed Lines

Commonly Used Commands

Command	Keys
New	Ctrl+N
Open	Ctrl+O
Save	Ctrl+S
Print	Ctrl+P
Help	F1
Insert New Slide	Ctrl+M

IDG BOOKS WORLDWIDE

...For Dummies: #1 Computer Book Series for Beginners

PowerPoint For Windows® 95 For Dummies®

Cheat Sheet

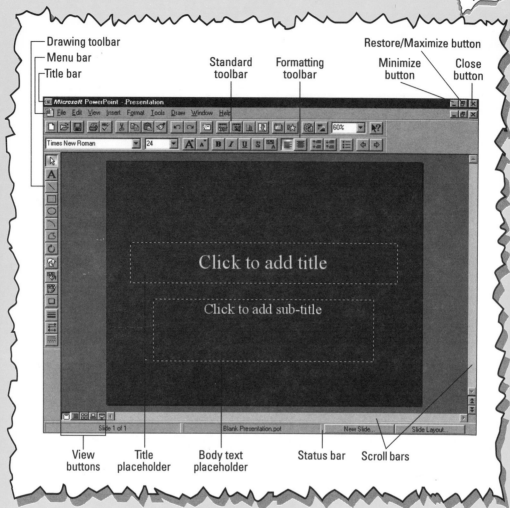

- Drawing toolbar
- Menu bar
- Title bar
- Standard toolbar
- Formatting toolbar
- Restore/Maximize button
- Minimize button
- Close button

Click to add title

Click to add sub-title

- View buttons
- Title placeholder
- Body text placeholder
- Status bar
- Scroll bars

Formatting Commands

Command	Keys
Bold	Ctrl+B
Italic	Ctrl+I
Underline	Ctrl+U
Center	Ctrl+E
Left align	Ctrl+L
Right align	Ctrl+R
Justify	Ctrl+J
Normal	Ctrl+spacebar

Editing Commands

Command	Keys
Undo	Ctrl+Z
Cut	Ctrl+X
Copy	Ctrl+C
Paste	Ctrl+V
Select All	Ctrl+A
Find	Ctrl+F
Replace	Ctrl+H
Duplicate	Ctrl+D

. . .For Dummies: #1 Computer Book Series for Beginners

Microsoft Graph is a separate program, not part of the PowerPoint program. The Microsoft Graph that comes with PowerPoint 95 is the same program that comes with Excel 95 and Office 95. So if you know how to use Excel to create graphs, you can pretty much skip this chapter: You already know everything you need to know.

Although Microsoft Graph is a separate program, it works from within PowerPoint in a way that makes it look like it isn't a separate program. When you create or edit a graph, Microsoft Graph comes to life. But rather than pop up in its own window, Microsoft Graph sort of takes over PowerPoint's window and replaces PowerPoint's menus and toolbars with its own. This magic is accomplished with an elaborate arrangement of smoke and mirrors known as *OLE 2.* If you don't have anything else to do, check out the sidebar "Stop me before I tell you about OLE" to find out more about this cool feature.

Microsoft Graph has its own Help system. To see Help information for Microsoft Graph, first call up Microsoft Graph by inserting a graph object or double-clicking an existing graph object. Then press F1 or use the Help menu.

Creating a Graph

To add a graph to your presentation, you have two options:

- ✔ Create a new slide by using an AutoLayout that includes a graph object.
- ✔ Add a graph object to an existing slide.

It's easier to create a new slide by using an AutoLayout because the AutoLayout positions other elements on the slide for you. If you add a graph to an existing slide, you probably have to adjust the size and position of existing objects to make room for the graph object.

Inserting a new slide with a graph

These steps show you how to insert a new slide that contains a graph:

1. **Move to the slide that you want the new slide to follow.**
2. **Click the New Slide button on the status bar.**

   The New Slide dialog box, shown in Figure 12-1, appears.

Stop me before I tell you about OLE

If you read anything about Windows these days, you can't avoid reading about OLE. Microsoft introduced OLE, which can be pronounced *oh-el-ee* or *ohlay* (rhymes with *Frito-Lay*), with Windows 3.1. A new version of OLE, however, known as OLE 2, was recently developed to overcome the many shortcomings in the original OLE. PowerPoint 4, Word for Windows 6, and Excel 5 are the first Microsoft application programs to take advantage of the new OLE 2 capabilities.

OLE stands for *Object Linking and Embedding.* The idea behind OLE is that it enables you to create documents that contain different kinds of data. Suppose that you want to include some spreadsheet data in a word processing document. With OLE, you simply insert a *spreadsheet object* in the word processing document. OLE remembers that the data was originally created by a spreadsheet program. If you want to edit the spreadsheet data, you just double-click it. OLE magically conjures up the spreadsheet program so that you can edit the data.

With the original OLE, a new window appeared when you double-clicked an embedded object to edit it. With OLE 2, embedded objects are not edited in separate windows. Instead, when you double-click an embedded object, the menus and toolbars from the embedded object's program appear to replace the main program's menus and toolbar. You can then directly edit the object. Click anywhere outside the object to restore the original program's menus and toolbars.

Some interesting tidbits about OLE follow:

- In OLE terminology, the document that contains an embedded object is called a *container,* and a program that creates a container document is called a *client.* An embedded object is called a *component,* and the program that creates it is called a *server.* These terms are important to the people who write OLE programs, but they're completely unimportant to normal people like you and me.

- Microsoft Graph isn't the only OLE program that can work with PowerPoint. Microsoft WordArt, Equation Editor, and Organization Graph are other examples of OLE, as is PowerPoint's capability to embed a Word for Windows table or an Excel worksheet.

Figure 12-1:
The New
Slide dialog
box.

(New Slide dialog box: "Choose an AutoLayout:" with OK, Cancel, and Graph buttons)

3. Choose the slide type you want and click OK.

Several slide types include graph objects. Choose the one you want and then click OK. PowerPoint adds a new slide of the chosen type. As you can see in Figure 12-2, the graph object is simply a placeholder; you have to use Microsoft Graph to complete the graph.

4. Double-click the graph object to conjure up Microsoft Graph.

PowerPoint awakens Microsoft Graph from its slumber, and the two programs spend a few moments exchanging news from home. Then Microsoft Graph takes over, creating a sample graph with make-believe data, as shown in Figure 12-3.

5. Change the sample data to something more realistic.

The *datasheet,* visible in Figure 12-3, supplies the data on which the graph is based. The datasheet is in a separate window and is not a part of the slide. Unfortunately, the datasheet window sits right on top of the graph, so you cannot see the graph until you close the datasheet window or move the window by dragging the title bar.

The datasheet works just like a spreadsheet program. For more information about using it, see the section "Working with the Datasheet," later in this chapter.

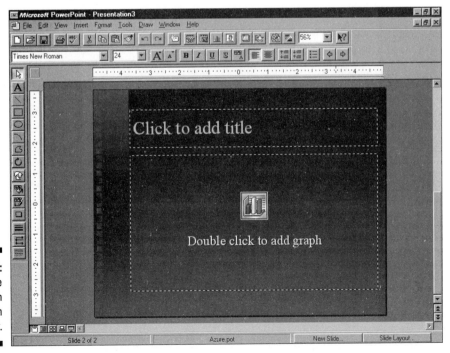

Figure 12-2:
A new slide
with a virgin
graph
object.

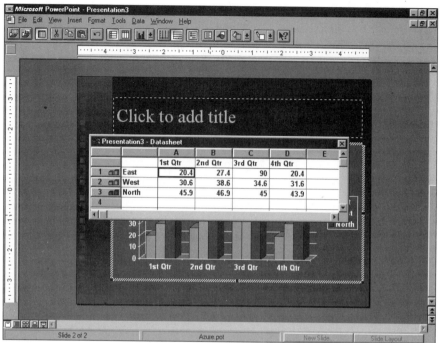

Figure 12-3:
Microsoft
Graph takes
over.

6. Return to the slide.

Click anywhere on the slide outside the graph or the datasheet to leave Microsoft Graph and return to the slide. You can then see the graph with the new numbers, as shown in Figure 12-4.

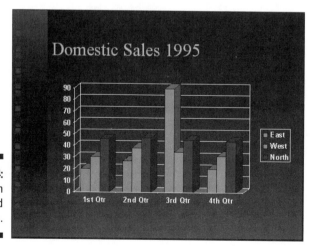

Figure 12-4:
A slide with
a finished
graph.

Inserting a graph in an existing slide

Remember that this method is the more difficult of the two methods of adding graphs to your slides. Use the preceding one unless you have already created your slide.

Follow these steps to add a graph to an existing slide:

1. **Move to the slide on which you want to place the graph.**

2. **Summon the Insert⇨Microsoft Graph command.**

   Or click the Insert Graph button (shown in the margin).

3. **Type your data in the datasheet.**

   Replace the sample data with your numbers.

4. **Click outside the graph to return to the slide.**

5. **Rearrange everything.**

   The graph undoubtedly falls on top of something else already on the slide. You probably need to resize and move the graph object and perhaps other objects on the slide to make room for the graph. Or you may want to delete any unnecessary text or clip art objects from the slide. See the next section, "Moving and Resizing a Graph," to find out how to move your graph around.

Moving and Resizing a Graph

You can move or resize graphs the same way you do any other PowerPoint object. To move a graph, just click the mouse anywhere in the graph and drag it to its new location. To resize a graph, click the object and then drag one of the eight love handles that appear.

Holding down the Ctrl key while resizing an object keeps the object centered over its original position. This rule also holds true for graphs.

If you drag one of the edge love handles (top, bottom, left, or right), the proportions of the graph are distorted. Depending on the graph type, this procedure may emphasize or de-emphasize differences between values plotted on the graph.

Working with the Datasheet

The datasheet contains the numbers plotted in your Microsoft Graph graph. The datasheet works like a simple spreadsheet program, with values stored in cells that are arranged in rows and columns. Like a spreadsheet, each column is assigned a letter, and each row is assigned a number. You can identify each cell in the datasheet, therefore, by combining the column letter and row number, as in A1 or B17. (Bingo!)

 Ordinarily, each series of numbers is represented by a row in the spreadsheet. You can change this orientation so that each series is represented by a column by clicking the By Column button on the toolbar (shown in the margin) or by using the Data⇨Series in Columns command.

The first row and column in the datasheet are used for headings and are not assigned a letter or number.

If you want to graph a large number of data values, you may want to increase the size of the datasheet window. Unfortunately, they forgot to put the maximize button on the datasheet window, but you can still increase the size of the datasheet window by dragging any of its corners.

 You can choose an entire column by clicking its column letter, or you can choose an entire row by clicking its row number. You also can choose the entire datasheet by clicking the blank box in the upper-left corner of the datasheet.

You can change the font used in the datasheet by using the Format⇨Font command. You also can change the numeric format with the Format⇨Number command. Changing the font and number format for the datasheet affects not only the way the datasheet is displayed but also the format of data value labels included in the graph.

Although the datasheet resembles a spreadsheet, you cannot use formulas or functions in a datasheet. If you want to use formulas or functions to calculate the values to be plotted, use a spreadsheet program, such as Excel, to create the spreadsheet and then import it into Microsoft Graph. (Or create the graph in Excel rather than in PowerPoint and then import the Excel Graph into the PowerPoint presentation by using the Insert⇨Object command or copy it into PowerPoint by way of the Clipboard.)

 If the datasheet disappears, you can summon it again by clicking the Datasheet button on the toolbar (shown in the margin).

 If you copy data from another application such as Excel and then paste it into the datasheet by using the Edit⇨Paste Link command, you are greeted with the *Graph wizard,* a dialog box that confronts you with simple questions such as

"Would you like a legend?" or "How about lunch?" Answer the questions to create a basic graph, but feel free to embellish the graph by using the ideas in the following sections.

Changing the Graph Type

Microsoft Graph enables you to create 14 basic types of graphs. Each type conveys information with a different emphasis. Sales data plotted in a column graph may emphasize the relative performance of different regions, for example, and the same data plotted as a line graph may emphasize the increase or decrease in sales over time. The type of graph that's best for your data depends on the nature of the data and which aspects of it you want to emphasize.

Fortunately, PowerPoint doesn't force you to decide the final graph type up front. You can easily change the graph type at any time without changing the graph data. These steps show you how:

1. **Double-click the graph to activate Microsoft Graph.**

2. **Summon the Format⊃Chart Type command.**

   Microsoft Graph displays the Chart Type dialog box, shown in Figure 12-5 and Figure 12-6. From this dialog box, you can choose the graph type you want to use. The graph types are arranged in two groups: two-dimensional and three-dimensional. Figure 12-5 shows the 2-D types; Figure 12-6 shows the 3-D types. To switch from the 2-D group to the 3-D group, click the 3-D radio button.

3. **Click the graph type that you want.**

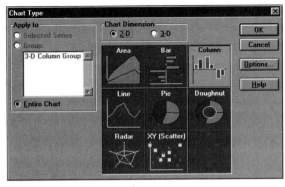

Figure 12-5: The Chart Type dialog box shows the 2-D chart types.

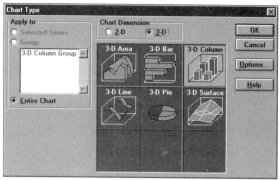

Figure 12-6:
The Chart
Type dialog
box shows
the 3-D
chart types.

4. **To use a variant of the graph type, click the <u>O</u>ptions button and choose the graph subtype.**

   For example, the 3-D column graph type has subtypes that enable you to place columns for the different series next to one another, on top of one another, or behind one another.

5. **Click OK, and you're done.**

Another way to summon the Chart Type dialog box is to double-click the graph object and then right-click the graph. When the quick menu appears, choose the <u>C</u>hart Type command.

You can change the graph type another way by using the Chart Type button on Microsoft Graph's toolbar. When you click the down arrow next to the button, a palette of graph types appears, as shown in Figure 12-7. All 14 basic graph types are available from this menu, but if you want to choose a subtype, you must use the F<u>o</u>rmat⇨<u>C</u>hart Type command.

One more way to change the graph type is to use an AutoFormat. See the section "Applying an AutoFormat" at the end of this chapter for more information.

Figure 12-7:
The Chart
Type button
is a shortcut
for
assigning
graph types.

If you choose one of the 3-D graph types, you can adjust the angle from which you view the graph by using the Format⇨3-D View command. Experiment with this one; it's kind of fun.

Unlike graph types, the characters in most modern novels come in only two-dimensional varieties.

Embellishing a Graph

Microsoft Graph enables you to embellish a graph in many ways: You can add titles, labels, legends, and who knows what else. You add these embellishments by using the Insert menu command.

Adding graph titles

Microsoft Graph enables you to add two types of titles to your graph: a graph title, which describes the graph's contents, and axis titles, which explain the meaning of each graph axis. Most graphs use two axes: the *value axis* and the *category axis*. Some 3-D graph types use a third axis called the *series axis*.

These steps show you how to add any of these title types:

1. Choose the Insert⇨Titles command.

The Titles dialog box, shown in Figure 12-8, appears.

Figure 12-8:
The Titles
dialog box.

2. Check the type of title that you want to insert and then click OK.

3. Click the title and type some text.

4. Move the title, if you want, by dragging it with the mouse.

5. Change the font, if you want, by using the Format⇨Font command.

In most cases, the slide title serves as a graph title for a graph included on a PowerPoint slide. If that's the case, there's no need to use a graph title.

The Value Axis title is sometimes handy for pointing out that sales are in thousands or millions or that the number of hamburgers served is in the billions. The Category Axis title is a good place to add a note, such as Sales by Quarter.

To remove a title, click it and press the Delete key. Or follow the steps in this section and uncheck the title you want to remove.

Adding a label

A *label* is the text that's attached to each data point plotted on the graph. You can tell Microsoft Graph to use the actual data value for the label, or you can use the category heading for the label.

To add a label, use the following steps:

1. **Conjure up the Insert⇨Data Labels command.**

2. **From the Data Labels dialog box, choose whether you want to create a label (from the headings in the data table) or use the actual data value for each point plotted on the graph. Then click OK.**

3. **To change the format used for the labels, choose a label and summon the Format⇨Selected Data Labels command. Then set the pattern, font, number format, and alignment that you want.**

4. **If a data label isn't positioned where you want it, move it by clicking it and then dragging it to a new location.**

For most slide types, data labels add unnecessary clutter without adding much useful information. Use labels only if you think that you must back up your graph with exact numbers.

Some graph types — such as pie graphs — enable you to display a percentage rather than an exact value as the label. This type of label is very helpful because percentages are often difficult to judge from an unlabeled pie graph.

To remove labels, follow the steps in this section, but check None when the Data Labels dialog box appears. Or click the label that you want to remove and press the Delete key.

Adding a legend

A *legend* explains the color scheme used in the graph. If you want a legend to appear in your graph, follow these steps:

1. **Invoke the Insert⇨Legend command.**

2. **Move the legend by dragging it with the mouse or resize it by clicking it and dragging one of its control handles.**

   To remove the legend, click it and press Delete.

To change the format of the legend, click the legend and then use the Format⇨Selected Legend command.

Microsoft Graph enables you to create a legend, but you're on your own if you need a myth or fable.

Applying an AutoFormat

Microsoft Graph's AutoFormats are a combination of a graph type and other graph elements, such as legends, labels, fonts, and colors. Think of AutoFormats as templates for graphs.

Each type of graph format is appropriate for a particular type of data. For example, if your data shows how expenses break down into various categories, use a pie graph. To show how sales have increased or decreased over time, use a column graph or a line graph. Use common sense to pick the graph type that's right for your data.

To apply an AutoFormat, follow these steps:

1. **Double-click the graph to edit it.**

2. **Use the Format⇨AutoFormat command.**

   The AutoFormat dialog box, shown in Figure 12-9, comes to life.

Figure 12-9:
The
AutoFormat
dialog box.

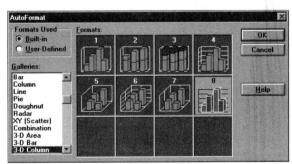

3. Choose the AutoFormat that you want to use.

The various formats are arranged in Galleries by graph type. First, choose the basic graph type from the Galleries list. Then choose the format you want to use.

4. Click OK, and you're done.

You can apply a different AutoFormat to a graph at any time. When you do, the graph type, color scheme, and other characteristics of the graph may change, but the data remains the same.

Chapter 13

Organization Chart (or, Who's in Charge Here?)

In This Chapter

▶ Creating an organizational chart

▶ Adding boxes

▶ Reorganizing your chart

▶ Adding fancy stuff

*O*rganizational charts — you know, those box-and-line charts that show who reports to whom, where the buck stops, and who got the lateral arabesque — are an essential part of many presentations. You can draw organizational charts by using PowerPoint's standard rectangle- and line-drawing tools, but that process is tedious at best. If Jones gets booted over to advertising, redrawing the chart can take hours.

Mercifully, Microsoft decided to toss in a program designed just for creating organizational charts. It calls it — hold on to your hat — Microsoft Organization Chart. It's not as tightly integrated with PowerPoint as Microsoft Graph is, but it gets the job done. (Because Microsoft Organization Chart is a bit of a mouthful, I'll call the program OrgChart from now on.)

Keep in mind that organizational charts are useful for more than showing employee relationships. You also can use them to show any kind of hierarchical structure. For example, back when I wrote computer programs for a living, I used organizational charts to plan the structure of my computer programs. They're also great for recording family genealogies, although they don't have any way to indicate that Aunt Milly hasn't spoken to Aunt Beatrice in 30 years.

OrgChart terms you can skip

OrgChart thrusts a bunch of specialized terminology in your face. This list explains some of the more important terms:

Manager: A box that has subordinate boxes reporting to it.

Subordinate: A box beneath a manager box that reports to that manager in a line relationship.

Co-worker: Two or more boxes that report to the same manager.

Assistant: A box that has a staff relationship to another box rather than a line relationship. Assistant boxes are drawn differently to indicate their different relationship to the chart.

Co-managers: Two or more boxes that share subordinates. Don't you feel sorry for those subordinates?

Group: All the boxes that report to a particular manager.

Group style: The way a group of boxes are drawn to show their relationships. OrgChart has several group style options you can choose. You can freely mix group styles within the same chart.

Branch: A box and all the boxes that report directly and indirectly to it.

Connecting line: A line that shows a relationship between two boxes.

Creating an Organizational Chart

You can add an organizational chart to a presentation in two ways:

- ✔ Create a new slide by using an AutoLayout that includes an organizational chart.
- ✔ Add an organizational chart to an existing slide.

The easier of the two methods is to create a new slide by using an AutoLayout. That way, the organizational chart is already positioned in the correct location on the slide. If you add an organizational chart to an existing slide, PowerPoint usually plops it down right on top of something else important, so you have to move things around to make room for the chart.

If you create an organizational chart with more than four or five boxes, it probably won't fit within the OrgChart window. To see the whole chart, maximize OrgChart by clicking the maximize button in the upper-right corner of the window.

Inserting a new slide with an organizational chart

Follow these steps to add a new slide with an organizational chart:

1. **Move to the slide that you want the new slide to follow.**
2. **Click the New Slide button on the status bar.**

   The New Slide dialog box, shown in Figure 13-1, shows its familiar face.

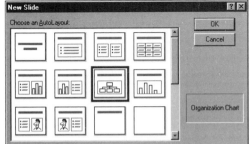

Figure 13-1:
The New
Slide dialog
box.

3. **Pick the OrgChart slide type and click OK.**

   PowerPoint adds a new slide with a placeholder for an organizational chart (see Figure 13-2).

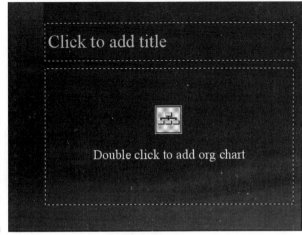

Figure 13-2:
A new slide
with an
organizational
chart
placeholder.

4. Double-click where it says *Double click to add org chart.*

PowerPoint launches Microsoft Organization Chart, which pops up in its own window and enables you to create the chart. OrgChart starts off with a simple four-box chart, as shown in Figure 13-3.

5. Draw the organizational chart.

Click the boxes that are already on the sample chart and type the names for your chart boxes. OrgChart enables you to type a name, title, and one or two comment lines for each box.

Subordinate: 🖰

If you want to add boxes, click the Subordinate button (shown in the margin) and then click the box you want the new box to be subordinate to. (For more information about adding boxes to a chart, see the steps listed later in this chapter, under the heading "Adding Boxes to a Chart.")

Figure 13-4 shows the OrgChart window after I finished creating a simple chart with seven boxes. For the first four boxes (Doc, Sneezy, Grumpy, and Bashful), I just replaced the text *Type name here* with the names I wanted to use. I added the other three boxes by using the Subordinate button.

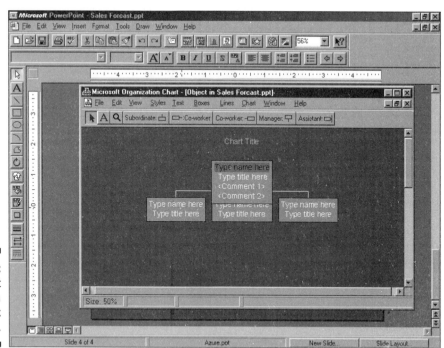

Figure 13-3:
OrgChart
starts with a
four-box
chart.

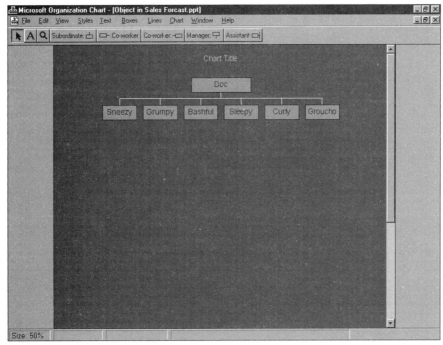

Figure 13-4:
A finished
organizational
chart.

6. Use the File⇨Exit and Return command to return to PowerPoint.

Back in PowerPoint, you can see your organizational chart in all its glory. Figure 13-5 shows how a finished organizational chart looks on the slide.

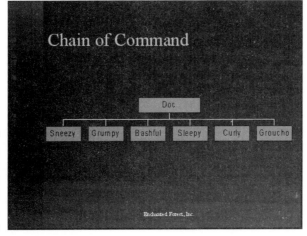

Figure 13-5:
A slide with
a finished
organizational
chart.

Inserting an organizational chart in an existing slide

These steps show you how to add an organizational chart to an existing slide:

1. **Move to the slide on which you want the chart placed.**

2. **Choose the Insert⇨Object command. When the Object dialog box appears, choose MS Organization Chart 2.0 and click OK.**

3. **Draw the chart.**

   Replace the text *Type here* with your own text and add new boxes by clicking the Subordinate button and then clicking the slide that you want the new box to be subordinate to.

4. **Invoke the File⇨Exit and Return command to return to PowerPoint.**

5. **Rearrange everything.**

   If the chart landed on top of something important, rearrange the objects on the slide so that everything is visible. Drag them, resize them, or delete them if you must.

Adding Boxes to a Chart

To add a new box to an organizational chart, you use one of the five box buttons listed in Table 13-1.

Table 13-1	OrgChart's Box Buttons
Box Button	**What It Does**
Subordinate:	Inserts a new box subordinate to the box you click.
:Co-worker	Inserts a co-worker to the left of the box you click. The new box is subordinate to the same box as the existing box you click.
Co-worker:	Inserts a co-worker to the right of the box you click. The new box is subordinate to the same box as the existing box you click.
Manager:	Inserts a manager box above the box you click.
Assistant:	Inserts an assistant box for the box you click.

Follow these general steps for adding a new box:

1. **Click the appropriate Box button for the type of box that you want to add.**

2. **Click the existing box that you want the new box related to.**

3. **Type the name and, if you want, the title and comments for the new box.**

   Press the Tab or Enter key to move from line to line within the box. Press the Esc key or click anywhere outside the box when you're finished.

To add several boxes, hold down the Shift key when you click the Box button. Then you can create several boxes without having to reset the Box button each time.

OrgChart automatically adjusts the size of the box based on the amount of text you type in the box. To keep the boxes small, type as little text as you can.

To insert a new manager box between an existing box and its subordinates, first select the boxes that you want to be subordinate to the new manager box. Then hold down the Ctrl key and click the Manager button.

Rearranging the Chart

Some companies continually rearrange their organizational charts. If you're the hapless chap responsible for keeping the chart up to date, you better study this section closely.

Selecting boxes

The easiest way to select a box is to click it with the mouse. To select several boxes, hold down the Shift key while clicking. Or if you're a keyboard junkie, you can use the shortcuts summarized in Table 13-2.

Table 13-2	Keyboard Shortcuts for Selecting Boxes
Keyboard Action	*What It Does*
Ctrl+G	Selects all the current box's co-workers (the boxes in the same group).
Ctrl+B	Selects an entire branch, beginning with the current box.
Ctrl+A	Selects all boxes in the chart.

(continued)

Table 13-2 *(continued)*

Keyboard Action	What It Does
Ctrl+←	Selects the box to the left of the current box.
Ctrl+→	Selects the box to the right of the current box.
Ctrl+↑	Selects the current box's manager.
Ctrl+↓	Selects the first box that reports to the current box.

Deleting chart boxes

To delete a box from an organizational chart, click the box to select it and press the Delete key. OrgChart automatically adjusts the chart to compensate for the lost box.

When you delete a box from an organizational chart, you should observe a moment of somber silence — or throw a party. It all depends on whose name was on the box, I suppose.

Moving a box

To move a box to a different position on the chart, drag the box with the mouse until it lands right on top of the box you want it to be subordinate to. OrgChart automatically rearranges the chart to accommodate the new arrangement.

Suppose that you want to recast the organizational chart shown in Figure 13-5 to introduce a new layer of management. Figure 13-6 shows the result. To create this chart, I dragged Sneezy and Bashful on top of Grumpy. Then I dragged Sleepy and Groucho on top of Curly.

Moving a box precisely on top of another box is a bit tricky. OrgChart clues you that you've made it by changing the color of the box. Release the mouse button as soon as you see the color change.

If you move a box by dragging it, any subordinate boxes are moved also. To move a box without moving its subordinates, select the box, press Ctrl+X to cut it to the Clipboard, select the box you want to move the cut box to, and press Ctrl+V to insert the box.

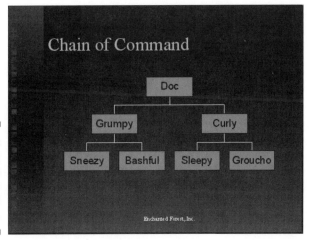

Figure 13-6:
Rearranging
the boxes
on an
organizational
chart.

Using group styles

OrgChart enables you to arrange groups of boxes in several different ways.
Suppose that you decide that the six boxes subordinate to Doc in Figure 13-5
cause the chart to be too wide. It's easy to rearrange those six boxes so that
they are shown as in Figure 13-7. All you have to do is apply a different
group style.

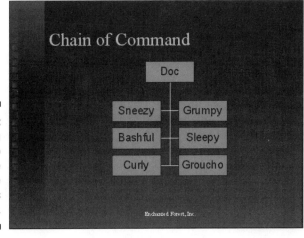

Figure 13-7:
Changing
the group
style
changes the
chart's
appearance.

Follow these steps to apply a group style:

1. Select all the boxes you want rearranged.

Hold down the Shift key while you click the boxes.

2. Choose the Styles menu command.

The Groups menu appears, as shown in Figure 13-8.

Figure 13-8:
The Groups
menu.

3. Click the group style you want.

OrgChart applies the style to the boxes you selected and adjusts the chart as necessary.

Made an oops? Don't forget about the Undo command (Ctrl+Z or Alt+Backspace).

You can mix and match group styles any which way you please to create some bizarre-looking charts. Figure 13-9 shows an organizational chart in which Bashful reports to Doc as a subordinate and has an assistant named Hawkeye and two subordinate workers named Grumpy and Sneezy. Pluto and Sleepy are comanagers over Curly, Groucho, and Fonzie.

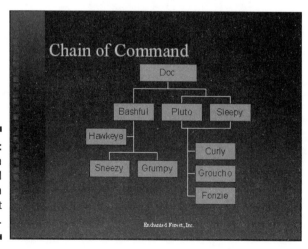

Figure 13-9:
An
organizational
chart with
different
group styles.

Formatting Chart Boxes

OrgChart enables you to apply fancy formatting options to the text in chart boxes, the boxes themselves, or the lines that connect the boxes.

Follow these steps to spruce up your boxes:

1. **Select the box or boxes whose format you want to change.**
2. **Use the following commands to format the box text:**
   - Text⇨Font: Changes the font and font characteristics for the box text.
   - Text⇨Color: Changes the text color.
   - Text⇨Left: Left-justifies the text.
   - Text⇨Right: Right-justifies the text.
   - Text⇨Center: Centers the text.
3. **Use the following commands to format the boxes:**
   - Boxes⇨Box Border: Assigns a border style for the box.
   - Boxes⇨Box Shadow: Creates a shadow effect for the box.
   - Boxes⇨Box Color: Sets the box color.

To add emphasis to the lines that connect the boxes, follow these steps:

1. **Select the line segments you want to emphasize.**
2. **Use the following commands to change the line segments:**
   - Boxes⇨Line Thickness: Sets the thickness of the lines.
   - Boxes⇨Line Style: Enables you to create dashed or solid lines.
   - Boxes⇨Line Color: Sets the line color.

Unfortunately, because OrgChart doesn't implement the expected keyboard shortcuts for text formatting, you can't italicize text by pressing Ctrl+I or bold it by pressing Ctrl+B.

One good use for these formatting options is to draw attention to a particular part of a chart. Figure 13-10 shows a chart that uses contrasting color to show the chain of command from Doc to Sneezy.

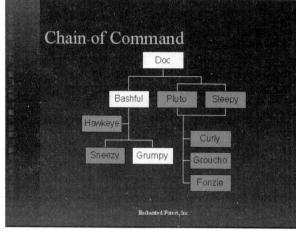

Figure 13-10:
Using box
formats to
draw
attention to
a certain
part of a
chart.

Chapter 14

Equations, WordArt, and Other Ornaments

● ●

In This Chapter

▶ The Equation Editor

▶ WordArt

▶ Word tables and Excel worksheets

● ●

*G*raphs and organizational charts aren't the only ornaments that you can add to your presentations. For the math nuts out there, PowerPoint comes with an Equation Editor that helps you create Einsteinian equations that make even the most resolute audience members hide under their chairs. For the typographers out there who would give their pica sticks to skew some text, there's WordArt. For all those Word for Windows and Excel zealots, PowerPoint includes OLE 2 links to both those programs so that you can stick a table or worksheet right in the middle of a slide. All these features are very useful — well, if you happen to need them. Otherwise, they just take up disk space.

Using Equation Editor

Steven Hawking has said that his editor told him that every mathematical equation he included in his book *A Brief History of Time* would cut the book's sales in half. So he included just one: the classic $e=mc^2$. See how easy that equation was to type? The only trick was remembering how to format the little *2* as a superscript.

My editor promised me that every equation I included in this book would double its sales, but I didn't believe her, not even for a nanosecond. Just in case, Figure 14-1 shows some examples of the equations you can create by using PowerPoint's handy-dandy Equation Editor program. You wouldn't even consider using ordinary text to try to create these equations, but they took me only a few minutes to create with Equation Editor. Aren't they cool? Tell all your friends about the cool equations you saw in this book so that they'll all rush out and buy copies for themselves.

$$\mu_{Y.X} = \overline{Y}_X \pm t_\alpha s_{Y.X} \sqrt{\frac{1}{n} + \frac{(X - \overline{X})^2}{\sum X^2 - n\overline{X}^2}}$$

$$I = \frac{\sum \left(\frac{P_n}{P_0} \times 100 \right) v}{\sum v}$$

$$t = \frac{\overline{X}_A - \overline{X}_B}{\sqrt{\frac{(n_A - 1)s_A^2 + ((n_B - 1)s_B^2}{n_A + n_B - 2}} \sqrt{\frac{1}{n_A} + \frac{1}{n_B}}}$$

$$f(x) = y = \sqrt[3]{\frac{x - 1}{x^2 + 1}}$$

$$\sigma_p = \sqrt{\frac{\pi(1 - n)}{n}} \sqrt{\frac{N - n}{N - 1}}$$

$$\sqrt{(x - h - c)^2 + (y - k)^2} = \left| h + \frac{c}{e^2} - x \right| e$$

$$t = \frac{b}{\frac{s_{Y.X}}{\sqrt{\sum X^2 - n\overline{X}^2}}}$$

$$d_1^* = -z_{\alpha/2} \sqrt{P_c (1 - P_c) \left(\frac{1}{n_A} + \frac{1}{n_B} \right)}$$

Figure 14-1:
Eight
equations
that will
probably not
affect the
sales of this
book one
way or
another.

Equation Editor is a special version of a gee-whiz math program called MathType, from Design Science.

Equation Editor also comes with Microsoft Word for Windows and Microsoft Office. If you have Word or Office and already know how to use its Equation Editor, you're in luck; they're identical.

You don't have to know anything about math to use Equation Editor. I don't have a clue what any of the equations in Figure 14-1 do, but they sure look great, don't they?

Don't forget to tell your friends how great the equations in Figure 14-1 are. They alone are worth the price of the book.

Equation Editor has its own complete Help system. After you're in Equation Editor, press F1 or use the Help command to call up complete information about using it.

Adding an equation to a slide

To add an equation to a slide, follow these steps:

1. Choose the Insert⇨Object command.

Alternatively, create a new slide by using one of the AutoLayouts that includes an Object placeholder. Then double-click the Object placeholder. Either way, the Insert Object dialog box appears, as shown in Figure 14-2.

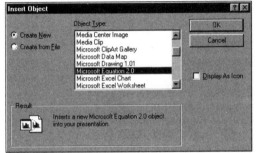

Figure 14-2:
The Insert
Object
dialog box.

2. Choose Microsoft Equation 2.0 from the Object Type list box and then click OK.

This step summons Equation Editor, which appears in its own window, as shown in Figure 14-3.

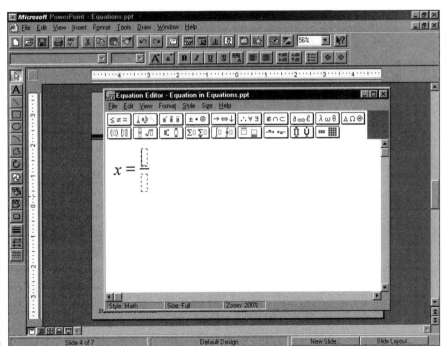

Figure 14-3:
Equation
Editor in
action.

3. **Start typing your equation.**

The variables and basic operators, such as plus and minus signs, are easy enough. But how do you get those fancy symbols, such as square root and summation? The answer lies in the Equation toolbar, dangling up by the top of the Equation Editor's window.

4. **To add a symbol that's not on the keyboard, use one of the buttons in the top row of the Equation toolbar.**

Each button yields a menu of symbols, most of which only Robert Oppenheimer could understand. There's nothing special about the tools in the top row of the Equation toolbar; they simply insert special characters into your equation. The magic of Equation Editor lies in the bottom row on the toolbar, which enables you to build the parts of the equation that have elements stacked on top of one another, such as fractions, superscripts, and roots.

5. **To add a stacked symbol, use one of the buttons in the bottom row of the Equation toolbar.**

Each button in the bottom row of the toolbar is attached to a menu of *templates,* which you use to create stacked symbols. Most templates include a symbol and one or more *slots,* in which you type text or insert other symbols. Back in Figure 14-3, for example, I used a template to create a fraction. You can see that the fraction template consists of a horizontal stroke with slots for the numerator above and the denominator below.

To complete this fraction, I can type a number in each slot. Or I can add another symbol or template to make the equation more interesting. Most equations consist of templates nestled within the slots of other templates. The beauty of it is that Equation Editor adjusts the equation on the fly as you add text or other templates to fill a slot. If you type something like ax^2+bx+c in the top slot, for example, Equation Editor stretches the fraction bar accordingly.

To move from one template slot to the next, press the Tab key.

6. **When you're done, choose File⇨Exit and Return.**

Equation Editor bows out and the equation is added to the slide. You can now drag the equation object to change its size or location.

Confused? I don't blame you. After you latch on to the idea behind templates and slots, you can slap together even the most complex equations in no time. But the learning curve here is steep. Stick with it.

The *denominator* is the bottom part of a fraction, not an Arnold Schwarzenegger movie.

Sometimes Equation Editor leaves behind droppings that obscure the clean appearance of the equation. When that happens, use the View⇨Redraw command to clean up the equation.

Spend some time exploring the symbols and templates available on the toolbar. There's enough stuff here to create a presentation on how to build your own atomic bomb. (None of the equations in Figure 14-1 has anything to do with atomic bombs. Honest.)

Editing an equation

To edit an equation, follow these steps:

1. **Double-click the equation.**

   This step summons Equation Editor.

2. **Make your changes.**

   For example, suppose that you just doubled the mass of Jupiter by typing a **4** when you meant 2. Just click the 4 to select the template that contains it, and then type a **2** in its place.

3. **Choose the File➪Exit and Return command.**

All the standard Windows editing tricks work in Equation Editor, including the Ctrl+X, Ctrl+C, and Ctrl+V shortcuts for cutting, copying, and pasting text, respectively.

Typing text

Equation Editor watches any text you type in an equation and does its level best to figure out how the text should be formatted. If you type the letter *x*, for example, Equation Editor assumes that you intend for the *x* to be a variable, so the *x* is displayed in italics. If you type **cos**, Equation Editor assumes that you mean the cosine function, so the text is not italicized.

You can assign several different text styles to text in an equation:

✔ **Math:** The normal equation style. When you use the Math style, Equation Editor examines text as you type it and formats it accordingly by using the remaining style types.

✔ **Text:** Text that is not a mathematical symbol, function, variable, or number.

✔ **Function:** A mathematical function such as *sin, cos,* and *log.*

✔ **Variable:** Letters that represent equation variables, such as *a, b,* or *x.* Normally formatted as italic.

✔ **Greek:** Letters from the Greek alphabet that use the Symbol font.

✔ **Symbol:** Mathematical symbols, such as +, =, and Σ. Based on the Symbol font.

✔ **Matrix-Vector:** Characters used in matrices or vectors.

You can change the text style by using the Style commands, but you should normally leave the style set to Math. That way, Equation Editor can decide how each element of your equation should be formatted.

On occasion, Equation Editor's automatic formatting doesn't work. Type the word **cosmic**, for example, and Equation Editor assumes that you want to calculate the cosine of the product of the variables *m, i,* and *c.* When that happens, highlight the text that was incorrectly formatted and use the Style⇨Text command.

Equation Editor's default text sizes are designed for use with Word for Windows, not PowerPoint. They are much too small. If you plan to use Equation Editor exclusively with PowerPoint, use the Size⇨Define command and double all the point sizes shown in the dialog box that's displayed. (You can always revert to the default sizes by using the Size⇨Define command and clicking the Defaults button.)

Don't use the spacebar to separate elements in an equation — let Equation Editor worry about how much space to leave between the variables and the plus signs. The only time you should use the spacebar is when you're typing two or more words of text formatted with the Text style.

The Enter key has an interesting behavior in Equation Editor: It adds a new equation slot, immediately beneath the current slot. This technique is sometimes a good way to create stacked items, but it's best to use an appropriate template instead.

Using WordArt

WordArt is a little program that takes a snippet of ordinary text and transforms it into something that looks like you paid an ad agency an arm and a leg to design. And the best part is that it's free! Figure 14-4 is an example of what you can do with WordArt in about three minutes. Pretty nifty, eh?

Once again, you're in luck if you already know how to use WordArt in Word for Windows. WordArt is the same in PowerPoint and Word for Windows.

Figure 14-4:
You too can
do this with
WordArt.

Follow these steps to transform mundane text into something worth looking at:

1. **Use the Insert⇨Object command.**

   Or insert a new slide by using one of the AutoLayouts that includes an Object placeholder and then double-click the placeholder. Either way, the Insert Object dialog box appears like a flash (refer back to Figure 14-2).

2. **Choose Microsoft WordArt 2.0 from the Object Type list box and then click OK.**

   A number of other object types may have infiltrated the list; if so, just scroll until you find WordArt 2.0. When you finally find it, click OK to conjure up WordArt. Like the other OLE 2 add-ons, WordArt and PowerPoint spend a few moments discussing who is really in charge here. Then WordArt takes over PowerPoint's menus and toolbars and replaces them with its own.

3. **Type some text in the Enter Your Text Here dialog box.**

4. **Pick a shape from the shape list, on the left side of the toolbar.**

   The text is skewed to conform to the shape you choose. Figure 14-5 shows how the screen looked after WordArt took over and I typed some text and picked a shape.

5. **Fool around with other WordArt controls.**

   The various controls available on the WordArt toolbar are summarized in Table 14-1. Experiment as much as you want until you get the text to look just right.

6. **Click anywhere outside the WordArt frame to return to the slide.**

Figure 14-5:
WordArt
takes
charge.

Table 14-1		WordArt Buttons
Button	*Name*	*What It Does*
B	Bold	Makes the text bold.
I	Italic	Makes the text italic.
Ee	Even Height	Makes all characters the same height, whether they are uppercase or lowercase.
◁	Flip	Flips letters on their sides.
⬧	Stretch	Stretches the text to fill the selected shape.
⬧	Align	Displays a menu of alignment choices (Center, Left, Right, plus three types of justification).

Button	Name	What It Does
	Spacing Between Characters	Displays a dialog box that enables you to adjust spacing.
	Rotate	Displays a dialog box that enables you to rotate the text.
	Shading	Selects a pattern or color for the text.
	Shadow	Selects one of several shadow types for the text.
	Border	Adjusts the thickness of the text outline.

Don't forget that, in PowerPoint's eyes, a WordArt object is not text. You can't edit it just by clicking it and typing. Instead, you have to double-click it to conjure up WordArt and then edit the text from within WordArt.

WordArt is used most often to create a company logo for the master slide or for the title slide.

Adding a Word Table or Excel Worksheet

If you want to create a slide that has columnar information, don't struggle with trying to line up the text by using PowerPoint's crude tab stops. Instead, take advantage of PowerPoint's capability to create an OLE 2 link with Word for Windows to embed a Word table. When you insert a Word table, all of Word's features for creating and editing a table are available to you from within PowerPoint.

Figure 14-6 shows an example of a Word table inserted into a PowerPoint slide. Notice the gridlines that mark the individual table cells. These were created by using Word's table-formatting commands, not PowerPoint's line-drawing button.

You can also insert an Excel worksheet into a PowerPoint presentation. This capability gives you access to Excel's advanced features for calculating values with sophisticated formulas and functions.

For these features to work, you must have Word for Windows or Excel installed on your computer. There's no such thing as a free lunch.

Figure 14-6:
A Word
table
inserted
into a
PowerPoint
slide.

Inserting a Word table

Follow these steps to insert a Word table:

1. **Create a new slide by using the Table AutoLayout and double-click the Table placeholder.**

   This step creates a slide with a placeholder for a Word table. Alternatively, you can use the Insert⇨Microsoft Word Table command or click the Insert Microsoft Word Table button on the Standard toolbar (shown in the margin). Either way, the Insert Word Table dialog box pops up, as shown in Figure 14-7.

Figure 14-7:
The Insert
Word Table
dialog box.

Insert Word Table	? ✕
Number of Columns:	OK
2	Cancel
Number of Rows:	
2	

2. **Dial the table size you want.**

   The default table size of two columns by two rows is undoubtedly too small. Increase the column and row settings as necessary.

3. **Click OK.**

   Microsoft Word and PowerPoint argue about health-care reform for a few moments and then Word plops down its menus and toolbars right on top of PowerPoint's and wraps a ruler around the table. Have a look at Figure 14-8 to see what I mean.

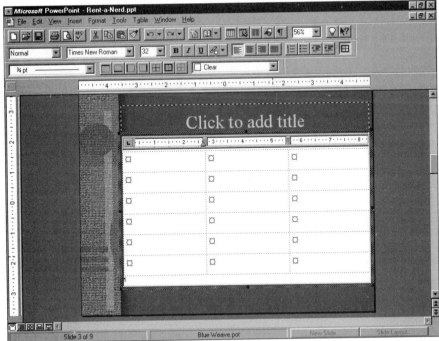

Figure 14-8:
Word has
completely
taken over!

4. **Type some text in the table cells.**

   Click the cell in which you want to type text or press the Tab key to move from cell to cell. To adjust the width of a column, drag the column marker on the ruler.

5. **Add a border if you're in a daring mood.**

   Select a cell or range of cells, and then use the Border toolbar to add borders to the selected cell or cells. If the Border toolbar isn't visible, click the Border button to summon it.

6. **Click anywhere outside the table to return to the slide.**

   Marvel at the greatness of your work.

Don't forget that even though it looks like text on-screen, PowerPoint thinks of the text as a Word table. To edit it, you have to double-click and wait while Word and PowerPoint get together. The OLE 2 link for embedding a Word table requires that you have Word for Windows Version 6 (or later) installed on your computer.

Don't try to cram more than four columns into a table. Remember that folks have to be able to read the table from the back of the room.

For the complete Lowe-down on using Word tables, run — don't walk — to the nearest computer store or bookstore and pick up a copy of *MORE Word For Windows 95 For Dummies* (IDG Books Worldwide, Inc.), by yours truly.

Inserting an Excel worksheet

Inserting an Excel Worksheet is similar to inserting a Word table. No AutoLayout format provides a placeholder for an Excel worksheet, however, nor does the Insert menu have an Excel Worksheet command.

The two options for inserting a worksheet are shown in this list:

✔ Use the Insert⇨Object command and browse the Object Type list box for Excel Worksheet.

✔ Click the Insert Microsoft Excel Worksheet button on the Standard toolbar (shown in the margin).

You must have Excel 5 or 95 for this feature to work.

After you insert the worksheet, you can toil with it by using Excel's worksheet-editing tools. When you're done, click anywhere outside the worksheet to return to the slide.

Chapter 15

Lights! Camera! Action! (Adding Sound and Video)

In This Chapter

▶ Adding burps, chortles, and gee-whizzes to your presentation

▶ Fiddling with video

*W*hat's all the rage about multimedia these days? You would think that some computer geek in Sunnyvale just invented talking movies. Multimedia technology has progressed almost to the point where a $3,000 computer can belch realistically and play six seconds of *The African Queen* almost as well as a $159 VCR can.

Oh, well. It's a trendy business, and I wouldn't be caught dead not including a chapter about multimedia gags in a PowerPoint book. Mercifully, this chapter is short because there's not really much you can do with sound and video in PowerPoint except paste them on a slide and play them when you run the slide show on your computer.

Adding Sound to a Slide

It used to be that the only sound you could get from your computer was a sterile *beep*. Nowadays, you can make your computer talk almost as well as the computers in the *Star Trek* movies. Or you can give them a sophomoric sense of audible distaste. At last, the computer can be as obnoxious as the user!

 There's a catch. Your computer must be equipped with a *sound card* to play these types of sounds. Apple Macintosh users love to brag that every Macintosh ever made has had sound capabilities built right in while poor PC users still have to purchase a separate sound card to make their computers burp as well as a Mac. Fortunately, sound cards are getting less and less expensive. Cheap ones can be had for about $50 nowadays, and fairly good ones go for about $150.

Adding sound capability to a Windows computer used to be a major undertaking. Now, thanks to Windows 95, adding sound capability is almost a no-brainer. Windows 95 automatically configures the sound card, so you don't have to mess around with driver files and other messy details.

All about sound files

Computer sounds are stored in *sound files*, which come in two varieties:

- **Wave files:** Contain digitized recordings of real sounds, such as Darth Vader saying, "I find your lack of faith disturbing" or DeForest Kelly (that's Dr. McCoy, for you non-Trekkers) saying, "He's dead, Jim." Windows comes with four WAV files: CHIMES.WAV, CHORD.WAV, DING.WAV, and TADA.WAV. Notice that these files all have names that end with WAV.

- **MIDI files:** Contain music stored in a form that the sound card's synthesizer can play. Windows comes with one: CANYON.MID. All MIDI files have names that end in MID.

To insert a sound into a PowerPoint presentation, all you have to do is paste one of these sound files into a slide. Then when you run the presentation in Slide Show view, you can have the sounds play automatically during slide transitions, or you can play them manually by clicking the Sound button.

You're more likely to use wave files than MIDI files in a PowerPoint presentation. MIDI files are great for playing music, but the wave files enable you to add truly obnoxious sounds to a presentation.

The four WAV sounds that come with Windows are pretty boring, but fortunately we have no national shortage of sound files. PowerPoint itself comes with a handful of useful sound files, including drum rolls, breaking glass, gunshots, and typewriter sounds. If you purchased PowerPoint along with the multimedia CD-ROM, you also get dozens of additional sounds to spice up your presentations.

You can also download sound files from just about any online system (such as The Microsoft Network, CompuServe, and America Online), purchase them in collections from computer software stores, or beg, borrow, or steal them from your computer-geek friends. Most computer geeks will gladly offer you a disk full of *Star Trek* sounds in exchange for a large bag of Cheetos.

If you have a microphone, you can plug into your sound card, and you can even record your own sounds. Move your computer into the living room some weekend and rent the following movies:

> ✔ *Star Wars*
>
> ✔ Any *Pink Panther* movie
>
> ✔ *The Great Muppet Caper*
>
> ✔ *Star Trek IV* and *Star Trek VI*
>
> ✔ *The African Queen*
>
> ✔ *2001: A Space Odyssey*
>
> ✔ *Annie Hall, Bananas,* or *Sleeper*

Have a ball!

Sound files consume large amounts of disk space. A typical two-second sound clip can take up 25K of precious disk real estate. It doesn't seem like much space, but it adds up.

Inserting a sound in PowerPoint

To make your PowerPoint presentation as obnoxious as possible, follow these steps:

1. Move to the slide to which you want to add the sound.

2. Choose the Insert⇨Sound command.

The Insert Sound dialog box appears, as shown in Figure 15-1.

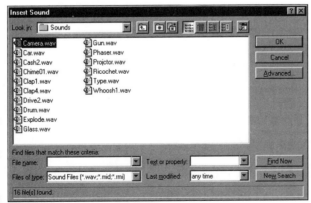

Figure 15-1:
The Insert
Sound
dialog box.

3. Find the sound file that you want to insert.

You may have to rummage through your hard disk until you find the file. Keep looking; it's there somewhere.

4. Click the OK button.

The sound is placed on the slide as an icon, as shown in Figure 15-2.

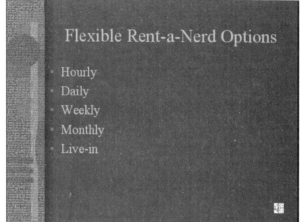

Figure 15-2:
A slide
with a
sound icon.

Playing an embedded sound

To play an embedded sound while working in Slide view, double-click the sound icon.

To play the sound during a slide show, only a single click is needed.

Removing a sound

If you finally come to your senses and realize that sounds are a bit frivolous, you can easily remove them. To remove a sound, click it and press the Delete key.

Using transition sounds

You can also use sounds to embellish slide transitions. This embellishing is covered in Chapter 16.

Working with Video

Welcome to the MTV era of computing. If your computer has the chutzpah, you can add small video clips to your presentations and play them at will. I'm not sure why you would want to, but hey, who needs a reason?

Adding a video clip to a slide is similar to adding a sound clip. There's a crucial difference, however, between video clips and sound bites: Video is meant to be *seen* as well as *heard.* An inserted video should be given ample space on your slide.

Oh, and you think that sound files are big? Wait till you see how big video files are. Ha! The whole multimedia revolution is really a conspiracy started by hard disk manufacturers.

Fortunately, Windows 95 handles most of the nasty setup and configuration details necessary to get videos to work. All you have to do is follow the steps outlined in the following sections, and you're on your way.

Adding a movie to a slide

These steps show you how to add a video clip to a slide:

1. **Find a good movie.**

   The hardest part about using video in a PowerPoint presentation is finding a video file that's worth showing. There are many good sources for video clips; the PowerPoint multimedia CD contains samples from several collections.

2. **Move to the slide on which you want to insert the movie.**

   Hopefully, you left a big blank space in the middle of the slide to put the movie in. If not, rearrange the existing slide objects to make room for the movie.

3. **Choose the Insert⇨Movie command.**

   The Insert Movie dialog box appears, as shown in Figure 15-3.

4. **Select the movie you want to insert and then click OK.**

   The movie is inserted on the slide, as shown in Figure 15-4.

Playing a movie

To play a movie, double-click it while in Slide view. In Slide Show view, a single click is sufficient to play the movie.

Figure 15-3:
The Insert
Movie
dialog box.

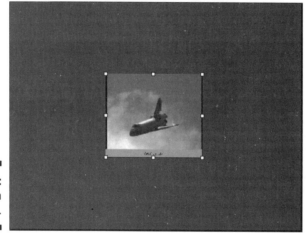

Figure 15-4:
A slide with
a movie.

When you play a movie, a set of controls appears at the bottom of the movie window, as shown in Figure 15-5. You can use these controls to stop the movie, pause it, or move forward or backward to any point in the movie.

Figure 15-5:
Movie
controls.

After a video has started playing, you can stop it by clicking the Stop button, or by clicking anywhere outside the movie's frame.

Hiding the video controls

You can hide the video controls at the bottom of an active movie window by following these steps:

1. **Right-click the movie and then choose the Edit Video Clip Object from the quick menu that appears.**

2. **Choose the Edit⬄Options command.**

   The Options dialog box appears, as shown in Figure 15-6.

Figure 15-6:
The Options
dialog box.

3. **Uncheck the Control Bar On Playback check box.**

4. **Click OK.**

5. **Click anywhere outside the movie frame to return to Slide view.**

Setting a movie to play automatically

You can set a movie so that it plays automatically when you display its slide during a slide show by following these steps:

1. **Click the movie that you want to play automatically to select it.**

2. **Choose the Tools⬄Animation Settings command.**

   The Animation Settings dialog box appears, as shown in Figure 15-7.

Figure 15-7:
The
Animation
Settings
dialog box.

3. Select Play in the Play Options list box.

4. Click the More button.

The More Play Options dialog box appears, as shown in Figure 15-8.

Figure 15-8:
The More
Play Options
dialog box.

5. Select the Automatically option, but leave the seconds field set to zero.

6. Click OK to return to the Animation Settings dialog box, and then click OK again.

Chapter 16

Transitions and Animation Effects

● ●

In This Chapter

▶ Using slide transitions

▶ Using builds

▶ Simple animations

▶ Self-running presentations

● ●

*I*f you plan to run your presentation on your computer's screen, you can use or abuse a bag full of exciting on-screen slide show tricks. Your audience probably won't be fooled into thinking that you hired Industrial Light and Magic to create your special effects, but they'll be impressed all the same. Using special effects is just one more example of how PowerPoint can make even the dullest content look spectacular.

You set up most of these special effects from PowerPoint's Slide Sorter view. In fact, aside from providing an easy way to rearrange the order of your slides, creating special effects is Slide Sorter view's main purpose in life.

Using Slide Transitions

A *transition* is how PowerPoint gets from one slide to the next during an on-screen slide show. The normal way to segue from slide to slide is simply to cut to the new slide. Effective, but boring. PowerPoint enables you to assign any of 45 different special effects to each slide transition. For example, you can have a slide scoot over the top of the current slide from any direction, or you can have the current slide scoot off the screen in any direction to reveal the next slide. And you can use various types of dissolves, from a simple dissolve to checkerboard or venetian-blind effects.

Keep these points in mind when using slide transitions:

✔ Transition effects look better on faster computers. The more powerful the computer, the more raw processing horsepower it has to implement the fancy pixel dexterity required to produce good-looking transitions.

✔ Some of the transition effects come in matched sets that apply the same effect from different directions. You can create a cohesive set of transitions by alternating among these related effects from slide to slide. For example, set up the first slide using Wipe Right, the second slide using Wipe Left, the third with Wipe Down, and so on.

✔ If you can't decide which transition effect to use, set all the slides to Random Transition. (Select all slides and then choose Random Transition from the toolbar.) Then PowerPoint picks a transition effect for each slide at random.

Slide transitions the easy way

Here's the easy way to assign transition effects:

1. Switch to Slide Sorter view.

Click the Slide Sorter View button (shown in the margin) or choose the View➪Slide Sorter command.

Figure 16-1 shows how PowerPoint displays a presentation in Slide Sorter view. Notice that the Formatting toolbar is replaced by the *Slide Sorter toolbar,* which enables you to apply special effects quickly for on-screen presentations.

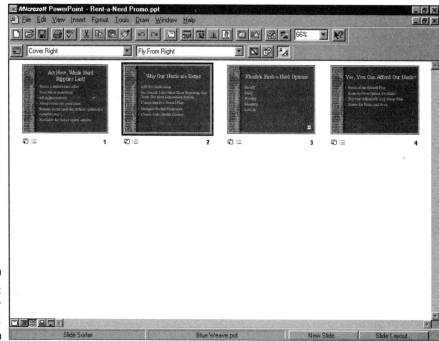

Figure 16-1:
Slide Sorter
view.

2. **Click the slide for which you want to create a transition.**

3. **Choose the transition effect you want from the drop-down list box.**

The Slide Sorter toolbar has two list boxes; the one on the left is for transition effects. In Figure 16-1, the transition is currently set to Cover Right.

When you assign a transition effect to a slide, an icon (shown in the margin) appears beneath the slide to indicate that the slide has a transition effect.

4. **Do it to other slides.**

The other slides will become jealous if you don't give them fancy transition effects, too. Repeat steps 2 and 3 to give transition effects to other slides.

To get an idea of what the transition looks like, click the transition effect button beneath the slide in Slide Sorter view. PowerPoint quickly replaces the slide with the preceding slide and then redisplays the slide using the transition effect you chose.

You can set the transition for several slides at once by selecting each slide to which you want the effect applied before choosing the effect. To select several slides, hold down the Ctrl or Shift key while clicking each slide.

Slide transitions the hard way

You can set slide transitions by using the menus also. Here's how:

1. **Head for Slide Sorter view.**

Use the View⇨Slide Sorter command or click the Slide Sorter View button (shown in the margin).

2. **Select the slide to which you want to add an effect.**

3. **Choose the Tools⇨Slide Transition command.**

Or, as a shortcut, click the Slide Transition button (shown in the margin) on the Slide Sorter toolbar. Either way, the Slide Transition dialog box, shown in Figure 16-2, appears.

4. **Choose the transition effect that you want from the Effect drop-down list box.**

5. **Choose the speed of the transition if you want.**

Fast is almost always best, unless you're trying to fill time and you don't really have anything to say.

6. **Choose a sound to accompany the transition.**

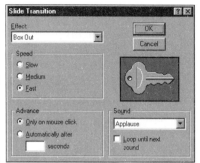

Figure 16-2:
The Slide
Transition
dialog box.

7. **Click OK or press Enter.**

PowerPoint demonstrates the transition effect you pick in the picture near the middle-right of the Slide Transition dialog box. Each time you pick a different effect, the picture changes from a dog to a key (or vice versa) to show you how the transition looks.

Using Builds

You can set up a *build effect* for any slide that contains a bulleted list. When a slide has a bulleted list, the bulleted items are added to the slide one at a time. The build effect dictates the entrance made by each bullet item. You can have them appear out of nowhere, drop from the top of the screen, march in from the left or right, or do a back somersault followed by two cartwheels and a double-twist flip (talc, please!).

The build effect you choose for a slide is used for all bullets on that slide. However, if you pick Random Effect, a different effect is used for each bullet. Your audience will be on the edge of their collective seats, waiting to see what bullet effect is next.

Like the transition effects, some of the bullet effects come in matched sets — for example: Fly from Left, Fly from Right, Fly from Top, and Fly from Bottom. Use these effects on consecutive slides to add some continuity to your presentation.

Experts refer to build effects as *progressive disclosure.* These same people refer to jumping jacks as *two-count side-step straddle hops.*

Build effects the easy way

Here's the easy way to assign a build effect:

1. **Switch to Slide Sorter view.**

   Use the View⇨Slide Sorter command or click the Slide Sorter View button (shown in the margin).

2. **Click the slide to which you want to add a build effect.**

3. **Choose the build effect from the drop-down list box.**

   The Slide Sorter toolbar has two list boxes (refer back to Figure 16-1); the one on the right is for build effects.

 When you use a build effect on a slide, PowerPoint displays an icon (shown in the margin) below the slide to help you remember that you've added the build effect. To remove the build effect from the slide, choose No Build Effect in the drop-down list box.

Build effects the hard way

You can add build effects by using the menus also. Follow these steps:

1. **Zip over to Slide Sorter view.**

   Use the View⇨Slide Sorter command or click the Slide Sorter View button (shown in the margin).

2. **Click the slide to which you want to add an effect.**

3. **Choose the Tools⇨Build Slide Text command and then choose Other.**

   The Animation Settings dialog box appears, as shown in Figure 16-3.

Figure 16-3:
The
Animation
Settings
dialog box.

4. **Select build By 1st Level Paragraphs in the Build Options drop-down list.**

   Other options in this list box allow you to build by lower-level paragraphs.

5. Choose a build effect by using the three drop-down list boxes in the build Effects group.

These three list boxes let you choose a build effect, specify how you want to apply the build effect to the entire paragraph (all at once, a word at a time, or one letter at a time), and indicate a sound effect to be played along with the build. Experiment with these different options to see how each one works.

6. Click OK or press Enter.

You can use the After Build Step list box to tell PowerPoint to dim each point after it has been built. This allows the audience to focus on each new point as it is displayed.

Animating Other Slide Objects

You can use animation effects with any object you have placed on a slide, not just with text objects. For example, suppose you include a clip art picture of a race car. Rather than just have it appear on the slide, you can apply an animation effect so that the car appears to drive onto the screen, complete with a race car sound effect. It isn't exactly Disney-quality animation, but it's kind of fun.

To animate an object, follow these steps:

1. In Slide View, click the object that you want to animate.

2. Choose the Tools⇨Animation Settings command.

The Animation Settings dialog box appears. (Refer to Figure 16-3.)

3. Choose Build for the Build Options list box.

4. Select an appropriate build type — such as Fly from Right.

The build types are listed in the first list box in the Effects group.

5. Select an appropriate sound — such as Drive By.

The sound effects are listed in the last list box in the Effects group.

6. Click OK.

Using the Predefined Animation Effects

PowerPoint 95 comes with an Animation Effects toolbar that includes several predefined animation effects. This toolbar saves you the trouble of wading through the Animation Settings dialog box to set the build type and sound effects manually.

To use the preset animation effects, click the Animation Effects button on the Standard toolbar. The Animation Effects toolbar appears, as shown in Figure 16-4. Then select the slide or object you want to animate and click the appropriate Animation buttons to apply a preset effect. Table 16-1 summarizes the buttons on the Animation Effects toolbar.

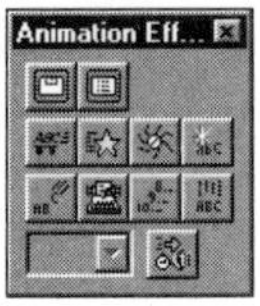

Figure 16-4:
The
Animation
Effects
toolbar.

Table 16-1   Buttons on the Animation Effects Toolbar

Button	Name	What It Does
	Animate Title	Causes the slide title to drop in from above.
	Build Slide Text	Applies a build effect to the slide text.
	Drive-In Effect	Applies the Fly From Right build effect and Screeching Brakes sound to the selected object.
	Flying Effect	Applies the Fly From Left build effect and Whoosh sound to the selected object.
	Camera Effect	Applies the Box Out build effect and Camera sound to the selected object.
	Flash Once	Applies the Flash Once (Medium) build effect to the selected object, with no sound.
	Laser Text Effect	Applies the Fly From Top Right, By Letter build effect and the Laser sound effect to the selected object.
	Typing Text Effect	Applies the Wipe Down, By Letter build effect and the Typewriter sound effect to the selected object.

(continued)

Table 16-1 *(continued)*

Button	Name	What It Does
 8.-- 9.-- 10.--	Reverse Text Build	Applies a simple Wipe Right build effect, with no sound, to the object so that paragraphs are built in reverse order. Use this effect for Top-Ten lists.
¡!¡ ABC	Drop-In Text Effect	Applies a Fly From Top, By Word build effect with no sound.
1 ▼	Animation Order	Lets you control the order in which objects are animated.
	Animation Settings	Summons the Animation Settings dialog box.

Setting Up a Presentation That Runs by Itself

You can use PowerPoint's slide transitions and animation effects to set up a slide show that runs completely by itself. Just follow these steps:

1. Switch to Slide Sorter view.

Use the View➪Slide Sorter command or click the Slide Sorter View button (shown in the margin).

2. Set the transitions and build effects however you wish.

Refer to the sections "Using Slide Transitions" and "Using Builds" for help with this step.

3. Press Ctrl+A to select all slides in the presentation.

4. Click the Slide Transition button (shown in margin).

The Slide Transition dialog box appears (refer to Figure 16-2).

5. Select the Automatically after check box and then select the number of seconds that you want to pause between each slide.

6. Click OK.

To run the slide show automatically, choose the View➪Slide Show command to summon the Slide Show dialog box. Select the Use Slide Timings option and check the Loop Continuously Until 'Esc' check box if you want the show to run continuously, all day long. Then click OK.

Part IV
Cool PowerPoint 95 Features

The 5th Wave   By Rich Tennant

"Oh sure, it's nice working at home, except my boss drives by every morning and blasts his horn to make sure I'm awake."

In this part...

This part covers a covey of PowerPoint for Windows 95 features that just don't fit anyplace else in this book. You can think of this part as "Miscellaneous PowerPoint 95 Features" if you want.

Chapter 17

Using AutoCorrect

In This Chapter

▶ Using PowerPoint's AutoCorrect feature

▶ Controlling what gets AutoCorrected and what doesn't

▶ Adding your own AutoCorrect entries

*A*utoCorrect was originally introduced with PowerPoint 4 and was so popular that Microsoft decided to add it to PowerPoint 95. AutoCorrect monitors your typing, carefully watching for common typing mistakes and fixing them quicker than you can say "Bob's Your Uncle." For example, type *adn* and AutoCorrect changes it to *and. Teh* becomes *the. Recieve* becomes *receive.* You get the idea.

Doing the AutoCorrect Thing

You control AutoCorrect from the Tools⇨AutoCorrect command, which brings up the dialog box shown in Figure 17-1. This dialog box lets you activate specific AutoCorrect features; in the figure, all AutoCorrect features are enabled, but you might find that one feature or another doesn't suit your fancy. If that's the case, use the Tools⇨AutoCorrect command to disable the feature you don't like.

Figure 17-1:
The
AutoCorrect
dialog box.

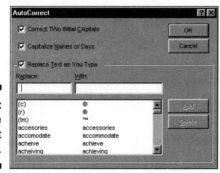

The Tools⇨Options command also has some options that seem like AutoCorrect options. For example, the option to automatically convert straight quotes to curly quotes is found under the Tools⇨Options command, not under AutoCorrect. Go figure.

The following sections describe each AutoCorrect option in detail.

Correct TWo INitial CApitals

If you're an average typist, you probably have the bad habit of once in a while leaving the Shift key down a bit too long when typing the initial capital letter of a sentence or proper noun. The result is that two letters of the word wind up being capitalized rather than just one. If this option is enabled, AutoCorrect watches for this mistake and changes the second capital letter to lowercase.

This is a very useful feature, unless of course you *want* to type the first two letters of a word in capitals. As an example, you'd have fun trying to prepare a presentation about using this feature. Every time you typed **Correct TWo INitial CApitals** on a slide, PowerPoint would change it to *Correct Two Initial Capitals*, politely correcting your double capitalization.

The simple solution is to just press Ctrl+Z (the Undo key, remember?) immediately after PowerPoint "corrects" your capitalization. Doing so restores the capitalization exactly as you typed it.

Capitalize Names of Days

If this option is enabled, PowerPoint always capitalizes the first letter of the names of days — Monday, Tuesday, Wednesday, and so on. Thus, if you type **thursday**, PowerPoint automatically changes it to *Thursday*.

 Unfortunately, PowerPoint provides no option for capitalizing the names of months (January, February, and so on). However, you can easily add AutoCorrect entries to capitalize month names. Just set up the following AutoCorrect entries:

Replace	*With*
january	January
february	February
march	March

And so on, through December. For instructions on setting up your own AutoCorrect entries, see the following section, "Replace Text as You Type."

Replace Text as You Type

This option is the heart of AutoCorrect; the other options are merely gravy. At its core, AutoCorrect is a list of replacements that should be made whenever certain words are typed. For example, whenever you type **adn**, PowerPoint should automatically substitute *and*. PowerPoint makes these substitutions only if the Replace Text as You Type checkbox is selected.

PowerPoint comes with an extensive list of built-in AutoCorrect entries. Some of these entries correct commonly misspelled words, such as *adn* for *and* and *teh* for *the*. Others provide a convenient way to quickly insert special symbols. These AutoCorrect entries are summarized in Table 17-1.

Table 17-1	Built-in AutoCorrect Entries for Creating Symbols
Replace	*With*
(c)	Copyright symbol: ©
(r)	Registered symbol: ®
(tm)	Trademark symbol: ™

You can use the Undo command to undo a change made by AutoCorrect. For example, if you type —> and do *not* want it converted to an arrow, press Ctrl+Z immediately after PowerPoint changes it to the arrow. The text is then restored to —>.

Creating AutoCorrect Entries

To add your own AutoCorrect entries, follow these steps:

1. **Call up the Tools⇨AutoCorrect command.**

   The AutoCorrect dialog box is displayed.

2. **Type the text you want to be replaced in the Replace field.**

3. **Type the text you want to replace it with in the With field.**

4. **Click OK.**

For example, if you want to set up an AutoCorrect entry so that every time you type **february**, PowerPoint replaces it with *February,* type **february** in the Replace field and **February** in the With field. Then click Add.

Deleting AutoCorrect Entries

To remove an entry from the AutoCorrect list, highlight the entry you want to remove and click the Delete button.

Chapter 18

Creating Notes Pages

. . . .

In This Chapter

▶ Creating speaker notes to get you through your presentation

▶ Adjusting the notes page to make long notes fit

▶ Adding a new slide from Notes Pages view

▶ Printing your notes pages

. . . .

*E*ver had the fear — or maybe the actual experience — of showing a beautiful slide, complete with snappy text and perhaps an exquisite chart, and suddenly forgetting why you included the slide in the first place? You stumble for words. "Well, as you can see, this is a beautiful chart, and, uh, this slide makes the irrefutable point that, uh, well, I'm not sure — are there any questions?"

Fear not! One of PowerPoint's slickest features is its capability to create speaker notes to help you get through your presentation. You can make these notes as complete or as sketchy as you want or need. You can write a complete script for your presentation or just jot down a few key points to refresh your memory.

The best part about speaker notes is that you are the only one who sees them. They don't actually show up on your slides for all the world to see. Instead, notes pages are printed separately. There's one notes page for each slide in the presentation, and each notes page includes a reduced version of the slide so that you can keep track of which notes page belongs to which slide.

To add speaker notes to a presentation, you must switch PowerPoint to Notes Pages view. Then you just type away.

Don't you think that it's about time for a short chapter? Although notes pages are one of PowerPoint's slickest features, creating notes pages isn't all that complicated — hence the brevity of this chapter.

Understanding Notes Pages View

Notes Pages view shows the speaker notes pages that are created for your presentation. There is one notes page for each slide in a presentation. Each notes page consists of a reduced version of the slide and an area for notes. Figure 18-1 shows an example of a presentation shown in Notes Pages view.

You can switch to Notes Pages view in two ways:

- ✔ Click the Notes Pages View button (shown in the margin) to the left of the horizontal scroll bar.

- ✔ Use the View➪Notes Pages command.

Unfortunately, no keyboard shortcut is available to switch directly to Notes Pages view. To add notes to a presentation, just click the notes text object and begin typing.

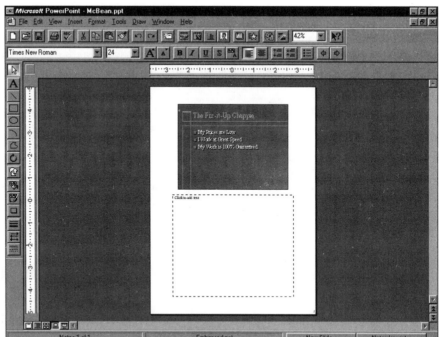

Figure 18-1:
A presentation in Notes Pages view.

When you first switch to Notes Pages view, the display probably will be too small for you to read the speaker notes. To enlarge the display, click the down arrow next to the zoom setting to reveal a list of zoom settings and pick the one that works best for you. A zoom factor of 66 or 75 percent is usually about right. (You can also type any zoom factor you like directly into the zoom size field.)

Adding Notes to a Slide

To add notes to a slide, follow this procedure:

1. **In Slide or Outline view, move to the slide to which you want to add notes.**

2. **Switch to Notes Pages view.**

3. **Adjust the zoom factor if necessary so that you can read the notes text.**

4. **Scroll the display if necessary to bring the notes text into view.**

5. **Click the notes text object, where it reads *Click to add text*.**

6. **Type away.**

The text you type appears in the notes area. As you create your notes, you can use any of PowerPoint's standard word processing features, such as cut, copy, and paste. Press the Enter key to create new paragraphs.

Figure 18-2 shows a notes page displayed with a zoom factor of 75 percent and with some notes typed.

After you have switched to Notes Pages view, you don't have to return to Slide view or Outline view to add notes for other slides. Use the scroll bar or the Page Up and Page Down keys to add notes for other slides.

My Notes Don't Fit!

If your notes don't fit in the area provided on the notes page, you have two options: Increase the size of the text area on the notes page or create a second notes page for a slide.

Increasing the size of the text area on a notes page

To increase the size of the text area on a notes page, follow this procedure:

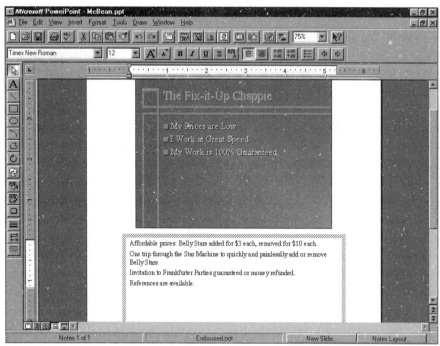

Figure 18-2:
Notes that
are enlarged
for your
reading
pleasure.

1. **Make the notes page slide object smaller by grabbing a corner of the slide object (by clicking it) and dragging it to a smaller size. After you shrink the slide, move it to the top of the page.**

2. **Increase the size of the notes page text area by clicking it and then dragging the top love handle up.**

Figure 18-3 shows a notes page with a smaller slide and a larger area for notes.

Changing the size of the slide and text areas while you're in Notes Page view changes those areas for only the current page; other pages are unaffected. To change the size of these areas for all notes pages, switch to Notes Master view and make the adjustment. (Masters were covered back in Chapter 8.)

To create the largest possible area for notes on a notes page, delete the slide area altogether. Just click it and press the Delete key. If you do that, you find that it's all too easy to get your notes pages mixed up so that you cannot tell which notes page belongs with which slide. Include page numbers on both your slides and your notes pages to help keep them in sync or type each slide's title at the top of the notes page. (You can set up page numbers for slides and notes pages by using the View⇨Header and Footer command.)

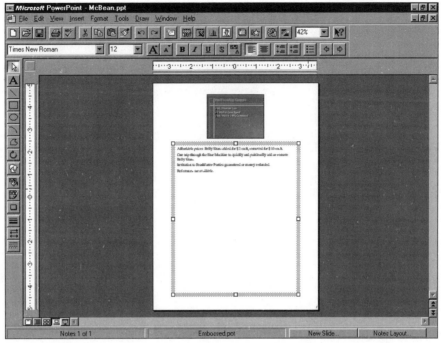

Figure 18-3:
A notes
page with
more room
for notes.

Adding an extra notes page for a slide

PowerPoint doesn't provide any way to add more than one page of notes for each slide. But these steps show a trick that accomplishes essentially the same thing:

1. **Create a new slide immediately following the slide that requires two pages of notes.**

   Do this step in Slide, Outline, or Notes Pages view.

2. **Switch to Notes Pages view and move to the notes page for the slide you just created.**

   Delete the slide object at the top of this notes page by clicking it and pressing the Delete key. Then extend the notes text area up so that it fills the page by clicking it and then dragging the top center love handle up.

3. **Type the additional notes for the preceding slide on this new notes page.**

   Add a heading, such as "Continued from slide 23," at the top of the text to help you remember that this portion is a continuation of notes from the preceding slide.

4. Use the <u>T</u>ools⇨<u>H</u>ide Slide command to *hide* the slide.

You can use this command from any view. The Hide Slide command hides the slide, which means that it isn't included in an on-screen slide show.

The result of this trick is that you now have two pages of notes for a single slide, and the second notes page doesn't have an image of the slide on it and is not included in your slide show.

If you're printing overhead transparencies, you may want to uncheck the Print <u>H</u>idden Slides check box in the Print dialog box. That way, the hidden slide isn't printed. Be sure to recheck the box when you print the notes pages, though. Otherwise, the notes page for the hidden slide isn't printed either — and the reason you created the hidden slide in the first place was so that you can print a notes page for it!

Think twice before creating a second page of notes for a slide. Do you really have that much to say about a single slide? Maybe the slide contains too much to begin with and should be split into two slides.

Adding a New Slide from Notes Pages View

If you're working on the notes for a slide and realize that you want to create a new slide, you don't have to return to Slide view or Outline view. Just click the New Slide button on the status bar or use the <u>I</u>nsert⇨New <u>S</u>lide menu command to add the new slide.

If you want to work on the slide's appearance or contents, however, you must switch back to Slide or Outline view. You cannot modify a slide's appearance or contents from Notes Pages view.

To revert quickly to Slide view from Notes Pages view, double-click the notes page's slide area.

Printing Notes Pages

Notes pages don't do you much good if you can't print them. These steps show you how to do so:

1. Summon the <u>F</u>ile⇨<u>P</u>rint command.

The Print dialog box appears.

2. **Use the Print <u>W</u>hat list box to choose the Notes Pages option.**

3. **Make sure that the Print H<u>i</u>dden Slides box is checked if you want to print notes pages for hidden slides.**

4. **Click the OK button or press the Enter key.**

Figure 18-4 shows the Print dialog box with the Notes Pages option selected so that notes pages rather than slides are printed.

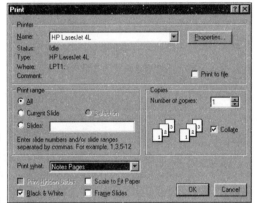

Figure 18-4:
The Print
dialog box.

If you have just printed slides on overhead transparencies, don't forget to reload your printer with plain paper. You probably don't want to print your speaker notes on transparencies!

More information about printing is in Chapter 5.

Random Thoughts about Speaker Notes

This section provides some ideas that may help you make the most of your notes pages.

If you're giving an important presentation for a large audience, you may want to consider using notes pages to write a complete script for your presentation. For less formal presentations, more succinct notes are probably better.

Use notes pages to jot down any anecdotes, jokes, or other asides you want to remember to use in your presentation.

If you prefer to hand-write your notes, you can print blank notes pages. Don't bother adding notes to your presentation, but use the File⇨Print command to print notes pages. The resulting notes pages have a reduced image of the slide at the top and a blank space in which you can hand-write your notes later.

You may also consider providing blank notes pages for your audience. The File⇨Print command can print audience handouts that contain two, three, or six slides per page, but these handout pages leave no room for the audience members to write notes.

Chapter 19
Making 35mm Slides

In This Chapter

▶ Using a local photo lab
▶ Preparing a file for Genigraphics
▶ Sending a file to Genigraphics

*Y*ou can convert PowerPoint slides easily to 35mm color slides, but unless you have your own photo processing equipment, you have to deal with a photo lab to get the job done. It isn't cheap (here in California, it costs $7–$10 per slide), but the slides look great.

This chapter briefly covers what you need to know to take your presentation to a local photo lab for processing. But most of the chapter is devoted to using Genigraphics — without a doubt the most convenient way to get 35mm slides out of PowerPoint.

Using a Local Photo Lab

One way to produce 35mm slides from a PowerPoint presentation is to take the presentation files to a local photo lab with the equipment to create the slides. Call the lab first to find out the cost and to check on any special requirements it may have, such as whether you need to embed TrueType fonts when you save the file and whether the lab prefers you to save the file to a $5^1/_4$ inch or $3^1/_2$ inch disk.

To be safe, always embed TrueType fonts and save the file to both $5^1/_4$ inch and $3^1/_2$ inch disks.

You'll find photo labs that can produce computer output listed in the Yellow Pages under Computer Graphics, or perhaps under Photo Finishing. Call several labs and compare costs and find out how quickly each can finish the job.

Use the PowerPoint File➪Save As command to save the presentation to disk. Take two copies of the presentation file — on separate disks — to the photo shop. Nothing is more frustrating than driving across town only to discover that something's wrong with your disk. Or if the shop has a modem, and you have a modem and know how to use it, you can probably zap your presentation to the lab over the phone.

Carefully proof your slides by using PowerPoint's Slide Show view. Run the spell checker. At $10 per slide, you don't want too many typos to slip by.

Using Genigraphics

Genigraphics is a company that specializes in computer graphics and managed to get its software bundled with PowerPoint. If you can't find a local shop that can do the job, Genigraphics is always available. You can send them your presentation on disk, or you can send it via modem. PowerPoint even comes with a built-in command that automatically sends your presentations to Genigraphics.

Genigraphics accepts major credit cards or can bill you COD. If you've got clout, you may convince them to open an account. For really big presentations, they offer convenient 15- or 30-year mortgages with fixed or adjustable rates.

Sending a presentation to Genigraphics for printing is easy. If you have a modem, follow these steps:

1. **Open your presentation.**

   Use the File➪Open command to find and open your file.

2. **Use the File➪Slide Setup command to set the slides to 35mm, Landscape. Click OK.**

3. **Choose the File➪Send to Genigraphics command.**

   The Genigraphics Wizard appears, as shown in Figure 19-1.

4. **Click Next.**

   The Wizard starts asking questions. See Figure 19-2, where the Wizard wants to know what kind of output you want to create: 35mm slides, transparencies, posters, and so on.

5. **Answer the questions and click Next.**

   More questions appear.

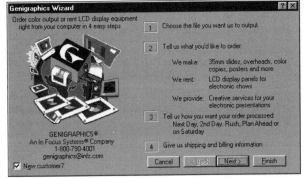

Figure 19-1:
The
Genigraphics
Wizard
comes to
life.

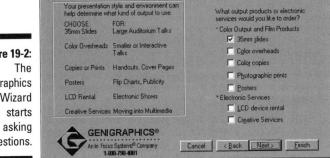

Figure 19-2:
The
Genigraphics
Wizard
starts
asking
questions.

6. Keep answering questions and clicking Next.

This process goes on for a while. Genigraphics needs a lot of information: how you want the slides created, how you want them shipped, where you want them shipped to, and — most importantly — how you're going to pay for them. There's no way around it: You're going to have to give them a credit card number.

One big decision you'll have to make is how quickly you need the slides. If you have procrastinated until the day before the big presentation, you'll have to pay a premium to get the slides processed overnight. At the time I wrote this, next-day processing cost $10.99 per slide. If you have a few days to spare, you can get by with second-day processing for $8.99 per slide. And if you have 7–10 days, you can use the Plan-Ahead method, which costs only $6.99 per slide.

Another important question you'll be asked is whether you want a separate slide for each build line. (A build displays bullet lines progressively, adding one line at a time.) This can make a huge difference in the cost. For example, suppose your presentation consists of 12 slides, and you put it off until the day before the big event. At $10.99 each, 12 slides will cost you about $132. But if each slide has five bullets, and you want a separate slide for each build, you're talking about 60 slides at a total of more than $650. Those build effects aren't cheap.

7. When you have answered all the questions, click Finish.

The Genigraphics Wizard fires up a program called GraphicsLink, which uses your modem to call into the Genigraphics computers and sends your presentation over the phone lines.

8. Watch for the FedEx truck.

The finished slides should appear at your doorstep within the stated delivery time.

If you don't have a modem, you can direct the Genigraphics Wizard to create a diskette containing your presentation. Then mail the diskette to Genigraphics for processing.

Chapter 20

Show Time!

In This Chapter

▶ Running a slide show

▶ Hiding slides

▶ Taking your show on the road

▶ The John Madden effect

▶ Using the Meeting Minder

▶ Giving presentations on the network

Starting a Slide Show

 To start a slide show immediately, click the Slide Show button (shown in the margin). PowerPoint replaces the entire screen with the first slide of the slide show. To advance to the next slide, press Enter, press the spacebar, or click the mouse button.

Alternatively, you can use the View⇨Slide Show command. Then the Slide Show dialog box shown in Figure 20-1 appears.

Figure 20-1:
The Slide
Show dialog
box.

With the options in the Slide Show dialog box, you can do the following:

- ✔ Choose <u>A</u>ll to include all slides in the slide show.
- ✔ Choose <u>F</u>rom and supply starting and ending slide numbers to display a range of slides.
- ✔ Choose <u>M</u>anual Advance to advance from slide to slide by pressing the Enter key, pressing the spacebar, or clicking the mouse button.
- ✔ Choose <u>U</u>se Slide Timings to advance automatically based on the timings specified for each slide.
- ✔ Choose <u>R</u>ehearse New Timings to have PowerPoint keep track of how long each slide is displayed as you rehearse your presentation.
- ✔ Choose <u>L</u>oop Continuously Until Esc if you want the entire slide show to loop from the end to the beginning automatically. You must use timings for this feature to work.

Keyboard tricks during a slide show

During an on-screen slide show, you can use the keyboard to control the sequence of your presentation. Table 20-1 lists the keys you can use.

Table 20-1	Keyboard Tricks for Your Slide Show
To Do This	*Press Any of These Keys*
Display next slide	Enter, spacebar, →, ↓, Page Down, N
Display preceding slide	Backspace, ←, ↑, Page Up, P
Display first slide	1+Enter
Display specific slide	*Slide number*+Enter
Toggle screen black	B, period
Toggle screen white	W, comma
Show or hide pointer	A, = (equals)
Erase screen doodles	E
Stop or restart automatic show	S, + (plus)
Display next slide even if hidden	H
Display specific hidden slide	*Slide number of hidden slide*+Enter
Ctrl+A	Change pen to arrow
Ctrl+P	Change arrow to pen
End slide show	Esc, Ctrl+Break (the Break key doubles as the Pause key), – (minus)

Mouse tricks during a slide show

Table 20-2 shows some tricks you can perform with your mouse during an on-screen slide show.

Table 20-2	Mouse Tricks for Your Slide Show
To Do This	*Do This*
Display next slide or build	Click
Call up menu of actions	Right-click
Display first slide	Hold down both mouse buttons for two seconds
Doodle	Press Ctrl+P to change the mouse arrow to a pen and then draw on-screen like John Madden. (If the doodle button does not appear, give your mouse a nudge.)

The John Madden effect

If you've always wanted to diagram plays on-screen the way John Madden does, try using the pen during a slide show. Here's how:

1. **Start a slide show.**

2. **When you want to doodle on a slide, press Ctrl+P.**

   The mouse arrow pointer changes to a pen shape.

3. **Draw away.**

   Figure 20-2 shows an example of a doodled-upon slide.

4. **To erase your doodles, press E.**

Drawing doodles like this requires good mouse dexterity. With practice, you can learn to create all kinds of interesting doodles. Work on circling text or drawing exclamation or question marks, smiley faces, and so on.

Keep these tasty tidbits in mind when doodling:

- To hide the mouse pointer temporarily during a slide show, press *A* or =. The pointer returns the moment you move the mouse, or you can press *A* or = again to summon it back.

- If you use the pen, be sure to say "Bam" and "Pow" a lot.

- To turn off the Doodle button, press the equals sign (=) on your keyboard.

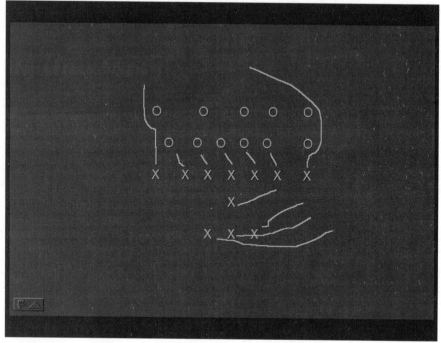

Taking Your Show on the Road

PowerPoint comes with a program called the *PowerPoint Viewer* that enables you to run a PowerPoint slide show on a computer that doesn't have a full-fledged copy of PowerPoint. You can't create, edit, or print presentations by using Viewer, but you can run on-screen slide shows just as if you were using the full PowerPoint program.

Using the Pack and Go Wizard

The easiest way to use the PowerPoint Viewer is to use the Pack and Go Wizard, a special PowerPoint command that copies a complete presentation onto a diskette, along with any supporting files required by the presentation — such as fonts — and a copy of the PowerPoint Viewer.

Here's the procedure for using the Pack and Go Wizard:

    1. Open the presentation you want to copy to diskette.

2. Choose the File⇨Pack and Go command.

The Pack and Go Wizard appears, as shown in Figure 20-3.

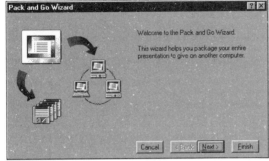

Figure 20-3:
The Pack
and Go
Wizard
comes
to life.

3. Click Next.

The Pack and Go Wizard asks which presentation you want to include, as shown in Figure 20-4. If you wish, check Other Presentations and click the Browse button.

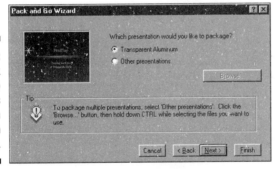

Figure 20-4:
The Pack
and Go
Wizard asks
which
presentation
to include.

4. Click Next.

The Pack and Go Wizard asks whether you want to copy the presentation to drive A or a different drive, as shown in Figure 20-5.

5. Change the drive letter if necessary, and then click Next.

The Pack and Go Wizard asks if you want to include linked files and TrueType fonts, as shown in Figure 20-6. It's usually a good idea to check both of these options.

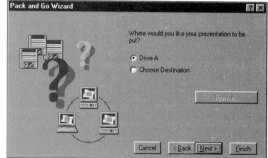

Figure 20-5:
The Pack
and Go
Wizard asks
which drive
to copy the
presentation
to.

Figure 20-6:
The Pack
and Go
Wizard asks
if it should
include
linked files
and
TrueType
fonts.

6. Click Next yet again.

This time, the Pack and Go Wizard asks whether you want the PowerPoint
Viewer included on the disk, as shown in Figure 20-7.

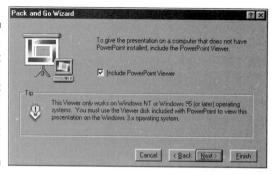

Figure 20-7:
Now it
wants to
know if it
should
include the
PowerPoint
Viewer.

7. **Click Next one more time.**

   Finally, the last screen of the Pack and Go Wizard appears.

8. **Insert a diskette in the diskette drive.**

9. **Click Finish.**

10. **Get a cup of coffee.**

    Copying the presentation and the PowerPoint Viewer to diskette can take a few minutes. Be patient.

Loading a packed presentation on another computer

You cannot run a presentation directly from the disk created by the Pack and Go Wizard. Instead, you must first copy the presentation from the diskette to another computer's hard drive. To do that, simply run the Pngsetup program, which the Pack and Go Wizard automatically copies to the diskette. After you run the Pngsetup program, you can run the presentation by using the Viewer, as described in the next section.

Running a slide show by using the Viewer

Here's the procedure for displaying a slide show using the Viewer:

1. **Start PowerPoint Viewer.**

   Double-click its icon, which should be found on the folder you copied the presentation to when you ran the Pngsetup program from the diskette.

2. **Select the presentation you want to show.**

   Figure 20-8 shows the dialog box that PowerPoint Viewer displays. Use it to rummage through your files until you find the presentation you want.

3. **Click Show.**

   On with the show. Break a leg, kid.

Once the show is underway, you can use any of the keyboard or mouse tricks described in the section "On with the Show." You can even doodle on-screen a la John Madden.

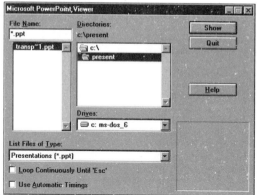

Figure 20-8:
The
PowerPoint
Viewer
dialog box.

If you have the full PowerPoint program, there's not much point in using the Viewer program instead. Viewer is designed for use on computers that don't have a copy of PowerPoint. Microsoft politely grants permission for you to copy the Viewer program to as many computers as you want. You can give it to your friends and associates. It would make a great birthday present for your mother-in-law.

If you use a desktop computer to create PowerPoint presentations and a laptop or notebook computer to run them, you don't have to install the full PowerPoint program on the laptop or notebook computer; just use the Pack and Go Wizard to transfer the presentation and the Viewer program to the notebook computer.

It's perfectly legal to give a friend a copy of the PowerPoint Viewer program along with a presentation. In fact, Microsoft specifically gives you permission to do so. This free-for-all applies only to PowerPoint Viewer, though. Don't make copies of the complete PowerPoint program for your friends unless you want to go to directly to jail (do not pass Go, do not collect $200).

If you want to set up a computer to run a slide show over and over again all day, click the Loop Continuously Until Esc box.

If you do set up an unattended presentation, be sure to hide the keyboard and mouse, or unplug them from the computer after you get the slide show going. Leaving a keyboard unattended is like inviting all the computer geeks within five miles to step up to your computer and find out which games you have.

If you're going to run a slide show on a computer other than the one you used to create the presentation, you need to make sure that the other computer has all the fonts that your presentation uses. If it doesn't, or if you're not sure, use the File⇨Save As command to save the file and check the Embed TrueType Fonts button. Doing so stores a copy of the fonts used by the presentation in the presentation file.

The Meeting Minder

PowerPoint 95 includes a nifty new feature called the *Meeting Minder,* which allows you to take notes during a presentation. To use the Meeting Minder, right-click the mouse during a slide show and choose the Meeting Minder command. The dialog box shown in Figure 20-9 appears.

Figure 20-9:
The Meeting
Minder.

As you can see, the Meeting Minder has three tabbed areas. You can use these areas as follows:

- ✔ **Notes Pages:** Click the Notes Pages tab, and then type any notes you would like to jot down for the slide currently displayed. Any notes you type are automatically added to the Notes page for that slide. You can print the Notes pages later by choosing the File⇨Print command. (See Chapter 18 for more information about Notes Pages.)

- ✔ **Meeting Minutes:** Click the Meeting Minutes tab to keep minutes during a meeting. When you are finished, you can then click the Export button and convert the minutes to a Word document.

- ✔ **Action Items:** Click the Action Items tab to record items that require action following the meeting. Anything you type here is added to the last slide of the presentation, titled "Action Items." That way, the action items are automatically displayed at the end of the presentation.

Running a Presentation over a Network

PowerPoint for Windows 95 allows you to run presentation conferences over a computer network, which basically means that you can run a slide show and invite other network users to view the slide show on their computers. Each person who participates in the conference must have PowerPoint for Windows 95 installed on his or her computer.

To start a presentation conference, open the presentation and choose the Tools⇨Presentation Conference command. PowerPoint asks you to supply the name of each computer you want to participate in the conference; be sure to first find out the network name of each of your colleagues' computers.

After you have begun the conference, others can join by choosing the Tools⇨Presentation Conference command on their computers.

When everyone has joined in the conference, you can begin the slide show. Anyone participating in the conference can use the Pen tool to draw annotations on the slide; those annotations are visible to everyone participating.

Part V
Working with Files

Arthur inadvertently replaces his mouse pad with an Ouija board. For the rest of the day, he receives messages from the spectral world.

YOU WILL FORGET YOUR PASSWORD. YOUR HARD DISK WILL CRASH AAAHAHAHAHA

In this part...

No matter how hard you try, you cannot avoid dealing with files. After all, the basic function of PowerPoint, and just about any other program for that matter, is to create files. If all you ever do is create files, pretty soon your hard disk resembles my feeble attempts at gardening: The good stuff is choked nearly to death by giant 8-foot weeds that you should have pulled out months ago. Like a garden, your hard disk — along with its directories and files — must be tended.

The chapters in this part are a file-management gardening guide. They explore the intricacies of working with PowerPoint files, making your files coexist peacefully with other types of files, keeping track of your files, and making sure that your files get adequate sunlight and nourishment.

Chapter 21

Juggling Multiple Presentations and Stealing Slides

• •

In This Chapter

▶ Editing several presentations all at once

▶ Stealing slides from another PowerPoint file

▶ Saving summary information

• •

S ure, you probably already know how to click the New button to create a new file, the Open button to retrieve an existing file, and the Save button to save a file. But there's much more to working with files than clicking these three buttons. This chapter covers the all-important and ever-so-boring topic of working with PowerPoint files. Have fun.

Editing More Than One Presentation at a Time

Some people like to do just one thing at a time: Start a task, work on it till it's done, and then put away their tools. These same people sort their canned goods by food group and have garages that look like the hardware department at Sears.

Then there are people like me, who work on no fewer than 12 things at a time, would just as soon leave canned goods in the bag arranged just the way the kid at the grocery store tossed them in, and haven't been able to park both cars in the garage since before the kids were born.

Apparently, a few of the latter type work at Microsoft because they decided to enable you to open a whole gaggle of PowerPoint files at a time. Now we're getting somewhere!

To open more than one presentation, just keep using the File⇨Open command. PowerPoint places each file you open in its own presentation window that's contained within the PowerPoint window. This presentation window is normally maximized to fill all the available space within the PowerPoint window, so you can see only one presentation window at a time. But you can switch between windows by choosing the window you want with the Window command or by pressing Ctrl+F6 to pop from window to window.

PowerPoint enables you to display the window for each open file in three ways:

- **Cascaded:** The presentation windows are stacked atop one another, as shown in Figure 21-1. This arrangement enables you to see the title bar of each window. To switch to a window other than the one on top, click its title bar or any other portion of the window you can see. This step sucks the window up to the top of the stack. To cause all presentation windows to fall into a cascaded stack, choose the Window⇨Cascade command.

- **Tiled:** The presentation windows are arranged side-by-side, as shown in Figure 21-2. This arrangement enables you to see a small portion of each presentation, though the more files you have open, the smaller this portion gets. To arrange all presentation windows in tiled form, use the Window⇨Arrange All command.

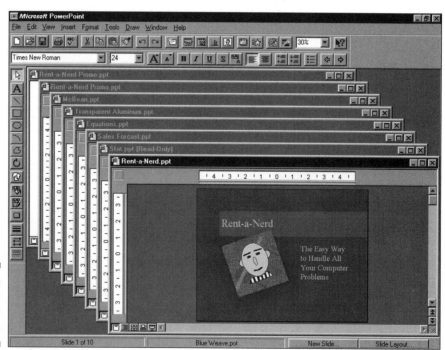

Figure 21-1: Cascaded presentation windows.

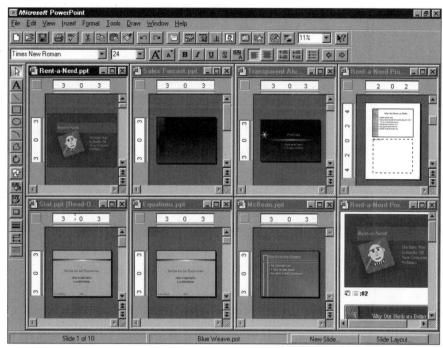

Figure 21-2:
Tiled
presentation
windows.

> ✔ **Minimized:** The windows become icons that appear within the PowerPoint window, as shown in Figure 21-3. To shrink a presentation window to an icon, click the window's minimize button. To restore the window, double-click the icon.

Even though you can open umpteen presentation windows, only one is active at a time. While you work on one presentation, the others lie dormant, praying to the ASCII gods that you won't neglect them forever.

To copy something from one file to another, switch to the first file's window, copy the object to the Clipboard (by using the normal Copy command), and then switch to the second file's window and paste away.

 Most other Windows programs that enable you to open multiple documents, including Word for Windows 7 and Excel 7, work the same as PowerPoint. So learning the menu commands and keyboard shortcuts for working with more than one presentation window in PowerPoint pays off because you use the same menu commands and keyboard shortcuts in other programs.

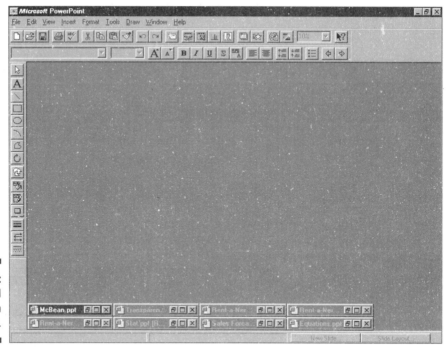

Figure 21-3:
Minimized
presentation
windows.

PowerPoint offers a handful of keyboard shortcuts for bouncing around between presentation windows. They're summarized for your reading pleasure in Table 21-1.

Table 21-1   Keyboard Shortcuts for Multiple Windows

Shortcut	What It Does
Ctrl+F6	Moves you to the next presentation window.
Shift+Ctrl+F6	Moves you to the previous presentation window.
Ctrl+F10	Maximizes a presentation window.
Ctrl+F5	Returns a window to its normal size.
Ctrl+F4	Closes a document window.

You can quickly change the size of a presentation window so that it's just big enough to show the entire slide at the current zoom factor by using the Window⇨Fit to Page command.

Here are a couple of tips for working with multiple windows:

- ✔ You can open more than one file with a single pass through the File⇨Open command. Just hold down the Ctrl key while you click each file you want to open or use the Shift key to select a block of files. When you click the OK button, all the files you selected open, each in its own window.

- ✔ Some men especially love to use the Ctrl+F6 shortcut to flip from one window to the next. They sit there at the computer, beer in hand, flipping incessantly from window to window and hoping to find a football game or a boxing match.

- ✔ If you want to shut down a window, use the File⇨Close command, press Ctrl+W, or click the window's close button. If the file displayed in the window contains changes that haven't been saved to disk, PowerPoint asks whether you want to save the file first.

Stealing Slides from Other Presentations

What do you do when you're plodding along in PowerPoint and realize that you want to copy slides from an old presentation into the one you're working on now? You steal the existing slides, that's what you do. No need to reinvent the wheel, as they say.

You can steal slides from other presentations in two ways. The easier method is to insert all the slides from an existing presentation into the file you're working on. PowerPoint has a menu command designed to do specifically that, so you don't have to think about it. If you need just a few slides from another file, you can open them both and copy slides individually from one file to the other. This technique takes a little more concentration, though.

Stealing a whole presentation

To steal all of an existing presentation and stash it in the presentation you're working on, follow these steps:

1. **Move to the slide you want the stolen slides to be placed after.**

2. **Conjure up the Insert⇨Slides from File command.**

   This step displays the dialog box shown in Figure 21-4.

3. **Snoop around on your hard disk until you find the presentation you want to steal. Highlight it and then click Insert.**

   You're done.

Don't bother reading this stuff about the Multiple Document Interface

If you're into Windows trivia, you may be interested to know that PowerPoint's capability to open more than one file at a time conforms to a Microsoft standard called *Multiple Document Interface,* lovingly abbreviated as *MDI.* Other programs that conform to MDI include Microsoft's Word for Windows and Excel.

A non-MDI program can open only one file at a time; every time you open a new file, the current file is closed. The Windows accessory programs, such as Notepad and Paint, are non-MDI programs. Most new full-figured programs use MDI,

but you still occasionally run across a non-MDI program. Just a few weeks ago I bought Microsoft Publisher, and guess what? No MDI. You can work on only one Publisher document at a time. Hmmm. Will they ever learn?

One side benefit of MDI is that all the mouse and keyboard shortcuts for working with document windows work the same for all programs that confess the MDI creed. So if you remember that Ctrl+F6 flips from window to window in PowerPoint, you already know how to flip from window to window in Word or Excel.

Figure 21-4:
The Insert File dialog box.

As the slides are copied into the presentation, they are adjusted to match the master slide layout for the new presentation. Embedded charts are even updated to reflect the new color scheme.

Stealing slides is a felony in most states, and if you transmit the presentation across state lines by way of a modem, the feds may get involved — which is good, because it pretty much guarantees that you'll get off scot-free.

The Insert➪Slides from File command copies all the slides in the file. You can't tell PowerPoint to copy just certain slides, but you can delete any slides you don't need after you copy the file. This technique is easiest to do in Slide Sorter or Outline view. If you need just a few slides, it may be easier to use the dragon-drop technique, described next.

Stealing just a few slides

The Insert➪Stolen Slides from Other Files command is good if you want to plant all the slides, or at least most of them, from an old presentation into a new one. If you want to borrow only a few slides, though, follow these steps:

1. **Open the new file and switch to Slide Sorter view.**

2. **Open the old presentation and switch to Slide Sorter view.**

3. **Use the Window➪Arrange All command to tile the windows.**

4. **Hold down the Ctrl key, click and drag the slide you want to steal right across the window boundary to the new presentation, and deposit it wherever you please.**

   This technique is affectionately known as *dragon-dropping* by perverted Windows junkies. Watch where you step.

If you don't hold down the Ctrl key when you drag the slide, the slide is *moved,* not copied. In other words, the slide is really stolen from the old presentation and relocated to the new presentation. This situation probably isn't what you want. Holding down the Ctrl key while doing a dragon-drop moves a *copy* of the slide to the new presentation.

To move several slides at a time, first select them by holding down the Shift key while you click each slide you want to steal. Then dragon-drop them into the new presentation.

Document Properties

PowerPoint stores summary information, known in Windows 95 lingo as *document properties,* with each PowerPoint presentation file you create. Document properties includes the filename and directory, the template assigned to the file, and some information you can type: the presentation's title, subject, author, keywords, and comments.

If you use PowerPoint much of the time and have trouble remembering which file is which, the summary info can help you keep your files sorted. It's also handy if you know that you created a presentation about edible spiders last year but can't remember the filename. Just use the File⇨Open command to search for all files with the keyword *spider* in the summary info. (Using the File⇨Open command to search for files is covered in Chapter 23.)

To view or set the document properties for a presentation, follow these steps:

1. Open the file, if it isn't already open.

2. Conjure up the File⇨Properties command.

The Properties dialog box appears, as shown in Figure 21-5.

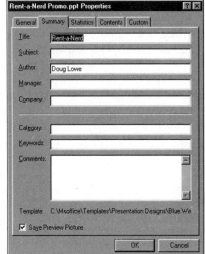

Figure 21-5:
The
Properties
dialog box.

3. Type whatever summary info you want to store along with the file.

The Title field in the Summary Info dialog box is automatically filled in with whatever you type in the first slide's title placeholder, and the Author field is filled in with your name. (PowerPoint asked for your name when you installed it, remember?)

4. Click OK.

5. Save the file (Ctrl+S or File⇨Save).

When you fill out the Summary Information, spend a few moments thinking about which keywords you may use to look for the file later on. Choosing descriptive keywords makes the file much easier to find.

Also, explore the other tabs on the Properties dialog box. You'll find all sorts of interesting information about your presentation there.

If you want to include summary information with every PowerPoint file you create, use the Tools⇨Options command and check the Prompt for File Properties option on the general tab (see Figure 21-6).

Figure 21-6:
The Options
dialog box,
where you
can set
the Prompt
for File
Properties
option.

Chapter 22

Sharing Information with Other Programs

In This Chapter

▶ Importing a text file
▶ Exporting a presentation to a word processor
▶ Saving a slide as a graphics file

*I*n the spirit of NAFTA, this chapter shows you how to exchange data with files created by other programs. Sure, it would be nice if you could build a brick-walled protectionist fortress around yourself and never even acknowledge the existence of other programs, but that wouldn't be — as a former president would say — prudent. Other programs are here to stay, so you had better learn to get along.

The technical term for loading a file created by some other program and converting it to PowerPoint format is, appropriately enough, *importing*. You can import all sorts of file types into PowerPoint: Word for Windows documents, other word processing documents, generic DOS text files, and files created by other presentation programs.

The converse of importing, naturally, is *exporting*. PowerPoint can import more file formats than it can export. I guess the folks at Microsoft want you to convert the competition's files to PowerPoint but not the other way around.

Importing a Foreign File

You have just spent three weeks writing a detailed proposal for a new project, and your boss has just decided that he wants *you* to make the presentation. He expects you to create top-quality 35mm slides based on the proposal, a 60-page Word for Windows document. What do you do?

If you have low self-esteem, you hide in the closet for a week or two. Otherwise, you just import the document into PowerPoint and get to work. With luck, PowerPoint's text-conversion routines recognize headings in the document and convert them to an outline suitable for presentation. It doesn't always work the way you hope, but it's a start, anyway.

PowerPoint can import not only Word for Windows files but also other file types. Here's the complete list of text file types PowerPoint admits:

- **Word for Windows:** PowerPoint works with Word for Windows' outline feature to convert a document to a presentation. Each level-1 heading starts a new slide, with lower-level headings converted to slide text. Paragraphs not assigned a heading style are ignored.

- **Other word processors:** To import a document created by another word processor, first use that word processor's conversion feature to store the document as a Rich Text Format (RTF) file. If the word processing program uses heading styles, they are properly converted to PowerPoint outline levels. If not, PowerPoint guesses at the outline structure by examining how paragraphs are indented.

- **DOS text files:** PowerPoint can read plain, old-fashioned DOS text files, sometimes called *ASCII files.* (ASCII is pronounced *ask-ee.*) Most word processors can save files in ASCII format, and the Windows Notepad program and the DOS Edit command work with ASCII files. PowerPoint looks for tabs at the beginning of each line to figure out how to construct an outline from the file.

- **Competitors' presentation files:** PowerPoint converts presentation files created by Harvard Graphics or Lotus Freelance.

Creating a presentation from a foreign file

This procedure shows you how to create a new presentation from a foreign file:

1. **Choose the File⇨Open command.**

   The File Open dialog box appears.

2. **Pick the file type.**

   Scroll through the List Files of Type list box until you find the one you want (see Figure 22-1).

3. **Choose the file you want to import.**

   You may have to rummage about to find it.

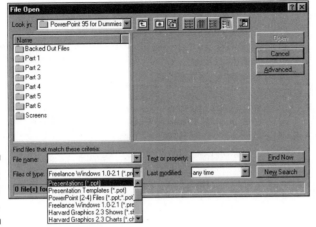

Figure 22-1:
Importing a
foreign file.

4. Click Open.

The file is imported. PowerPoint does its best to construct a reasonable outline from the file.

5. Apply a template.

Choose the Format⇨Apply Designer Template command and select an appropriate template.

6. Edit the outline.

The outline imported from the file probably needs a bit of work. Have fun.

Can't convert the file? It may be that you (or someone else) decided to leave out the text-conversion filters when PowerPoint was installed. Grab your original installation diskettes or CD-ROM disk and fire up the PowerPoint Setup program. Check to see that the text converters and the presentation converters are installed. Or, better yet, offer a bag of Doritos to your local computer guru. He or she will gladly install the missing converter, do a back flip, and may even recite *The Walrus and the Carpenter* from *Alice in Wonderland*. (*Real* computer gurus have committed most of the poetry in *Alice in Wonderland* to memory.)

Don't expect perfection when you import a document. PowerPoint does its best to guess at the outline structure of the document, but sometimes it gets confused. Be patient and be prepared to do some heavy editing.

The PowerPoint customs officers don't allow immigrant word processing files to bring their graphics with them. You have to copy any charts or pictures you want to include in the presentation. The easiest way to do that is to fire up both the word processor and PowerPoint at the same time and then copy graphics from the word processing document to PowerPoint by way of the Clipboard. (You press Ctrl+C to copy and Ctrl+V to paste, remember?)

Inserting slides from an outline

You can insert slides from an outline directly into an existing presentation by using the Insert➪Slides from Outline command. Here's the procedure:

1. **Move to the slide that you want your new slides to follow.**

   For best results, switch to Outline view or Slide Sorter view.

2. **Activate the Insert➪Slides from Outline command.**

   The Insert Outline dialog box, shown in Figure 22-2, appears.

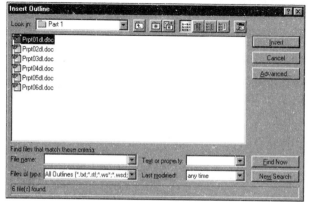

Figure 22-2:
The Insert
Outline
dialog box.

3. **Find the file that contains the outline you want to copy.**

4. **Click OK.**

5. **Review the outline and edit as necessary.**

   It probably won't work exactly as you expect, but it should be close.

The outline can be a Word for Windows document, a document exported from another word processor in Rich Text Format (RTF), or a plain ASCII file.

PowerPoint formats the new slides using the master slide that's already in place.

Exporting an Outline

PowerPoint enables you to save a presentation's outline by using Rich Text Format (RTF), a format for word processing documents that is recognized by just about every word processing program ever written. Here's the procedure:

1. **Activate the File⇨Save As command.**

   The Save As dialog box appears.

2. **Choose Outline/RTF (*.rtf) in the Save Files as Type list box.**

   See Figure 22-3.

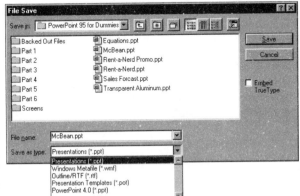

Figure 22-3:
Creating an
outline file.

3. **Type a filename.**

4. **Click Save.**

To open the outline file by using Microsoft Word for Windows, just use the File⇨Open command. Choose RTF as the file type to search for. Word automatically recognizes that the file is stored in RTF format and offers to convert it.

To open the outline file with other word processors, you may have to use an Import command or a separate conversion program.

Saving Slides as Graphic Files

Just spent hours polishing a beautiful slide and wish that you could find a way to save the slide as a graphics file so that you can import it into another program, such as Word for Windows or a desktop publishing program? You've come to the right place. Fancy that.

PowerPoint has the capability to save any slide in a presentation as a separate graphics file by using the Windows MetaFile (WMF) format. Just follow these steps:

1. **Open the presentation and move to the slide you want to save as a graphic.**

   You can do this in Slide view or in Slide Sorter view — whatever suits your fancy.

2. **Choose the File⇨Save As command.**

3. **Pick Windows MetaFile as the file type.**

4. **Type a filename without the extension.**

   The extension WMF is automatically appended to the end of the filename, so you don't have to type it.

5. **Click Save.**

   The slide is saved as a Windows MetaFile, suitable for framing in Word, Publisher, CorelDRAW!, PageMaker, or any other program that can import WMF files.

Chapter 23
Managing Your Files

In This Chapter

▶ Using filenames you can remember

▶ Using folders wisely

▶ Finding lost files

▶ Copying files

▶ Creating new folders

▶ Deleting files

▶ Creating new folders

▶ Backing up your files

My first computer had two disk drives; each drive held 360K of data. A year later, I had a gargantuan 10MB hard disk and wondered how I would keep track of two or three hundred files that I would store on the disk. (I never thought I would fill it up, either.) Today I have more than 1,200MB of disk space, with more than 20,000 files. It's a miracle I can find anything.

This chapter talks about the mundane task of managing your files: keeping track of where they are, giving them names that help you remember what they contain, and — perhaps most important — backing them up so that you have a spare copy for safekeeping.

Organizing Your Files

The first step in managing your files is organizing them so that you can find them when you need them. You must do only two things to organize your files, but you must do them both well: use filenames you can remember and use folders wisely.

Using filenames that you can remember

One of the best things about Windows 95 is that you have finally been freed of the sadistic eight-character file-naming conventions foisted upon you by the DOS moguls many years ago. With Windows 95, filenames can be as long as you want or need them to be (within reason), so instead of names like CNEXPO96.PPT, you can give your presentations names like COMPUTER NERD EXPO 96.PPT.

The best advice I can offer about using long filenames is to start using them right away. Most people are in the habit of assigning short, cryptic names to their files. Breaking that habit takes some conscious effort. Using long filenames will seem strange at first, but trust me: You'll get used to them.

The biggest problem with using long filenames is that not everyone has Windows 95 yet, so not everyone can use them. If you assign a long filename to a file and then copy that file to a diskette and take it to a computer that doesn't have Windows 95, the long filename will seem to have vanished, replaced by a cryptic eight-character approximation of the long filename. For example, COMPUTER NERD EXPO 96.PPT becomes COMPUT~1.PPT. The file is still accessible, but the long filename is not.

Whenever possible, you might want to try to jam as much important information as possible into the first six characters of the filename. For example, suppose you have two files: COMPUTER NERD EXPO 95.PPT and COMPUTER NERD EXPO 96.PPT. The short-form filenames for these two files will be COMPUT~1.PPT and COMPUT~2.PPT. From these filenames, it's hard to tell which is the '95 version and which is for '96. Suppose, however, that you had named the files 95 COMPUTER NERD EXPO.PPT and 96 COMPUTER NERD EXPO.PPT. Then the short filenames would be 95COMP~1.PPT and 96COMP~1.PPT.

Here are a few additional file-naming pointers:

✔ Be consistent about how you name files. If AREXPO94.PPT is the presentation file for Arachnid Expo '94, use AREXPO95.PPT for next year's Expo.

✔ As tempting as it may be, don't use filename extensions other than PPT for PowerPoint presentations. That's just asking for trouble.

✔ If your presentation includes speaker notes, add the filename to the bottom of the page on the Notes master. That way, the filename is printed on each speaker notes page, which makes it easier to file later.

Using folders wisely

The biggest file-management mistake most beginners make is to dump all their files in one folder. This technique is the electronic equivalent of storing all your tax records in a shoe box. Sure, all the files are there, but finding anything is next to impossible. Show the shoe box to your accountant on April 14, and you'll be lucky if she or he stops laughing long enough to show you how to file for an extension.

Use folders to impose organization on your files. Don't just dump all your files into one folder. Instead, create a separate folder for each project and dump all the files for each project into its folder. Suppose that you're charged with the task of presenting a market analysis every month. You can create a folder named MARKET ANALYSIS to store the PowerPoint files for these reports. Then each month's PowerPoint file is named by using the month and year: JANUARY 96.PPT, FEBRUARY 96.PPT, MARCH 96.PPT, and so on. (If you're not up to snuff on how folders work, see the sidebar, "Don't read this folder stuff if you can avoid it.")

Windows 95 enables you to create folders within folders to give your hard disk even more organization. Carrying our market-analysis presentation one step further, suppose that quite a few files are required to assemble each report: perhaps a master PowerPoint presentation file, several Excel worksheet files, a Word document or two, and who knows what else. To keep these files separate, you can create subfolders named JANUARY 96, FEBRUARY 96, MARCH 96, and so on within the MARKET ANALYSIS folder. All the files required for a given month's market analysis are stored in the appropriate subfolder. Very slick, eh?

You can read the steps for creating a new folder later in this chapter, under the heading "Creating a new folder." Isn't that clever?

This list includes some tips for working with folders:

✔ Every disk has a *root directory,* a special folder that should not be used to store files. The root directory is kind of like a fire lane, which should be kept free for emergency vehicles at all times.

✔ Don't store PowerPoint presentation files in the \POWERPOINT folder. The \POWERPOINT folder is where all PowerPoint's program files belong. You don't want your own files mingling with them.

✔ There's no reason you can't store files that belong to different application programs together in the same folder. Each file's extension identifies the program that created the file. No need to segregate.

✔ Don't forget to clean out your folders periodically by deleting files that you no longer need.

✔ There is no limit to the number of files you can store in a folder, nor is there a limit to the number of folders you can create. The only exception to this rule is that the root folder can have no more than 254 files and folders. That's why you should keep the root folder free from unnecessary files.

Don't read this folder stuff if you can avoid it

A *folder* is the means by which Windows keeps track of the files on your hard disk. Without folders, your hard disk would resemble the yarn basket after the cat ran amok.

The terms *directory* and *folder* are used interchangeably because until Windows 95, folders were called directories. The good folks at Microsoft thought that changing the name *directory* to *folder* would somehow make Windows 95 easier to use. Go figure.

Every file on a disk must have a *directory entry*,

which is nothing more than a notation in a folder that lists the file's name and its location on disk. Think of the folder as a guest registry for a bed-and-breakfast, and you have the idea. The guest registry lists the name of each occupant and the occupant's room number. In a similar way, a disk folder lists each file by name and its disk "room number."

Every disk has a least one folder, called the *root directory*. You can create additional folders to impose structure on your files.

Using the File⇨Open Command

The most direct way to open a presentation is to use the File⇨Open command. There are three ways in which you can summon this command:

- ✔ Choose the File⇨Open command from the menus.
- ✔ Click the Open button in the standard toolbar.
- ✔ Press Ctrl+O or Ctrl+F12. Ctrl+O is the more intuitive keyboard shortcut for the File⇨Open command — *O* is for *Open* — but Ctrl+F12 is left over from the early days of Windows, before Microsoft programmers decided that keyboard shortcuts should make sense. Rather than drop an antiquated and senseless keyboard shortcut in favor of one that makes sense and is consistent across all Windows applications (or at least is supposed to be), the Word developers at Microsoft decided to leave *both* keyboard shortcuts in place.

However you do it, the File Open dialog box shown in Figure 23-1 appears. If you're an experienced PowerPoint 4 user, you'll notice right away that this dialog box has changed substantially to accommodate the Windows 95 way of accessing documents. In particular, long filenames are supported.

Changing views

The File Open dialog box lets you switch among four different views of your documents. The four view buttons at the top of the File Open dialog box let you make the switch:

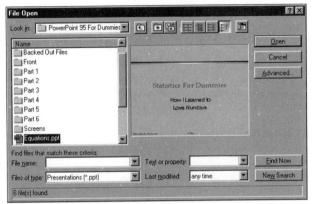

Figure 23-1:
The File
Open dialog
box.

✔ **List:** Displays a list of folders and documents with icons.

✔ **Details:** Displays a list of folders and documents with details, including the filename, type, size, and creation date.

✔ **Properties:** Displays a panel showing various properties for the selected file, including the title, author, template, word count, and other useful information.

✔ **Preview:** Displays a preview of the selected file.

Deleting and renaming files and folders

You can delete and rename files and folders from the File Open dialog box. Here's how:

✔ To delete a file or folder, simply select the file or folder and press the Delete key.

✔ To rename a file or folder, select the file or folder by clicking it once, and then click the filename again. A text editing box appears around the file or folder name, allowing you to edit the name. (Don't click too quickly, or PowerPoint will think that you double-clicked and will open the file or folder.)

Playing favorites

Some of the most useful additions to the File Open dialog box are the Favorites buttons, Look in Favorites and Add to Favorites. These buttons let you access commonly used folders on your hard disk so that you can locate the presentations you use most often with just a few mouse clicks.

The File Open dialog box has two buttons that make the Favorites feature work:

- ✔ **Look in Favorites:** Click this button, and you're instantly whisked away to a folder named \WINDOWS\FAVORITES, which contains icons for your favorite folders and presentation files.

- ✔ **Add to Favorites:** Click this button to add an icon for a folder or presentation file to the \WINDOWS\FAVORITES folder.

When you click the Add to Favorites button, a menu appears with two commands:

- ✔ **Add "folder" to Favorites** creates a shortcut to the current folder in \WINDOWS\FAVORITES. Use this command when you're looking at presentations in a folder, and you suddenly realize that you use the presentations frequently and would like the entire folder to be accessible from FAVORITES.

- ✔ **Add Selected Item to Favorites** creates a shortcut to the selected item — be it a presentation or a folder — in \WINDOWS\FAVORITES. Use this command when you've clicked a presentation or folder and want to add that presentation or folder to FAVORITES.

Finding Lost Files

In PowerPoint 4, you use a separate File➪Find File command to locate documents based on information in the document summary. In PowerPoint 7, the Find File command's capabilities have been enhanced and merged into the File Open dialog box, so PowerPoint 7 no longer offers a separate Find File command.

You can perform simple document searches by using fields that are available right on the File Open dialog box. The following paragraphs describe these fields:

- ✔ **File name:** Ordinarily, this field is left blank so that PowerPoint displays all the files in the folder that meet the criteria specified in the File of type, Text or property, and Last modified fields. You can, however, type a wildcard filename in this field to limit the files that are displayed. A *wildcard* filename includes an asterisk that stands for one or more unknown portions of the filename. For example, if you type **bob*** and press the Enter key, only those documents whose filenames begin with the letters *bob* are displayed.

- ✔ **Files of type:** This field lets you select the type of files to be listed in the File Open dialog box.

✔ **Text or property:** This field allows you to quickly display only those files that contain a certain word or phrase. For example, to show only those files that contain the name McBean, type **McBean** in the Text or property field.

✔ **Last modified:** This drop-down list lets you display only those files that have been modified today, yesterday, this week, last week, this month, last month, or any time. The last modified date is updated each time you save a document.

Copying Files

Both the File➪Open and File➪Save As commands let you make copies of your files. All you have to remember are the ubiquitous Ctrl+C and Ctrl+V shortcuts for Copy and Paste. Follow these easy, step-by-step instructions:

1. **Conjure up the File➪Open or File➪Save As command.**

2. **Press Ctrl+C to copy the file.**

3. **Navigate to the folder to which you want the file copied.**

4. **Press Ctrl+V to paste the file into the folder.**

Creating a New Folder

It happens to me all the time: I'm working on a new presentation, and when I'm ready to save it, I decide that I want to create a new folder for it. Back in the old Windows 3.1 days, you had to switch to Program Manager, launch File Manager, create the new folder, exit File Manager, and then switch back to PowerPoint and save the file in the new folder. Bother.

 Mercifully, PowerPoint 7 now allows you to create a new folder right in the File Save dialog box. All you have to do is click the New Folder button and type a name for the new folder, and — *voilà!* — no more File Manager.

Deleting Files

Don't need a file anymore? Free up the valuable disk space it occupies by deleting it. All you have to do is select the file in the Open or Save As dialog box and press the Delete key. Poof! The file is history.

Backing Up Your Files

When was the last time you changed the oil in your car, took your dog for a walk, or backed up the files on your hard disk? The neglect of any of these three tasks can have disastrous consequences. This isn't the time or place for a stern lecture about the importance of backing up, though, so I'll spare you the soapbox lecture.

One way to back up a file is to use PowerPoint's Save As command to save a copy of the file to a floppy disk.

But the best way to back up your files is to use an Official Backup Program. Fortunately, Windows 95 comes with a fairly decent backup program that can back up your files to diskettes or to a tape drive, if you're lucky enough to have one. You'll find the Windows 95 backup program buried in the Start menu under Programs, Accessories, System Tools.

Keep in mind these hints about backing up your files:

- Remember what I said about this not being the time or place for a lecture? I lied. Back up your files every day. You never know when a stray asteroid will strike your city and possibly wipe out all human life and erase your files, too. So don't put it off! Back up today!

- Always have plenty of disks on hand for backups.

- You don't have to back up every file on your hard disk every day. Just back up the files you changed that day. Microsoft Backup has a slick feature called *incremental backup* that does precisely that, and it does it automatically so that you don't even have to think about it.

- Not lucky enough to have a tape drive? With prices what they are, you should seriously consider it. You can purchase a tape drive capable of backing up 350MB of data on a single tape for under $150 these days.

- You'll sleep much better tonight if you back up your files today.

Part VI
The Part of Tens

"A STORY ABOUT A SOFTWARE COMPANY THAT SHIPS BUG-FREE PROGRAMS ON TIME, WITH TOLL-FREE SUPPORT, AND FREE UPGRADES? NAAAH – TOO WEIRD."

In this part...

PowerPoint is great at creating bulleted lists, so how fitting indeed that this book should end with a bevy of chapters that aren't much more than glorified bulleted lists. Each chapter in this part covers ten (more or less) things worth knowing about PowerPoint. Without further ado, here they are, direct from the home office in Fresno, California.

Chapter 24
Ten PowerPoint Commandments

*B*ut the hapless Windows user said, "Who am I to make this presentation? For I am not eloquent, but I am slow of speech and of tongue, and my charts runneth over." And Microsoft answered, "Fear not, for unto you this day is given a program, which is PowerPoint, and it shall make for you slides, which shall bring forth outlines and notes and yea, even handout pages."

— Presentations 1:1

And so it came to pass that these ten PowerPoint commandments were passed down from generation to generation. Obey these commandments and it shall go well with you, your flip chart, and your overhead projector.

I. Thou Shalt Frequently Saveth Thy Work

Every two or three minutes, press Ctrl+S. Saving your file takes only a second, and you never know when a meteor may drop in your backyard.

II. Thou Shalt Storeth Each File in Its Proper Folder

Whenever you save a file, double-check the folder in which you're saving the file. It's all too easy to save the file in the wrong folder and then spend hours searching for the file later.

III. Thou Shalt Not Abuseth Thy Programs' Formatting Features

Yes, PowerPoint enables you to set every word in a different font, use 92 different colors on a single slide, and fill every last pixel of empty space with clip art. If you want a ransom-note look, go ahead. Otherwise, keep it simple. Use the Style Checker to identify font abuse.

IV. Thou Shalt Not Stealeth Thy Neighbor's Clip Art

It's not yours. Your neighbor paid for it, which gives her or him the right to use it. If you want to use it, buy your own copy.

V. Thou Shalt Not Departeth from the Way of Thy Color Scheme; Neither Shalt Thou Departeth from the Pattern of Thine AutoLayout

Microsoft hired a crew of out-of-work artists to pick the colors for the color schemes, arrange things on the AutoLayouts, and design beautiful backgrounds for the templates. Humor them. They know what they're doing.

VI. Thou Shalt Not Fondle Thy INI and Registry Files

These files are off-limits. If you break this commandment, you had better keep the next one.

If you don't know what the INI files or the registry are, good for you. Keep it that way.

VII. Remember Thy Computer Gurus, to Keep Them Happy

Throw them an occasional Twinkie or bag of Cheetos. Treat them like human beings, no matter how ridiculous that seems. You want them to be your friends.

VIII. Thou Shalt Backeth Up Thy Files Day by Day

Yes, every day. One of these days, you'll come to work only to discover a pile of rubble where your desk used to be. If you back up every day, you won't lose more than one day's work.

IX. Thou Shalt Fear No Evil, for Ctrl+Z Is Always with Thee

March boldly ahead. Not sure what that button does? Click it! If you don't like it, you can always press Ctrl+Z to undo it.

X. Thou Shalt Not Panic

You're the only one who knows that you're nervous. You'll do just fine. Imagine the audience naked if it helps.

Chapter 25

Ten Things That Often Go Wrong

· ·

*T*here are probably closer to 10,000 things that can go wrong, but these 10 are among the things that go wrong most often.

I Can't Find My File!

You spent hours polishing that presentation and now you can't find the file. You know that you saved it, but it's not there! The problem is probably one of two things: Either you saved the file in a folder other than the one you thought you did, or you used a different name to save it than you intended. The solution? Use the File⇨Open command's search features. See Chapter 23 for detailed procedures.

I've Run Out of Memory!

Many computers with only 4MB of internal memory are running Windows these days. That's not enough to run PowerPoint. Microsoft officially says that you need 6MB of RAM to run PowerPoint, but even that's stretching it. 8MB is a more reasonable minimum, and even 12MB or 16MB isn't an outrageous amount of memory these days.

Short of purchasing more computer memory (which isn't a bad idea), avoid running more than one Windows program at a time. Also, try removing fonts that you don't need. The more fonts you have installed on your computer, the less memory you have free for other programs. (To remove fonts, fire up the Control Panel and click the Fonts icon. Choose the fonts you don't need and then press the Delete key.)

I've Run Out of Disk Space!

Nothing is more frustrating than creating a fancy PowerPoint presentation and then discovering that you're completely out of disk space. What to do? Start up a My Computer window and rummage through your hard disk, looking for files you don't need. Delete enough files to free up a few megabytes and then press Alt+Tab to move back to PowerPoint and save your file. I did this just a few days ago; I had to delete a bunch of sound files I recorded from the movie *Young Frankenstein.* (It was either them or the Word for Windows document files for the first few chapters of this book. Not an easy decision.)

If your disk is full and you can't find more than a few files to delete, you might consider activating the Windows 95 disk-compression program, DriveSpace.

PowerPoint Has Vanished!

You're working at your computer, minding your own business, when suddenly — whoosh! — PowerPoint disappears. What happened? Most likely, you clicked some area outside the PowerPoint window or you pressed Alt+Tab or Alt+Esc, which whisks you away to another program. To get PowerPoint back, press Alt+Tab. You may have to press Alt+Tab several times before PowerPoint comes back to life.

PowerPoint can also vanish into thin air if you use a screen saver program. Try giving the mouse a nudge to see whether PowerPoint reappears.

I Accidentally Deleted a File!

Just learned how to delete files and couldn't stop yourself, eh? Relax. It happens to the best of us. Odds are that you can get the deleted file back if you act fast enough. Double-click the Recycle Bin icon that sits on your desktop. There, you'll probably find the deleted file. Copy it back to the folder where it belongs.

It Won't Let Me Edit That!

No matter how hard you click the mouse, PowerPoint won't let you edit that doohickey on-screen. What gives? The doohickey is probably a part of the Slide Master. To edit it, use the View⇨Master⇨Slide Master command. This step displays the Slide Master and enables you to edit it.

Something Seems to Be Missing!

You just read the chapter about Equation Editor, but nothing happens when you try to use it. You, or whoever installed PowerPoint on your computer, probably decided not to install it. To correct this oversight, gather up your original installation disks and launch the PowerPoint Setup program. (This problem can happen with many optional components of PowerPoint, including Microsoft Chart, clip art, and templates.)

What Happened to My Clip Art?

You just purchased and installed an expensive clip art collection that has 500 stunning photographic-quality images from the 1994 USA Synchronized Swimming Championships, but you can't find them in the ClipArt Gallery. Where did they go? Nowhere. You just have to tell ClipArt Gallery about them. Fire up the Gallery by clicking the Insert Picture button or by double-clicking a clip art object. Then click the Organize button. Then click Add and tell PowerPoint where the new picture files are located.

One of the Toolbars Is Missing!

You reach for the Bold button, but it's not there. In fact, the whole Formatting toolbar seems to be missing. What gives? Somehow the view got messed up. It happens all the time, so don't feel bad. Just look in the mirror and say to yourself, "It's not my fault that the toolbar disappeared. It happens even to experts like that nice Mr. Lowe, who wrote a whole book about PowerPoint. I shouldn't blame myself. After all, I'm good enough, I'm smart enough, and, doggone it, people like me."

Then use the View⇨Toolbars command to reactivate the missing toolbar.

All the Text Is the Same!

This problem happens in Outline view when you click the Show Formatting button. Just click Show Formatting again to restore text formatting, such as font, point size, italics, and so on.

Chapter 26

Ten PowerPoint Shortcuts

• •

*Y*ou can do just about anything you can do with PowerPoint by hacking your way through the menus or clicking the correct toolbar button. But a few shortcuts are worth knowing about.

Shift+Click the View Buttons to Display Masters

You can use the View⇨Masters command to display the Slide, Notes Pages, Handout, or Outline Masters. But an easier way is to hold down the Shift key while clicking the status bar buttons. The following table shows the buttons.

Button Combination	Master
▢	Slide Master
▤	Outline Master
▦	Handout Master
▣	Notes Pages Master

Right-Click Anywhere to Get a Quick Menu

You can right-click just about anything with the mouse button to get a quick menu of common things you can do to the object. Try it — it's kind of fun.

Ctrl+X, Ctrl+C, or Ctrl+V to Cut, Copy, or Paste

Just about all Windows applications respond to these keyboard shortcuts.

Shortcut	Action
Ctrl+X	Cuts the selection to the Clipboard.
Ctrl+C	Copies the selection to the Clipboard.
Ctrl+V	Inserts the contents of the Clipboard.

Note: Before you use Ctrl+X or Ctrl+C, select the object you want to cut or copy.

Ctrl+Z to Undo a Mistake

Oops! Didn't mean to double-click there! Don't panic. Press Ctrl+Z, and whatever you did last is undone.

Ctrl+B or Ctrl+I for Bold or Italics

Like most Windows applications, PowerPoint accepts the following keyboard shortcuts for text formatting:

Shortcut	Action
Ctrl+B	Bold
Ctrl+I	Italic
Ctrl+U	Underline
Ctrl+spacebar	Return to normal format

Note: Before using these shortcuts, highlight the text that you want to format.

Ctrl+S to Save a File

Press Ctrl+S to save the current presentation to a file. The first time you save a new file, PowerPoint displays the Save As dialog box, in which you can assign a name to the file. Thereafter, Ctrl+S saves the file by using the same name.

Ctrl+G to Show the Guides

Need help aligning drawn objects? Press Ctrl+G to display the guides. You can then drag the guidelines around and snap objects to them.

Shift While Drawing to Constrain Objects

If you hold down the Shift key while drawing an object, the object is drawn as straight as an arrow. Circles will be circles, squares will be squares, and lines will stick to 45-degree angles.

Alt+Esc, Alt+Tab, or Ctrl+Esc to Switch to Another Program

This isn't really a PowerPoint shortcut; it's a Windows one. To switch to another application, use one of these keyboard combinations:

- **Alt+Esc:** Switches to the next program in line.
- **Alt+Tab:** Displays the name of the next program in line. While holding down the Alt key, keep pressing Tab until the name of the program you want appears. Release both keys to switch to that program.
- **Ctrl+Esc:** Pops up the Start menu, from which you can start other programs.

F1: The Panic Button

Stuck? Press F1 to activate PowerPoint's Help. With luck, you can find enough information to get you going. The help is *context sensitive,* which means that it tries to figure out what you were doing when you pressed F1 and gives you specific help for that task.

Chapter 27

Ten Tips for Creating Readable Slides

● ●

*T*his chapter gives you a few random tips and pointers that help you produce readable slides.

Try Reading the Slide from the Back of the Room

The number-one rule of creating readable slides is that everyone in the room should be able to read them. If you're not sure, there's one sure way to find out: Try it. Put the slide in the projector, walk to the back of the room, and see whether you can read it. If you can't, you have to make some adjustments.

Five Bullets, Tops

Ever notice that David Letterman uses two slides to display each of his Top Ten lists? Dave's producers know that ten items are too many for one slide. Five are just right. Take a cue from Dave's show and limit yourself to no more than five bullet points per slide.

Avoid Small Text

If you can't read a slide from the back of the room, it's probably because the text is too small. The rule of thumb is that 24 points is the smallest you should go for slides, and 18 points for overheads. Twelve-point type may be perfectly readable in a word processing document, but it just doesn't cut it on an overhead or slide.

Avoid Excessive Verbiage Leading to Excessively Lengthy Text That Is Not Only Redundant but Also Repetitive and Reiterative

This heading could have been "Be Brief." Get the point?

Use Consistent Wording

Whenever possible, be consistent in the way you word your bulleted lists. Consider this list:

- Profits will be improved
- Expanding markets
- We must reduce the amount of overseas competition
- Production increase

Each sentence uses a different grammatical construction. The same points made with consistent wording have a more natural flow:

- Improved profits
- Expanded markets
- Reduced overseas competition
- Increased production

See what I mean?

Stick to the Color Scheme

With all the professionally chosen color schemes packed into PowerPoint's templates, there's no reason to try to create your own. The color schemes combine colors that work well together. Why spoil the party?

Stick to the AutoLayouts When You Can

You can't, at least not always. But try to if you can. The AutoLayouts include various placeholder objects that are already lined up for best readability.

Keep the Background Simple

Don't splash a bunch of distracting clip art on the background unless it is essential. The purpose of the background is to provide a well-defined visual space for the slide's content. Avoid templates that have beach scenes in the background, for example. For overheads, light-colored backgrounds are best. Dark backgrounds work well with slides.

Use Only Two Levels of Bullets

Sure, developing your subpoints into sub-subpoints and sub-sub-subpoints is tempting, but no one can follow you. Don't make your slides more confusing than they need to be. If you need to make sub-sub-subpoints, you probably need a few more slides.

Keep Graphs Simple

Microsoft Graph can create elaborate graphs that even the best statisticians will marvel at. But the most effective graphs are pie charts with three or four slices and column charts with three or four columns.

If you remember only one rule when creating your presentation, remember this one: *Keep it simple, clean, and concise.*

Chapter 28

Ten New Features in PowerPoint 95

● ●

*I*f you're an experienced PowerPoint 4 user just upgrading to PowerPoint 7 (the Windows 95 version of the program), you probably turned to this chapter first. It lists the ten most important new features in PowerPoint for Windows 95.

Long Filenames

Windows 95 frees you from the tyranny of eight-character filenames, but long filenames aren't much use unless you also have programs such as PowerPoint 95 that support Windows 95 long filenames.

With PowerPoint 95, you can use filenames such as 1996 SALES CONFERENCE.PPT instead of 96SLSCNF.PPT. Enough said.

The Style Checker

PowerPoint 95 includes a new Style Checker feature that not only corrects your spelling errors but also lets you know if you have used too many fonts, tried to cram too much information onto a single slide, or committed some other stylistic gaffe. I describe the Style Checker in Chapter 4.

AutoCorrect

AutoCorrect is a feature that was introduced in Microsoft Word a few years back and is just now catching on in other programs. It automatically corrects the most common spelling errors as you type them. For example, if you type *adn*, AutoCorrect automatically changes it to *and* without even asking. I describe AutoCorrect in Chapter 17.

AutoClipArt

Hmpfh. I don't really think much of this feature, but it's new, so I'd better mention it. AutoClipArt scans through your presentation, looking for key words that might suggest clip art that can illustrate your point. Unfortunately, its success depends on your using the vocabulary by which Microsoft chose to index its clip art. For example, if you use the word *Accomplishment* in your presentation, AutoClipArt suggests that you use a clip art image of a reward certificate. But if you use the word *Achievement,* no clip art is suggested.

AutoClipArt is a nice idea, but it doesn't work in practice. So I wouldn't bother with it.

Title Masters

PowerPoint 95 now has a new type of Master — called a *Title Master* — that allows you to set up a different format for title slides. All the templates that come with PowerPoint 95 use the Title Master to give title slides a layout that complements the presentation's basic slide layout. I discuss Title Masters, along with other Masters, in Chapter 8.

New Fill Options

Besides filling objects or slide backgrounds with colors, patterns, and shading, PowerPoint 95 also allows you to fill objects or slide backgrounds with textures, as shown in Figure 28-1. In addition, you can now use two-color shading, in which one color gradually fades into another. You'll find details on using these new fill options in Chapter 9.

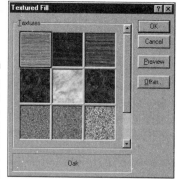

Figure 28-1:
PowerPoint 95 provides several background textures.

Simpler Transitions and Animations

PowerPoint 95 allows you to combine build effects with sound to create interesting animations. For example, you can drop in text one letter at a time, accompanied by typing sounds, to create an interesting typewriter effect. Or you can quickly slide in a clip art picture of an automobile from the right edge of the screen, accompanied by the sound of screeching brakes.

PowerPoint provides a new Animation Effects toolbar, shown in Figure 28-2, so that you can quickly apply some of the more common animation effects. More information about these effects is found in Chapter 16.

Figure 28-2:
The new
Animation
Effects
toolbar.

Meeting Minder

The Meeting Minder is a little window that you can open up during an electronic presentation and use to record minutes, action items, or other notes. Meeting Minder is pictured in Figure 28-3.

Truthfully, a yellow pad and a Number 2 pencil might be a better alternative to the Meeting Minder in many cases. But if you're looking for a high-tech way to keep notes during a meeting, Meeting Minder is the solution. I cover Meeting Minder in Chapter 20.

Figure 28-3:
PowerPoint's
new
Meeting
Minder lets
you keep
notes
during a
presentation.

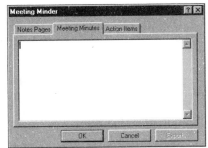

Presentation Conferencing

PowerPoint now lets you hold meetings without reserving a conference room. Assuming that everyone who wants to participate in the meeting has a networked computer with a copy of PowerPoint installed, you can conduct a presentation on the network! The presentation's slides are displayed on each participant's computer. Each participant can scribble on the slides by using the John Madden pen, and each participant's scribbling is visible on all participant's computers (color coded, of course).

Hmph. We'll see how popular this turns out to be. Microsoft still hasn't figured out a way to send coffee and donuts over the network, so I think face-to-face meetings will remain a popular option.

Genigraphics Wizard

With the preceding version of PowerPoint, sending a presentation to Genigraphics, a service bureau that creates 35mm slides, overhead transparencies, and other types of fancy computer output, was a chore. You had to set up a special Genigraphics print driver, then use the driver to print the presentation to a file, and then use a special program to send the file to Genigraphics over a modem. Bother.

Microsoft fixed that by creating a special Send to Genigraphics command. Now, you just fire up this command and answer a few simple questions (not the least of which is, "How are you gonna pay for all this?"), and the presentation is automatically sent to Genigraphics.

Customizable Toolbars

Don't like the way the toolbars are laid out in PowerPoint? No problemo. Just fire up the Tools⇨Customize command and change them. You can add new buttons, drop buttons, rearrange buttons, and create entirely new toolbars.

PowerPoint picked this idea up from Word for Windows, which lets you customize not only toolbars but also menus and keyboard shortcuts. Maybe you'll get to customize keyboard shortcuts and menus in the next version of PowerPoint; for now, you'll have to settle for customized toolbars.

Chapter 29

Ten Cool Things on the PowerPoint Multimedia CD-ROM

● ●

*P*owerPoint for Windows 95 comes on a CD-ROM disk that includes not only the PowerPoint program but also a special "Value Pack" of added multimedia goodies. These goodies are all found in the VALUPACK folder on the CD, and they're described in the following sections.

Sounds

In the VALUPACK\AUDIO folder, you'll find two collections of sound files: one by Cambium Development, Inc., the other by Network Music, Inc. The Cambium collection includes a program called Cambium Sound Choice Lite, plus 23 sound files that feature music that you can use to enhance your presentations. The Network collection includes 93 sound files that provide effects such as barking dogs and airplanes, plus several music files.

Clip Art

A collection of several hundred clip art files can be found in the VALUPACK\CLIPART folder. The best way to use these files is to add them to ClipArt Gallery, as described in Chapter 10.

Microsoft Imager

Wow. Microsoft Imager is a secret program that's found on the CD. It lets you manipulate bitmap picture files, often producing results that are drastically different from the original picture. For example, Figure 29-1 shows two versions of a lion. The first is a photograph that Microsoft Imager supplies as a sample. The second is the same image after it's been run through Imager. Imager can transform photographs in many ways: You can increase the contrast, change the color hues, soften or sharpen the focus, and more.

Figure 29-1:
Imager can
convert a
photograph
to a picture
that looks
hand-drawn.

To install Imager, switch to the VALUPACK\IMAGER folder on the CD-ROM and then run the Setup program.

Photos

In the VALUPACK\PPPHOTOS folder, you'll find two sample collections of photographs that you can insert into your presentations:

- ✔ PhotoDisc, one of the largest suppliers of digitized photographs, has provided more than 100 photos in the VALUPACK\PPPHOTOS\PHOTODSC folder. These photos are samples of the tens of thousands of photos that you can purchase from Photodisc.

- ✔ Sense Interactive Multimedia has provided 33 images from several of its collections in the VALUPACK\PPPHOTOS\SENSE folder.

PhotoDisk and Sense Interactive Multimedia have also both provided short PowerPoint presentations that you can run to learn about the various photograph collections that are available and how you can order them.

Samples

The VALUPACK\PPSAMPLES folder contains five sample PowerPoint presentations:

- ✔ CALENDAR.PPT includes 36 months of calendars, up through December 1997. Figure 29-2 shows the calendar for February 1996.
- ✔ FLOWCHRT.PPT includes symbols for constructing flowcharts. See Figure 29-3.
- ✔ PRINTME.PPT contains color matching samples that you can print.
- ✔ TABLES.PPT contains elements that you can paste together to create attractive tables, as shown in Figure 29-4.
- ✔ TIMELINE.PPT contains symbols that you can piece together to make timelines, as shown in Figure 29-5.

More Templates

If the designer templates that are installed with PowerPoint aren't enough for you, you'll find 58 additional templates in the VALUPACK\PPTMPL folder on the CD-ROM.

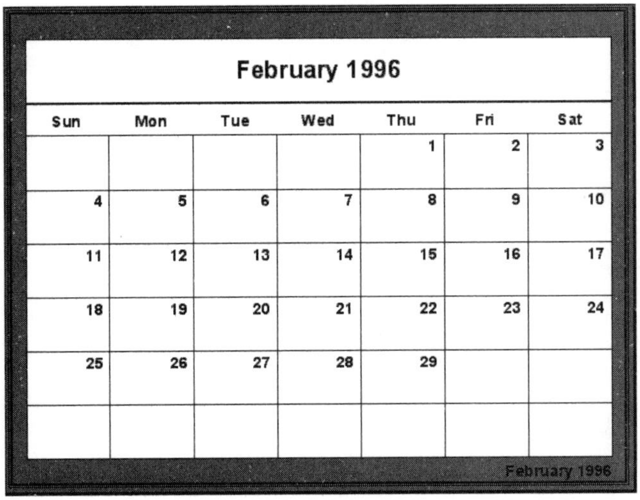

Figure 29-2:
You can
find this
calendar,
CALENDAR.
PPT, in the
VALUPACK\
PPSAMPLES
folder.

February 1996						
Sun	**Mon**	**Tue**	**Wed**	**Thu**	**Fri**	**Sat**
				1	2	3
4	5	6	7	8	9	10
11	12	13	14	15	16	17
18	19	20	21	22	23	24
25	26	27	28	29		

February 1996

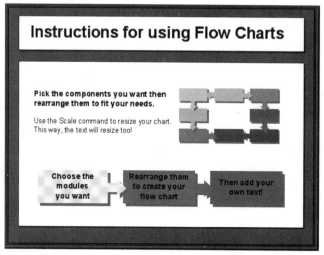

Figure 29-3:
The
FLOWCHRT.
PPT file
contains
symbols for
creating
flowcharts.

Figure 29-4:
The
TABLES.PPT
file contains
pieces of
tables.

Videos

The VALUPACK\VIDEOS folder contains two collections of multimedia files:

- ✔ TC Visual (VALUPACK\VIDEOS\TCVISUAL) contains several samples of animated clip art that you can order directly from TC Visual. A PowerPoint presentation is included to demonstrate the animated clip art.

- ✔ Four Palms (VALUPACK\FOURPALM) contains several sample video files, including images of the space shuttle landing, trucks driving, and more. A PowerPoint presentation that demonstrates the samples and explains how you can order additional videos from Four Palms is included.

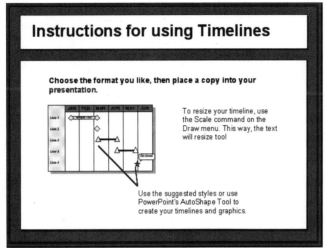

Figure 29-5:
The
TIMELINE.
PPT file
lets you
construct
timelines.

Chapter 30

Ten Ways to Keep Your Audience Awake

● ●

*N*othing frightens a public speaker more than the prospect of the audience falling asleep during a speech. This chapter lists some things you can do to prevent that from happening. (Yawn.)

Don't Forget Your Purpose

Too many presenters ramble on and on with no clear sense of purpose. The temptation is to throw in every clever quotation and every interesting fact you can muster that is even remotely related to the purpose of your presentation. The reason that this temptation is so strong is that you most likely haven't identified what you hope to accomplish with your presentation. In other words, you haven't pinned down your *purpose*.

Don't confuse a presentation's title with its purpose. Suppose that you're asked to give a presentation to a prospective client on the advantages of your company's new, improved ChronoSimplastic Infindibulator. Your purpose in this presentation is not to convey information about the new Infindibulator but to persuade the client to buy one of the $65 million beasties. The title of your presentation may be *Infindibulators for the '90s,* but the purpose is "to convince these saps to buy one, or maybe two."

Don't Become a Slave to Your Slides

PowerPoint makes such beautiful slides that you may be tempted to let them be the show. That's a big mistake. *You* are the show, not the slides. The slides are merely visual aids, designed to make your presentation more effective.

Dimming the lights, hiding behind the lectern, and letting your slides do the talking for you is tempting. Keep the slides in their place.

Don't Overwhelm Your Audience with Unnecessary Detail

"On November 19, 1863, a crowd of 15,000 gathered in Gettysburg to hear Edward Everett, one of the nation's most eloquent orators, speak for two hours about the events that had transpired during the famous battle. When Everett finished, Abraham Lincoln rose to deliver a brief two-minute postscript that has since become the most famous speech in American history . . . ."

If PowerPoint had been around in 1863, Everett probably would have spoken for four hours. PowerPoint practically begs you to say too much. After you get cranking on that outline, the bullets just fly, one after the other. Pretty soon, you have 40 slides for a 20-minute presentation. That's about 35 more than you probably need. Try to shoot for one slide for every two to four minutes of your presentation.

Don't Neglect Your Opening

As they say, you get only one opportunity to make a first impression. Don't waste it by telling a joke that has nothing to do with your presentation, apologizing for your lack of preparation, or listing your credentials. Don't pussyfoot around; get right to the point.

The best openings are those that capture the audience's attention with a provocative statement, rhetorical question, or compelling story. A joke is okay, but only if it sets the stage for the subject of your presentation.

Be Relevant

The objective of any presentation is to lead your audience to say, "Me too." Unfortunately, far too many presentations leave the audience thinking, "So what?"

The key to being relevant is to give your audience what it needs, not what you think is interesting or important. The most persuasive presentations present solutions to real problems rather than opinions about contrived problems.

Don't Forget the Altar Call

You've spent hours putting your presentation together. Don't forget to ask for the order. Invite your audience to respond and show them how. Make them an offer they can't refuse. Tell 'em your 800 number. Roll the pen across the table. Give the altar call. (The buses will wait.)

Practice, Practice, Practice

Somehow a rumor got started that Abraham Lincoln hastily wrote the Gettysburg Address on the train, just before pulling into Gettysburg. In truth, Lincoln agonized over every word of the address.

Practice, practice, practice. Work through the rough spots. Polish the opening, the altar call, and all the awkward transitions in between. Practice in front of a mirror or with a tape recorder. Time yourself.

Don't Panic

Don't worry! Be happy! Even the most gifted public speakers are scared silly every time they step up to the podium. Whether you're speaking to one person or 10,000, relax. In 20 minutes, it will all be over.

No matter how nervous you are, no one knows it except you. That is, unless you tell them. The number-one rule of panic avoidance is "Never apologize for your fears." Behind the podium, your knees may be knocking hard enough to bruise yourself. But no one else knows. After you swab down your forehead and wipe the drool off your chin, people will say, "Weren't you nervous? You seemed so calm!"

Expect the Unexpected

Expect things to go wrong, because they will. The light bulb in the overhead projector will burn out. The microphone won't work. You'll drop your notes as you approach the podium. Who knows what else could happen?

Above All Else, Don't Be Boring

An audience can overlook almost anything, but one thing they cannot overlook is being bored. Above all, you must never bore your audience.

This guideline doesn't mean that you have to tell jokes, jump up and down, or talk fast. Jokes, excessive jumping, and rapid speech can be as boring as formatting disks. If you obey the other commandments — if you have a clear-cut purpose and stick to it, avoid unnecessary detail, and address real needs — you'll never be boring. Just be yourself and have fun. If you have fun, so will your audience.

Appendix

Installing PowerPoint

· ·

Throughout this book, I've assumed that PowerPoint already lives on your computer. If you're not so lucky, this appendix guides you through the tedious process known as *installation,* a form of torture devised by sadistic programmers back in the early days of computing.

If you are faced with the prospect of installing PowerPoint on your computer, you have two choices:

  ✔ Do it yourself.

  ✔ Bribe your friendly neighborhood computer guru to do it for you.

A one-pound bag of M&Ms and a six-pack of Jolt Cola are usually sufficient to persuade a computer guru to do the installation for you. You can probably pull it off yourself, though. It's tedious but not overly complicated.

System Requirements

To run PowerPoint, you need three things:

  ✔ A computer that runs Windows 95

  ✔ At least 6MB (megabytes) of RAM, but 8MB is better

  ✔ About 35MB of free disk space

Yes, I said 35MB of disk space. That's how much disk space PowerPoint consumes if you install all its options. (If you're tight on space, you can instruct PowerPoint to leave out some of its lesser-used features, like import filters, fonts, or applets that you don't plan on using.)

Installing PowerPoint

To install PowerPoint, follow these steps:

1. **Cancel all appointments.**

   Installing PowerPoint takes half an hour or so, but then you will want to fire it up and play with it awhile. I suggest that you set aside the better part of an afternoon to indulge yourself.

2. **Find the PowerPoint installation disks.**

   I assume that you have your own set of PowerPoint disks. If you are "borrowing" someone else's copy of PowerPoint, shame on you! That's stealing, it's against the law, and it just isn't nice. Put this book down right now and march straight over to your local computer store to buy your own copy of PowerPoint. You'll sleep much better tonight.

3. **Start your computer.**

4. **Stick the PowerPoint Setup disk (disk 1) in the disk drive.**

   If you have just one floppy drive, it is called drive A. If you have two floppy drives, one atop the other, the one on top is usually drive A, and the one on the bottom is drive B. If you have two floppy drives side by side, the one on the left is usually drive A and the one on the right is drive B.

5. **Choose the Start⇨Run command.**

   Click the Start button and then choose Run. This step calls forth the Run dialog box, in which you can run a DOS command. The command you want to run here is SETUP, on either the A or B drive, depending on in which drive you inserted Disk 1. For drive A, type the following line in the Open field:

   a:setup

   For drive B, type this line:

   b:setup

   No spaces and no period at the end. Just the letter A or B followed by a colon and the single word *setup*. Figure A-1 shows the Run dialog box with the correct command for the A drive.

Figure A-1:
The Run
dialog box.

Run	? ✕

Type the name of a program, folder, or document, and Windows will open it for you.

Open: a:setup

OK   Cancel   Browse...

6. Press the Enter key.

You hear the floppy drive churn back and forth for an unbearably long time. Finally, just when you're about to give up, the Microsoft PowerPoint for Windows 95 Setup dialog box appears, as shown in Figure A-2. From this point on, just follow the instructions on-screen.

These pointers can help to get you through the day:

✔ Read and follow instructions carefully.

✔ Setup asks you for the path where you want to install PowerPoint. If you just press Enter here, PowerPoint is installed in a directory named MSOFFICE\POWERPOINT on drive C. Change this setting only if you know what you're doing. Otherwise, simply press Enter.

✔ When asked to choose which type of installation to perform, pick Complete. This option installs everything, including the Ginsu knives, cheese shredder, and optional rotisserie attachment. It requires about 35MB of disk space. Setup displays a list of components to be installed. If you don't have enough disk space available for all of them, you can omit certain components by unchecking them. For example, if you don't plan on lecturing about advanced hydrophysics, you may leave out the Equation Editor.

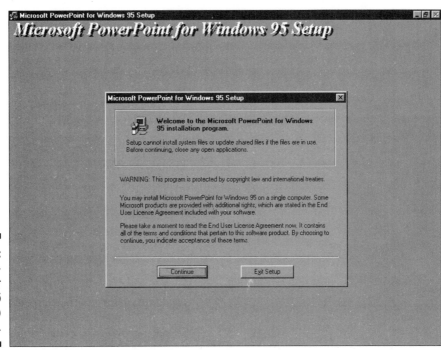

Figure A-2:
The Power-
Point for
Windows 95
Setup
program.

✔ When Setup says to swap disks, take the old disk out of the drive and place it face down on top of the discard pile. Then draw a new disk from the top of the kitty, insert it in the drive, and press Enter.

✔ When PowerPoint tells you its serial number, don't bother writing it down. You can see the serial number at any time by starting PowerPoint and choosing the Help➪About PowerPoint command.

✔ Now is a good time to fill out the registration card.

✔ When you're done, don't forget to remove the last disk from the floppy drive. Gather up the spent installation disks and store them someplace safe. You never know when you may need them again.

Index

• Symbols •

3-D graphs, 180
35mm color slides, converting
    PowerPoint slides, 247
/ (slash) key, 64
©, creating with AutoCorrect, 237
®, creating with AutoCorrect, 237
™, creating with AutoCorrect, 237

• A •

accent color in color schemes, 128
Action Items tab, 259
Add to Favorites button, 283–284
Align button in WordArt, 212
Align commands, 173–174
Align Left button, 104
Align Right button, 105
Alignment command, 104
Alt+Backspace (erase), 160
Alt+Esc (program switching), 299
Alt+F4 (exit), 33
Alt+H (help), 86
Alt+Shift+1 (collapse presentation), 63
Alt+Shift+↓ (move text down), 62
Alt+Shift+← (promote paragraph), 59
Alt+Shift+→ (demote paragraph), 59
Alt+Shift+↑ (move text up), 62
Alt+Shift+A (expand presentation), 63
Alt+Tab (program switching), 294, 299
altar call in presentations, 317
Animate Title button, 231
animation aids for Help topics, 89
animation effects, 230–232
Animation Effects button, 231
Animation Effects toolbar, 230–232, 307
Animation Order button, 232
Animation Settings button, 232
Animation Settings dialog box,
    223–224, 229
Answer Wizard, 91–92
Apply Design Template dialog box,
    122, 123
Apply Designer Template command, 275
Apply Object Style command, 140
Arc button, 160, 162
arcs, drawing, 162
Arrange All command, 264
arrow button on the Drawing toolbar, 38
arrow keys, moving within text objects, 41
arrowheads on line or arc objects, 168
ASCII files, importing, 274
assistant boxes, 194, 198
Assistant button, 198
attributes of objects, 167–168
audience handout pages. *See* handouts
audiences, keeping awake, 315–318
AUDIO folder in VALUPACK, 309
AutoClipArt, 306
AutoContent Wizard, 17–22
AutoContent Wizard option, 16–17
AutoCorrect, 235, 305
    adding entries, 237–238
    deleting entries, 238
AutoCorrect dialog box, 235–236
AutoFormat dialog box, 191–192
AutoFormats in Microsoft Graph, 191–192
AutoLayouts, sticking to, 303
Automatic Word Selection option,
    disabling, 44
AutoShapes button, 160, 165
AutoShapes toolbar, 165, 166
axes, 180

• B •

B&W View button, 40.
    See also Black & White check box
baby word processor, 40–44
Back button in Help, 88
background, keeping simple, 303
background color in color schemes, 128
background effects, custom, 135–136
Background Fill drop-down list, 134
background objects
    hiding, 117
    removing some but not all, 118
background shading in slides, 133–135
background slide color, adjusting, 113
Backspace key, 42, 43
backup program in Windows 95, 286
bitmap picture images, selecting for
        background, 136
Black & White check box, 82
Black & White view, switching to, 40
Blank layout, 28
Blank Presentation option, 17
BLANK PRESENTATION.POT default
        template, 124–125
blocks of text
    copying, 45
    cutting, 45
    deleting, 44
    replacing, 44
BMP (bitmap) format, 155
body text, 11
Bold button
    on Formatting toolbar, 96, 97
    in WordArt, 212
Border button in WordArt, 213
Box buttons, 198–199
Box Out build effect, 231
boxes
    adding to organizational charts, 198–199
    deleting from organizational charts, 200
    formatting, 203–204
    formatting text in, 203–204
    moving in organizational charts, 200–201

selecting in organizational charts,
        199–200
boxing clip art, 146–147
branch box, 194
Bring Forward command, 172
Bring to Front command, 172
Build command, with slides, 81
build effects, 228
    adding with menus, 229–230
    assigning, 228–229
    combining with sound, 307
    removing, 229
Build Slide Text button, 231
Build Slide Text command, 229
builds. *See* build effects
Bullet button, 102
bullet character, 40
Bullet dialog box, 103
Bulleted List layout, 27, 61
bullets, 102
    adding to paragraphs, 102
    changing color of, 103
    levels for, 303
    maximum number on a slide, 301
By Column button, 186

• C •

CALENDAR.PPT, 311
calendars, in PPSAMPLES, 311
Cambium Sound Choice Lite program, 309
Camera Effect button, 231
capitalization, checking with Style
        Checker, 73
Capitalize Names of Days option, 236–237
capitalizing text, 70–71
capitals, correcting two initial, 236
cascaded presentation windows, 264
Case and End Punctuation options, 73–74
category axis, 189
CD-ROM
    adding pictures from, 153
    VALUPACK folder, 309

CDR (CorelDRAW!) format, 155
Center button, on Formatting toolbar, 104
centered text, 104
Centers command, 174
CGM (Computer Graphic Metafile) format, 155
Change Case command, 70–71
Change Case dialog box, 70–71
character formatting. *See* text formatting
characters. *See also* text
  changing look of, 95–102
chart boxes. *See* boxes
Chart Type button, 188
Chart Type dialog box, 187–188
charts. *See* graphs
circles, drawing, 163
Clear command, 43, 46
clicking, 14, 16
clicking and dragging, 16
client, 182
clip art. *See also* pictures
  colorizing, 150–151
  converting to shape objects, 148
  drawing a box around, 146–147
  editing, 147–150
  inserting in presentations, 142–144
  locating, 295
  moving, 145
  sizing, 145
  stretching, 145
Clip Art button, 112
Clip Art command, 142
clip art files on CD-ROM, 309
CLIPART folder, 141
  in VALUPACK folder, 309
ClipArt Gallery, 142, 143–144
  adding pictures to, 151–152
Clipboard, 44
  copying text to, 45
  copying to, 298
  cutting to, 298
  inserting contents of, 298
Close command, 32, 267

closing presentations, 32
co-manager boxes, 194
co-worker boxes, 194, 198
Co-worker button, 198
Collapse Selection button, 56, 64
collapsing
  outlines, 63–64
  presentations, 63
  slides, 63–64
Collate check box, 81
color, changing text, 100–101
color-coding slides, 130
Color menu in Font dialog box, 137, 138
Color Scheme dialog box, 129–130, 131–132
color schemes, 127–129
  changing, 113, 129–130
  changing colors, 131–133
  overriding, 130–131
  sticking to, 159, 302
color slides, printing in black and white, 82
colorizing clipart, 150–151
colors
  applying to text, 137–138
  changing in color schemes, 131–133
  copying from existing objects, 139–140
Colors and Lines dialog box, 139, 146–147, 168
commandments for PowerPoint, 289–291
commands. *See specific commands and buttons*
component, 182
computer, turning off, 33
computer memory, conserving, 293
connecting line, 194
consistent wording, 302
container, 182
Contents tab, 87
context-sensitive help, 85, 299
Copies, printing more than one, 80–81
Copy button, 45
Copy command, 44

Copyright symbol (©), creating with
    AutoCorrect, 237
Correct TWo INitial CApitals option, in
    AutoCorrect, 236
Ctrl+↓ (down one paragraph), 42
Ctrl+↓ (select first box), 200
Ctrl+← (left one word), 42
Ctrl+← (select box to left), 200
Ctrl+→ (right one word), 42
Ctrl+→ (select box to right), 200
Ctrl+↑ (delete current box's
    manager), 200
Ctrl+↑ (up one paragraph), 42
Ctrl+A (select all boxes), 199
Ctrl+B (bold), 24, 96, 97, 298
Ctrl+B (select boxes in same branch), 199
Ctrl+Backspace (delete from cursor), 43
Ctrl+Break (end slide show), 252
Ctrl+C (copy), 24, 44, 45, 48, 298
Ctrl key, 42
  drawing, 161
  rotating objects, 170
  sizing objects, 40
Ctrl+D (duplicate), 46, 58, 61, 171
Ctrl+Delete (delete from cursor), 43
Ctrl+E (center), 104
Ctrl+End (move to end of text), 42
Ctrl+Enter (insert new slide), 61
Ctrl+Esc (Start menu), 299
Ctrl+F (find), 48
Ctrl+F4 (close document window), 266
Ctrl+F6 (next presentation window),
    264, 266, 267
Ctrl+F10 (maximize presentation
    window), 266
Ctrl+F12 (open), 31, 282
Ctrl+G (display guides), 173, 299
Ctrl+G (select boxes in same group), 199
Ctrl+H (replace), 50
Ctrl+Home (move to beginning of text), 42
Ctrl+I (italic), 24, 96, 98, 298
Ctrl+J (justify), 105
Ctrl+key combinations, 42, 48
Ctrl+L (align left), 104

Ctrl+M (insert new slide), 26, 61
Ctrl+O (open), 31, 282
Ctrl+P (doodle with Pen tool in a slide
    show), 253
Ctrl+P (print), 29, 78
Ctrl+R (align right), 105
Ctrl+S (save), 30, 159, 289, 299
Ctrl+Shift+< (decrease point size), 96, 99
Ctrl+Shift+> (increase point size), 96, 99
Ctrl+Shift+F (font), 96, 100
Ctrl+Shift+F6 (preview presentation
    window), 266
Ctrl+Shift+F12 (print), 29, 78
Ctrl+Shift (drawing), 161
Ctrl+Shift+P (change point size), 96, 99
Ctrl+spacebar (normal format), 96, 298
  clearing text attributes with, 117
Ctrl+U (underline), 96, 98–99, 298
Ctrl+V (paste), 24, 44, 46, 48, 298
Ctrl+W (close), 32, 267
Ctrl+X (cut), 24, 44, 45, 48, 298
Ctrl+Y (redo), 47
Ctrl+Z (undo), 47, 48, 160, 298
current selection, 44
current slide, printing, 80
cursor keys. *See* arrow keys
curved lines, drawing, 162
Custom Background command, 113,
    135–136
Custom Background dialog box, 117–118,
    134
custom dictionaries, 70
CUSTOM.DIC file, 70
Customize command, 308
Cut button, 45
Cut command, 44–45

• *D* •

dashed lines outlining objects, 168
Data Labels command, 190
Datasheet button, 186
datasheets, 180, 183, 186–187

date area, 111, 119
dates, adding to slides, 119
days, capitalizing names of, 236
Decrease Font Size button, 96, 99
Decrease Paragraph Spacing button, 108
default template, creating, 124–125
Delete key, 43, 46, 52
Delete Slide command, 47, 52
Demote button, 56, 59
demoting paragraphs, 58, 59
denominator, 208
design templates. *See* templates
desktop presentation program, 10
Details view button, 283
DIB (Device Independent Bitmap)
    format, 155
dictionaries, 70
directories. *See* folders
directory entry, 282
disk space, running out of, 294
diskettes, copying presentations onto,
    254–257
document properties, 269–271
documents, saving, 30–31
Don't Show on Title check box, 120
doodles, drawing in slide shows, 253–254
DOS commands, accessing in
    Windows 95, 79
DOS text files, importing, 274
double-clicking, 16, 161
dragging, 16, 62–63
"dragon-drop" technique for copying
    slides, 269
drawing shortcuts, 161
Drawing toolbar, 22, 23
Drawing+ toolbar, activating, 158, 159
drawing tools, 160
Drive-In Effect button, 231
Drop-In Text Effect button, 232
DRW (Micrografx Designer or Draw)
    format, 155
Duplicate command, 46, 58, 61
DXF (AutoCAD) format, 155

• E •

editing slides, 35
Ellipse button, 160, 162
embedded objects, 37
embedded sounds, 220
Embossed shadow type, 168
embossed text, 101–102
EMF (Windows metafile) format, 155
End (end of line) key, 42
Enter key
    creating new slides, 61
    in Equation Editor, 210
    in Outline view, 60
entries
    built-in for AutoCorrect, 237
    creating AutoCorrect, 237–238
EPS (Encapsulated PostScript) format,
    155
Equation Editor, 205–210
    changing default text size, 210
    Enter key in, 210
Equation Editor window, 207
Equation toolbar, 208
equations
    adding symbols to, 208
    adding to slides, 206–209
    editing, 209
    typing, 208
    typing text in, 209–210
erasing pen doodles in slide shows, 253
Esc in slide shows, 252
Even Height button in WordArt, 212
Excel worksheets, inserting into
    PowerPoint, 213, 216
Exit command, 33
exiting
    Help system, 88
    PowerPoint, 32, 33
Expand Selection button, 56, 64
expanded help contents, 87
expanding presentations, 63
exporting files, 273

• F •

F1 (help), 85, 299
face, drawing a funny, 171
FAVORITES folder, 284
File Open dialog box, 282–283
filenames
  long, 12, 280, 305
  wildcards with, 284
files. *See also* foreign files
  backing up, 286
  copying, 285
  deleting, 283, 285
  deleting accidentally, 294
  finding, 293
  finding lost, 284–285
  importing foreign, 273–276
  managing, 279–286
  naming, 280
  opening, 24, 31–32
  opening multiple, 264
  organizing, 279–282
  printing, 24
  printing to, 79–80
  refreshing, 294
  renaming, 283
  retrieving presentations from, 31–32
  saving, 24, 30–31, 299
  summary information for, 270
Fill Color button, 138–139
fill color in color schemes, 128
fill color of objects, 138–139, 167
filters, 154
Find command, 48–50, 91
Find dialog box, 49
Find File command, 282–283
find index, building, 90
Find tab, 90
Fit to Page command, 266
Flash Once button, 231
Flash Once (Medium) build effect, 231
Flip button in WordArt, 212
Flip Horizontal button, 169

Flip Vertical button, 169
flowcharts, symbols for constructing, 311, 312
FLOWCHRT.PPT, 311
flush left, aligning text, 104
Fly From Left build effect, 231
Fly From Right build effect, 231
Fly From Top, By Word build effect, 232
Fly From Top Right, By Letter build effect, 231
Flying Effect button, 231
folders, 282
  creating new, 285
  deleting, 283
  organizing files with, 280–281
  renaming, 283
  tips about, 281
Font control, 96, 100
Font dialog box, 95–96, 137, 138
font size, 99
fonts
  changing existing, 99–100
  removing, 293
footer area, 111, 119
footers
  displaying, 119
  editing placeholders directly, 121
  in Slide and Title Masters, 119–121
foreign files. *See also* files
  creating presentations from, 274–275
  importing, 273–276
Format Painter, 139–140
formats
  picture files, 155
  presentations, 20, 21
formatting hidden text, 64
formatting shortcuts. *See* shortcut keys
Formatting toolbar, 22, 23
FOURPALM folder, 312
Frame Slides check box, 82
Free Rotate button, 160, 169–170
Freeform button, 160, 163–164
freeform lines, drawing, 164, 165

Full Screen mode, 23
Function equation style, 209
funny face, drawing, 171

• *G* •

General presentation type, 18, 19
Genigraphics, 248–250, 308
Genigraphics Wizard, 248–250, 308
GIF (Graphic Interchange Format) format, 155
graph objects, 180
graph titles, adding, 189–190
graph types, 180, 187–189
Graph wizard, 186–187
graphics files. *See also* picture files
  saving slides as, 277–278
graphics filters, 154
GraphicsLink program, 250
graphs, 180
  adding labels, 190
  adding legends, 190–191
  adding titles, 189–190
  changing the type, 187–189
  creating, 181–185
  embellishing, 189–191
  inserting into existing slides, 185
  inserting new slides with, 181–184
  keeping simple, 303
  moving, 185
  resizing, 185
grayed commands on menus, 32
Greek equation style, 209
group boxes, 194
Group button, 174
Group command, 174
group style options, for boxes, 194
group styles, applying to organizational
  charts, 201–202
grouping objects, 149
groups, creating, 174–175
Groups menu, 202

guides
  activating, 173
  displaying, 299

• *H* •

handles, 38–40. *See also* love handles
  around clip art, 144, 145
  with AutoShape buttons, 166
Handout Master, 110, 115–116
Handout Master command, 115
handouts
  adding headers or footers, 120–121
  Header and Footer dialog box, 121
  printing, 81–82
Harvard Graphics presentation files,
  importing, 274
header area, 119
Header and Footer dialog box
  for notes and handouts, 121
  for slides, 120
headers
  editing placeholders directly, 121
  in Slide and Title Masters, 119–121
Help, activating, 299
Help contents, expanding, 87
Help menu, 86
Help system, 85–92
  exiting, 88
  in Windows 95, 86–88
Help topics
  animation in, 89
  displaying, 87–88
  searching for, 89–91
HGL (HP Graphic Language) format, 155
hidden slides, printing, 82
Hide Slide command, 82, 244
hiding, text formatting, 64–65
Home (beginning of line) key, 42
hot keys, 3
hovering over icons, 86

• I •

I-beam cursor, 25
icons, hovering over, 86
Imager, 309–310
IMAGER folder in VALUPACK, 310
importing files, 273
Increase Font Size button, 99
Increase Paragraph Spacing button, 108
incremental backup, 286
indent settings for paragraphs, 105–107
Index tab, 89–90
INI files, 290
Insert Clip Art button, 142, 153
Insert File dialog box, 268
Insert Graph button, 185
Insert key, 40
Insert Microsoft Excel Worksheet button, 216
Insert Microsoft Word Table button, 214
insert mode, 40
Insert Movie dialog box, 221, 222
Insert New Slide button, 26, 61
Insert Object dialog box, 207
Insert Outline dialog box, 276
Insert Picture dialog box, 136, 154
Insert Sound dialog box, 219
Insert Word Table dialog box, 214
insertion pointer, 25
installation, 319
internal memory, conserving, 293
Italic button
  on Formatting toolbar, 96, 98
  in WordArt, 212

• J •

JPG (JPEG files) format, 155
justified text, 105

• K •

keyboard
  controlling slide shows, 252
  moving text up or down, 62
keyboard hot keys, 3
keyboard shortcuts. *See* shortcut keys

• L •

labels, adding to graphs, 190
Landscape mode, 82
Laser Text Effect button, 231
laser transparencies, printing, 30
layers, changing for objects, 172
left justified text, 105
left-arrow key (←) compared to
  backspace, 42
Legend command, 191
legends for graphs, 180, 190–191
levels for bullets, 303
Line button, 160, 162
line color of objects, 167
line objects, 37
line segments, changing in boxes, 203
Line Spacing dialog box, 108
line style of objects, 167
lines
  adjusting spacing between, 107–108
  changing color, 162
  drawing freeform, 164, 165
List View button, 283
long filenames, 12, 280, 305
Look in Favorites button, 283–284
Loop Continuously Until Esc option, 252
Lotus Freelance presentation files,
  importing, 274
love handles, 38–40. *See also* handles
  with AutoShape buttons, 166
lowercase, changing to, 71
lowercase letters in searches, 49

• *M* •

main points in body text, 11
manager box, 194, 198
Manager button, 198
manual advance of slides, 252
marking text, 43–44
Master color scheme
    changing, 113
    overriding, 130–131
master slide, 46
master text style, overriding, 117
Masters, 109, 116–118
    calling up quickly, 110
    displaying by Shift+clicking, 297
Math equation style, 209
MathType, 206
Matrix-Vector equation style, 210
maximize button, 23
MDI (Multiple Document Interface), 268
Meeting Minder, 259, 307
Meeting Minutes tab, 259
memory, conserving, 293
menu bar, 22
menus, grayed commands on, 32
mice. *See* mouse
Microsoft Graph, 179, 180–181
Microsoft Graph command, 185
Microsoft Imager, 309–310
Microsoft Network, The, getting help
    on, 92
Microsoft Organization Chart, 193
Microsoft software, version numbers, 13
Microsoft Word Table command, 214
Middles command, 174
MIDI files, 218
minimized presentation windows, 265, 266
misspelled words, finding, 67–70
months, capitalizing names of, 236
More Play Options dialog box, 224
mouse
    clicking, 16
    clicking and dragging, 16
    double-clicking, 16

dragging, 16
moving, 16
moving text up or down with, 62–63
operating, 16
pointing, 16
promoting or demoting with, 60
right-clicking, 16
tricks for slide shows, 253
triple-clicking, 16
mouse pad, 16
Move Up button, 56, 62
movies
    adding to slides, 221
    playing, 221–223
    setting to play automatically, 223–224
MSN (The Microsoft Network), getting
    help on, 92
Multiple Document Interface (MDI), 268

• *N* •

networks, running presentations over,
    259–260, 308
New Folder button, 285
New Slide button, 26, 56, 61
New Slide command, 61
New Slide dialog box, 27, 52, 181–182, 195
notes
    adding headers or footers, 120–121
    adding to slides, 241
    creating pages for, 239
    Header and Footer dialog box, 121
    increasing the area for, 241–243
Notes Background dialog box, 117
Notes Master, 110, 116
notes pages
    adding extra, 243–244
    hiding background objects, 117
    printing, 244–245
Notes Pages command, 240
Notes Pages tab, 259
Notes Pages view, 24, 240
    adding new slides from, 244
Notes Pages View button, 240

notes text style, 117
Num Lock key, 41
Number Area, in Slide Master, 111, 119
Number of copies field, 80–81

• O •

Object command, 207
Object Linking and Embedding (OLE), 182
objects, 11, 37
    animating in slides, 230
    attributes, 167–168
    changing fill color, 138–139
    changing size, 39
    constraining with Shift key, 299
    copying colors from, 139–140
    creating semi-transparent, 139
    cutting to Clipboard, 46
    dashed lines outlining, 168
    deleting, 46
    duplicating, 46
    fill color, 167
    filling with textures, 306
    flipping, 169
    grouping, 149
    layering, 172
    line color, 167
    line style, 167
    moving to another slide, 46
    rotating 90 degrees, 169
    selecting, 38
    shadow on, 167
    types, 37, 161
    ungrouping, 149
OLE (Object Linking and Embedding), 182
online service from Microsoft, 92
Open an Existing Presentation option, 17
Open button, 31
Open command, 24, 31, 264
Open dialog box, 31–32
open shapes, drawing, 164
openings for presentations, 316

Options dialog box, 223, 271
organizational chart boxes. *See* boxes
organizational charts, 193
    adding boxes, 198–199
    applying group styles, 201–202
    creating, 194–198
    deleting boxes, 200
    inserting into existing slides, 198
    inserting slides, 195
    moving boxes, 200–201
    rearranging, 199–202
Organize ClipArt dialog box, 151–152
Organize dialog box, 153
OrgChart slide type, 195
orientation, changing, 82
outline box, 40
Outline menu command, 55
Outline toolbar, 56, 57
Outline view, 24, 28–29, 56–57
    compared to Slide view, 56–57
    presentations in, 56
    switching to, 55–56
Outline View button, 55
outlines
    collapsing, 63–64
    exporting, 276–277
    inserting slides from, 276
    printing, 82
output
    of presentations, 20, 21
    selecting for printing, 81–82
overhead transparencies, printing, 30, 82

• P •

Pack and Go Wizard, 254–257
packed presentations, loading to other
        computers, 257
Page Down key, 26, 36
page numbers, adding to speaker notes,
        116
Page Up key, 26, 36
panic avoidance during presentations, 317

paragraphs
  adding, 60
  adding bullets, 102
  copying, 58
  cutting, 58
  deleting, 58
  demoting, 58, 59
  dragging to new levels, 60
  editing, 58
  indent settings, 105–107
  marking, 44
  moving, 62
  pasting, 58
  promoting, 58, 59
  promoting to highest level, 61
  selecting, 58
Paste button, 46
Paste command, 44–45, 45–46
Pattern Fill dialog box, 135
PCD (Kodak's Photo CD) format, 155
PCT (Macintosh PICT file) format, 155
PCX (variant bitmap file) format, 155
periods, adding or removing, 71–72
Periods command, 71
Periods dialog box, 71–72
photo labs, using local for slides, 247–248
PhotoDisc, photos on CD-ROM, 310
PHOTODSC folder, 310
Pick Up Style command, 140
Picture command, 155
picture files. *See also* graphics files
  formats for, 155
picture images, selecting for background,
    136
pictures. *See also* clip art
  adding from CD-ROM, 153
  adding to ClipArt Gallery, 151–152
  drawing complicated, 170–175
  general tips for drawing, 157–160
  inserting directly, 153–155
  thumbnail, 152
placeholder message in text objects, 25
placeholders for repeating text, 119
Pngsetup program, 257
point, 147

pointing, the mouse, 16
polygons, drawing, 163–164
Portrait mode, 82
POT extension, 122
PowerPoint, 10
  clip art, 141–142
  commandments, 289–291
  disappearance of, 294
  exiting, 32, 33
  features, 10
  Help system, 85–92
  inserting Excel worksheets, 213, 216
  inserting sounds, 219–220
  inserting Word tables, 213, 214–216
  installing, 319, 320–322
  names for, 13
  new features for Windows 95, 305–308
  setup program, 321
  shortcuts, 297–299
  starting, 12–14
  system requirements, 319
  troubleshooting, 293–295
  Windows 95, Version 7, 12, 13
PowerPoint dialog box, 15–17
POWERPOINT folder, storing files in, 281
PowerPoint screen, 22–24
PowerPoint support forum on MSN, 92
PowerPoint Viewer, 254
  running slide shows with, 257–258
PowerPoint Viewer dialog box, 258
PPPHOTOS folder in VALUPACK folder, 310
PPSAMPLES folder in VALUPACK folder,
    311
PPT extension, 11
PPTMPL folder, 311
predefined animation effects, 230–232
Presentation Conference command, 260
presentation files, 11
presentation software, 8
presentation templates. *See* templates
presentation windows
  closing, 267
  shortcut keys for switching among
    multiple, 266
  switching between, 264

presentations, 10, 11
  automatic, 232
  changing color schemes, 129–130
  checking spelling, 67–70
  clip art in, 142–144
  closing, 32, 317
  collapsing, 63
  collating printing of, 81
  copying entire, 267–269
  copying onto diskettes, 254–257
  copying slides from other, 267–269
  creating with AutoContent Wizard, 17
  creating from foreign files, 274–275
  editing multiple, 263–267
  format, 20, 21
  keeping simple, 303
  moving through, 36
  on networks, 308
  opening, 316
  opening existing, 17
  opening multiple, 264
  output, 20, 21
  panic avoidance during, 317
  practicing, 317
  printing, 77–83
  printing part of, 80
  purpose of, 315
  relevancy of, 316
  retrieving from disk files, 31–32
  running over networks, 259–260
  sample on CD-ROM, 311
  saving, 30–31
  sending to Genigraphics, 248–250
  setting up unattended, 258
  types, 18
  visual styles, 20
PRESENTATIONS DESIGNS folder, 122
  storing templates in, 124
Preview View button, 283
Print button, 29, 77
Print command, 24, 78
Print dialog box, 29, 78, 244–245
Print Hidden Slides check box, 82
Print to File check box, 79–80

Print what field, 81–82
printers
  changing, 79–80
  problems with, 83
printing slides, 29–30
PRINTME.PPT, 311
programs, switching, 299
progressive disclosure. *See* build effects
Promote button, 56, 59
promoting paragraphs, 58, 59
Prompt for File Properties option, 271
Properties dialog box, 270
Properties View button, 283
punctuation, checking with Style
    Checker, 73
purpose of presentations, 315

question mark in dialog boxes, 86
question mark mouse pointer, 86
quick menu, right-clicking for, 297

• *R* •

ragged left text, 105
ragged right text, 105
RAM (random access memory), 30
Random Effect, 228
Random Transition, setting slides to, 226
ranges of slides, printing, 80
readable slides, creating, 301–303
Recolor Picture dialog box, 150
Rectangle button, 160, 162
rectangles, drawing, 162
recurring text, adding to slides, 112
Recycle Bin icon, 294
Redo button, 47
Redo command, 47
Redraw command, cleaning up equations
    with, 208
Registered symbol (®), creating with
    AutoCorrect, 237

registry, 290
Regroup command, 175
Rehearse New Timings option, 252
repeating text, placeholders for, 119
Replace command, 50
Replace dialog box, 50
Replace Text as You Type option, 237
Reverse Text Build button, 232
Rich Text Format (RTF)
   exporting outlines in, 276–277
   files, importing, 274
right justified text, 105
right-clicking
   the mouse, 16
   for quick menus, 297
root directory, 281, 282
Rotate button in WordArt, 213
Rotate Left button, 169
Rotate Right button, 169
RTF (Rich Text Format). *See* Rich Text
   Format (RTF)
ruler, 106, 158
Run command, 320
Run dialog box, 320

• S •

Save As command, 24
Save As dialog box, 299
Save button, 30
Save command, 24, 30
Scale to Fit Paper check box, 82
screen, maximizing, 23
scroll bars, 23
scroll box, dragging to move through
   slides, 26
Seal AutoShape button, 166
Selected Legend command, 191
Selection button, 38, 160
semi-transparent objects, creating, 139
Send Backward button, 171
Send Backward command, 172

Send to Back command, 172
Send to Genigraphics command, 308
SENSE folder, 310
Sense Interactive Multimedia, photos on
   CD-ROM, 310
series, 180
series axis, 189
Series in Columns command, 186
server, 182
Setup program for PowerPoint, 321
Shaded Fill dialog box, 134–135
Shading button in WordArt, 213
shadow
   applying, 163
   embossed, 168
   on objects, 167
Shadow button, 101, 213
shadow color in color schemes, 128
Shadow command, 147
Shadow dialog box, 147, 168
Shadow On/Off button, 147, 163
shape objects, 37, 148
Shift+F12 (save), 30
Shift+Tab (promoting paragraphs), 59
Shift key
   Box buttons with, 199
   drawing with, 161, 299
   restricting rotation angle, 170
   sizing objects with, 40
shortcut keys
   Alt+Backspace (erase), 160
   Alt+H (help), 86
   Alt+Shift+1 (collapse presentation), 63
   Alt+Shift+↓ (move text down), 62
   Alt+Shift+← (promote paragraph), 59
   Alt+Shift+→ (demote paragraph), 59
   Alt+Shift+↑ (move text up), 62
   Alt+Shift+A (expand presentation), 63
   Ctrl+↓ (down one paragraph), 42
   Ctrl+↓ (select first box), 200
   Ctrl+← (left one word), 42
   Ctrl+← (select box to left), 200
   Ctrl+→ (right one word), 42

(continued)

shortcut keys *(continued)*
  Ctrl+→ (select box to right), 200
  Ctrl+↑ (select current box's
    manager), 200
  Ctrl+↑ (up one paragraph), 42
  Ctrl+A (select all boxes), 199
  Ctrl+B (bold), 24, 96, 97, 298
  Ctrl+B (select boxes in same branch),
    199
  Ctrl+C (copy), 24, 44, 45, 48, 298
  Ctrl+D (duplicate), 46, 58, 61, 171
  Ctrl+E (center), 104
  Ctrl+Enter (insert new slide), 61
  Ctrl+F (find), 48
  Ctrl+F4 (close document window), 266
  Ctrl+F6 (next presentation window), 264,
    266, 267
  Ctrl+F10 (maximize presentation
    window), 266
  Ctrl+F12 (open), 31, 282
  Ctrl+G (display or hide guides), 173, 299
  Ctrl+G (select boxes in same group), 199
  Ctrl+H (replace), 50
  Ctrl+I (italic), 24, 96, 98, 298
  Ctrl+J (justify), 105
  Ctrl+L (align left), 104
  Ctrl+M (insert new slide), 26, 61
  Ctrl+O (open), 31, 282
  Ctrl+P (doodle), 253
  Ctrl+P (print), 29, 78
  Ctrl+R (align right), 105
  Ctrl+S (save), 30, 159, 289, 299
  Ctrl+Shift+< (decrease point size), 96, 99
  Ctrl+Shift+> (increase point size), 96, 99
  Ctrl+Shift+F (font), 96, 100
  Ctrl+Shift+F6 (preview presentation
    window), 266
  Ctrl+Shift+F12 (print), 29, 78
  Ctrl+Shift+P (change point size), 96, 99
  Ctrl+spacebar (normal format), 96,
    117, 298
  Ctrl+U (underline), 96, 98–99, 298
  Ctrl+V (paste), 24, 44, 46, 48, 298
  Ctrl+W (close), 32, 267
  Ctrl+X (cut), 24, 44, 45, 48, 298
  Ctrl+Y (redo), 47
  Ctrl+Z (undo), 47, 48, 160, 298
  F1 (help) key, 85
  for multiple windows, 266
  Shift+F12 (save), 30
  slash (/) key, 64
shortcuts in PowerPoint, 297–299
Show All button, 56, 63
Show Formatting button, 56, 64
Show Titles button, 56, 63
showing text formatting, 64–65
Shut Down command, 33
slash key (/), 64
slide backgrounds
  filling with textures, 306
  shading, 133–135
Slide Color Scheme command, 113, 129,
    130, 131
slide icon in Outline view, 56, 58
slide layouts, 27–28, 37
Slide Master, 11, 110
  changing, 110–113
  displaying, 294
Slide Master command, 110
slide numbers, adding, 119
slide objects, 11, 37
slide pages. *See* slides
Slide Show button, 251
Slide Show dialog box, 251–252
Slide Show view, 24
slide shows, 11
  automatic, 232
  controlling with the keyboard, 252
  erasing in, 253
  looping continuously, 252
  mouse tricks, 253
  running with PowerPoint Viewer,
    257–258
Slide Sorter command, 51
Slide Sorter toolbar, 226, 227
Slide Sorter view, 24, 51–53, 226
Slide Sorter View button, 226, 227, 229, 232
slide text style, changing, 117

slide titles, demoting, 59
Slide Transition button, 227, 232
Slide Transition command, 227
Slide Transition dialog box, 227, 228, 232
slide transitions, 225
Slide view, 24, 28
  compared to Outline view, 56–57
slides, 10
  adding, 51, 52
  adding data, 119
  adding equations, 206–209
  adding extra notes pages, 243–244
  adding movies, 221
  adding new, 26–28, 61, 244
  adding notes, 241
  adding recurring text, 112
  adding sounds, 217–220
  advancing manually, 252
  animating objects in, 230
  collapsing single, 63–64
  color-coding, 130
  converting to 35mm color slides, 247
  copying from other presentations,
    267–269
  copying specific, 269
  copying to Clipboard, 58
  creating readable, 301–303
  cutting to Clipboard, 58
  deleting, 47, 51, 52, 58
  displaying footers, 119
  drawing borders, 82
  duplicating, 58
  editing one paragraph on, 35
  editing entire, 58
  expanding single, 64
  Header and Footer dialog box, 120
  hiding, 82, 244
  hiding background objects for
    selected, 117
  inserting from outlines, 276
  inserting graphs into existing, 185
  inserting new with graphs, 181–184
  inserting in organizational charts, 195
  inserting organizational charts, 198

  keeping in their place, 315
  lining up text, 104–105
  maximum number of bullets, 301
  moving, 51
  moving forward and backward, 26, 36
  not being a slave to, 315
  number needed, 316
  printing, 29–30, 80
  rearranging, 51, 51–53
  saving as graphics files, 277–278
  saving in Windows MetaFile (WMF)
    format, 277–278
  selecting entire, 57–58
  shading background of, 133–135
  viewing entire, 25
Slides from File command, 267, 269
Slides from Outline command, 276
slots, 208
Snap to Grid command, 172–173
sound card, 217
Sound command, 219
sound files, 218, 309
sounds
  adding to slides, 217–220
  combining with build effects, 307
  inserting, 219–220
  playing embedded, 220
  removing, 220
spacing
  adjusting between lines, 107–108
  adjusting between paragraphs, 108
Spacing Between Characters button in
    WordArt, 213
speaker notes
  adding page numbers, 116
  creating, 239
  thoughts about, 245–246
spell checker, 67–70
Spelling command, 24
Spelling dialog box, 68–69
spelling dictionaries, 70
spreadsheet objects, 182
squares, drawing, 163
stacked symbols in equations, 208

stacking order, changing for objects, 172
standard dictionary, 70
Standard toolbar, 22, 23
Start button, 13–14
Start menu, 14
starting PowerPoint, 12–14
status bar, 22, 23
straight lines, drawing, 162
Stretch button in WordArt, 212
Style Checker, 67, 72–75, 305
Style Checker dialog box, 72
subordinate boxes, 194, 198
Subordinate button, 196, 198
subpoints in body text, 11
summary information for files, 270
Symbol equation style, 210
symbols
   for constructing flowcharts, 311, 312
   for constructing timelines, 311, 313
   inserting special with AutoCorrect, 237
   selecting for equations, 208
system requirements for PowerPoint, 319

● *T* ●

Tab key
   demoting paragraphs, 59
   selecting objects, 38
tab stops
   removing, 107
   setting, 105–107
tables, elements of, 311, 312
TABLES.PPT, 311
TCVISUAL folder, 312
Template option, 17
templates, 17, 109, 121–122
   applying different, 122–123
   on CD-ROM, 311
   color schemes with, 127–129
   creating new, 123–124
   creating new default, 124–125
   in equations, 208

ten PowerPoint commandments, 289–291
text. *See also* characters
   adding recurring to slides, 112
   aligning flush left, 104
   applying color, 137–138
   avoiding small, 301
   capitalizing, 70–71
   centering, 104
   copying, 24
   creating embossed, 101–102
   cutting, 24
   deleting, 43
   deleting blocks, 44
   dragging up or down, 62–63
   editing, 25–26
   finding, 48–50
   formatting in boxes, 203–204
   lining up on slides, 104–105
   marking, 43–44
   moving in Outline view, 62
   moving up or down, 62–63
   pasting, 24, 45–46
   replacing, 44, 50–51
   typing in equations, 209–210
Text & Clip Art layout, 27
text area for notes, increasing size,
   241–243
text attributes, clearing all, 117
text blocks, 45
Text button, 160
text color, changing, 100–101
Text Color button, 96, 100–101, 137
text file types for importing, 274
text fonts, changing existing, 99–100
text formatting, hiding, 64–65
text objects, 11, 25–26, 37
   editing, 40–44
   selecting, 38
   setting tags or indents, 106–107
text ruler, 158
text shadow, adding, 101
text sizes, changing default in Equation
   Editor, 210

text styles
  changing in slides, 117
  for equations, 209–210
Text Tool button, 112
text-and-lines color in color schemes, 128
Textured Fill dialog box, 136, 306
textures, fill options, 306
TGA (Targa files) format, 155
35mm color slides, converting
    PowerPoint slides, 247
3-D graphs, 180
thumbnail pictures, 152
TIF (Tagged Image) format, 155
tiled presentation windows, 264–265
TIMELINE.PPT, 311
timelines, symbols for, 311, 313
Tip of the Day, 14–15
tips, 14–15
title bar, 23
Title Case option, 71
Title layout, 37
Title Master command, 114
Title Masters, 110, 113–114, 306
title text color in color schemes, 128
titles
  adding to graphs, 189–190
  for slides, 11
Titles dialog box, 189
tOGGLE cASE option, 71
toolbars, 22
  customizing, 308
  reactivating, 295
Trademark symbol (™), creating with
    AutoCorrect, 237
transition effects, 225
transitions for slides, 225
transparencies, printing, 30, 82
triple-clicking, 16
troubleshooting PowerPoint, 293–295
typeover mode, 40
Typing Text Effect button, 231

• *U* •

Underline button, 96, 98–99
Undo button, 47
Undo command, 47
Ungroup button, 174
Ungroup command, 148, 174
ungrouping objects, 149
UPPERCASE, changing to, 71
uppercase letters in searches, 49

• *V* •

value axis, 189
VALUPACK folder on CD-ROM, 309
Variable equation style, 209
Version 7 of PowerPoint, 13
versions of Microsoft software, 13
vertical scroll bar, 36
video, adding, 221–224
video controls, hiding, 223
video files, samples from Four Palms, 312
VIDEOS folder in VALUPACK, 312
view buttons, 23, 24
  displaying Masters with, 297
Viewer. *See* PowerPoint Viewer
views, 11
  switching among, 24, 282–283
visual clarity
  checking for, 73
  setting options for, 73, 74–75
visual styles for presentations, 20

• *W* •

WAV files, 218
wildcard filenames, 284
Windows 95
  accessing DOS commands, 79
  adding sound, 218
  backup program, 286
  Help system, 86–88

Windows MetaFile (WMF) format. *See* WMF (Windows MetaFile format)
Wingdings, collection of bullets, 103
Wipe Down, By Letter build effect, 231
Wipe Right build effect, 232
WMF (Windows MetaFile)
  extension, 278
  format, saving slides in, 277–278
word processor, 40–44
Word tables, inserting into PowerPoint, 213, 214–216
Word for Windows outline files, importing, 274
WordArt, 210–213
wording, consistent, 302
words
  finding misspelled, 67–70
  finding whole, 49
  marking, 44
  replacing entire, 51
work, saving, 30–31
WPG (DrawPerfect) format, 155
WYSIWYG, 55

X-axis, 180
X Box, clicking, 33

Y-axis, 180

• Z •

Zoom command, 25
Zoom control, 52
zoom factor
  adjusting, 25
  increasing for drawing, 158

The Internet For Macs® For Dummies® 2nd Edition	by Charles Seiter	ISBN: 1-56884-371-2	$19.99 USA/$26.99 Canada
The Internet For Macs® For Dummies® Starter Kit	by Charles Seiter	ISBN: 1-56884-244-9	$29.99 USA/$39.99 Canada
The Internet For Macs® For Dummies® Starter Kit Bestseller Edition	by Charles Seiter	ISBN: 1-56884-245-7	$39.99 USA/$54.99 Canada
The Internet For Windows® For Dummies® Starter Kit	by John R. Levine & Margaret Levine Young	ISBN: 1-56884-237-6	$34.99 USA/$44.99 Canada
The Internet For Windows® For Dummies® Starter Kit, Bestseller Edition	by John R. Levine & Margaret Levine Young	ISBN: 1-56884-246-5	$39.99 USA/$54.99 Canada

MACINTOSH

Mac® Programming For Dummies®	by Dan Parks Sydow	ISBN: 1-56884-173-6	$19.95 USA/$26.95 Canada
Macintosh® System 7.5 For Dummies®	by Bob LeVitus	ISBN: 1-56884-197-3	$19.95 USA/$26.95 Canada
MORE Macs® For Dummies®	by David Pogue	ISBN: 1-56884-087-X	$19.95 USA/$26.95 Canada
PageMaker 5 For Macs® For Dummies®	by Galen Gruman & Deke McClelland	ISBN: 1-56884-178-7	$19.95 USA/$26.95 Canada
QuarkXPress 3.3 For Dummies®	by Galen Gruman & Barbara Assadi	ISBN: 1-56884-217-1	$19.99 USA/$26.99 Canada
Upgrading and Fixing Macs® For Dummies®	by Kearney Rietmann & Frank Higgins	ISBN: 1-56884-189-2	$19.95 USA/$26.95 Canada

MULTIMEDIA

Multimedia & CD-ROMs For Dummies® 2nd Edition	by Andy Rathbone	ISBN: 1-56884-907-9	$19.99 USA/$26.99 Canada
Multimedia & CD-ROMs For Dummies® Interactive Multimedia Value Pack, 2nd Edition	by Andy Rathbone	ISBN: 1-56884-909-5	$29.99 USA/$39.99 Canada

OPERATING SYSTEMS:

DOS

MORE DOS For Dummies®	by Dan Gookin	ISBN: 1-56884-046-2	$19.95 USA/$26.95 Canada
OS/2® Warp For Dummies® 2nd Edition	by Andy Rathbone	ISBN: 1-56884-205-8	$19.99 USA/$26.99 Canada

UNIX

MORE UNIX® For Dummies®	by John R. Levine & Margaret Levine Young	ISBN: 1-56884-361-5	$19.99 USA/$26.99 Canada
UNIX® For Dummies®	by John R. Levine & Margaret Levine Young	ISBN: 1-878058-58-4	$19.95 USA/$26.95 Canada

WINDOWS

MORE Windows® For Dummies® 2nd Edition	by Andy Rathbone	ISBN: 1-56884-048-9	$19.95 USA/$26.95 Canada
Windows® 95 For Dummies®	by Andy Rathbone	ISBN: 1-56884-240-6	$19.99 USA/$26.99 Canada

PCS/HARDWARE

Illustrated Computer Dictionary For Dummies® 2nd Edition	by Dan Gookin & Wallace Wang	ISBN: 1-56884-218-X	$12.95 USA/$16.95 Canada
Upgrading and Fixing PCs For Dummies® 2nd Edition	by Andy Rathbone	ISBN: 1-56884-903-6	$19.99 USA/$26.99 Canada

PRESENTATION/AUTOCAD

AutoCAD For Dummies®	by Bud Smith	ISBN: 1-56884-191-4	$19.95 USA/$26.95 Canada
PowerPoint 4 For Windows® For Dummies®	by Doug Lowe	ISBN: 1-56884-161-2	$16.99 USA/$22.99 Canada

PROGRAMMING

Borland C++ For Dummies®	by Michael Hyman	ISBN: 1-56884-162-0	$19.95 USA/$26.95 Canada
C For Dummies® Volume 1	by Dan Gookin	ISBN: 1-878058-78-9	$19.95 USA/$26.95 Canada
C++ For Dummies®	by Stephen R. Davis	ISBN: 1-56884-163-9	$19.95 USA/$26.95 Canada
Delphi Programming For Dummies®	by Neil Rubenking	ISBN: 1-56884-200-7	$19.99 USA/$26.99 Canada
Mac® Programming For Dummies®	by Dan Parks Sydow	ISBN: 1-56884-173-6	$19.95 USA/$26.95 Canada
PowerBuilder 4 Programming For Dummies®	by Ted Coombs & Jason Coombs	ISBN: 1-56884-325-9	$19.99 USA/$26.99 Canada
QBasic Programming For Dummies®	by Douglas Hergert	ISBN: 1-56884-093-4	$19.95 USA/$26.95 Canada
Visual Basic 3 For Dummies®	by Wallace Wang	ISBN: 1-56884-076-4	$19.95 USA/$26.95 Canada
Visual Basic "X" For Dummies®	by Wallace Wang	ISBN: 1-56884-230-9	$19.99 USA/$26.99 Canada
Visual C++ 2 For Dummies®	by Michael Hyman & Bob Arnson	ISBN: 1-56884-328-3	$19.99 USA/$26.99 Canada
Windows® 95 Programming For Dummies®	by S. Randy Davis	ISBN: 1-56884-327-5	$19.99 USA/$26.99 Canada

SPREADSHEET

1-2-3 For Dummies®	by Greg Harvey	ISBN: 1-878058-60-6	$16.95 USA/$22.95 Canada
1-2-3 For Windows® 5 For Dummies® 2nd Edition	by John Walkenbach	ISBN: 1-56884-216-3	$16.95 USA/$22.95 Canada
Excel 5 For Macs® For Dummies®	by Greg Harvey	ISBN: 1-56884-186-8	$19.95 USA/$26.95 Canada
Excel For Dummies® 2nd Edition	by Greg Harvey	ISBN: 1-56884-050-0	$16.95 USA/$22.95 Canada
MORE 1-2-3 For DOS For Dummies®	by John Weingarten	ISBN: 1-56884-224-4	$19.99 USA/$26.99 Canada
MORE Excel 5 For Windows® For Dummies®	by Greg Harvey	ISBN: 1-56884-207-4	$19.95 USA/$26.95 Canada
Quattro Pro 6 For Windows® For Dummies®	by John Walkenbach	ISBN: 1-56884-174-4	$19.95 USA/$26.95 Canada
Quattro Pro For DOS For Dummies®	by John Walkenbach	ISBN: 1-56884-023-3	$16.95 USA/$22.95 Canada

UTILITIES

Norton Utilities 8 For Dummies®	by Beth Slick	ISBN: 1-56884-166-3	$19.95 USA/$26.95 Canada

VCRS/CAMCORDERS

VCRs & Camcorders For Dummies™	by Gordon McComb & Andy Rathbone	ISBN: 1-56884-229-5	$14.99 USA/$20.99 Canada

WORD PROCESSING

Ami Pro For Dummies®	by Jim Meade	ISBN: 1-56884-049-7	$19.95 USA/$26.95 Canada
MORE Word For Windows® 6 For Dummies®	by Doug Lowe	ISBN: 1-56884-165-5	$19.95 USA/$26.95 Canada
MORE WordPerfect® 6 For Windows® For Dummies®	by Margaret Levine Young & David C. Kay	ISBN: 1-56884-206-6	$19.95 USA/$26.95 Canada
MORE WordPerfect® 6 For DOS For Dummies®	by Wallace Wang, edited by Dan Gookin	ISBN: 1-56884-047-0	$19.95 USA/$26.95 Canada
Word 6 For Macs® For Dummies®	by Dan Gookin	ISBN: 1-56884-190-6	$19.95 USA/$26.95 Canada
Word For Windows® 6 For Dummies®	by Dan Gookin	ISBN: 1-56884-075-6	$16.95 USA/$22.95 Canada
Word For Windows® For Dummies®	by Dan Gookin & Ray Werner	ISBN: 1-878058-86-X	$16.95 USA/$22.95 Canada
WordPerfect® 6 For DOS For Dummies®	by Dan Gookin	ISBN: 1-878058-77-0	$16.95 USA/$22.95 Canada
WordPerfect® 6.1 For Windows® For Dummies® 2nd Edition	by Margaret Levine Young & David Kay	ISBN: 1-56884-243-0	$16.95 USA/$22.95 Canada
WordPerfect® For Dummies®	by Dan Gookin	ISBN: 1-878058-52-5	$16.95 USA/$22.95 Canada

IDG BOOKS WORLDWIDE

Order Center: **(800) 762-2974** *(8 a.m.–6 p.m., EST, weekdays)*

9/1?

Quantity	ISBN	Title	Price	Total

Shipping & Handling Charges

	Description	First book	Each additional book	Total
Domestic	Normal	$4.50	$1.50	$
	Two Day Air	$8.50	$2.50	$
	Overnight	$18.00	$3.00	$
International	Surface	$8.00	$8.00	$
	Airmail	$16.00	$16.00	$
	DHL Air	$17.00	$17.00	$

*For large quantities call for shipping & handling charges.
**Prices are subject to change without notice.

Ship to:

Name _____

Company _____

Address _____

City/State/Zip _____

Daytime Phone _____

Payment: ☐ Check to IDG Books Worldwide (US Funds Only)

       ☐ VISA   ☐ MasterCard   ☐ American Express

Card # _____ Expires _____

Signature _____

Subtotal _____

CA residents add
applicable sales tax _____

IN, MA, and MD
residents add
5% sales tax _____

IL residents add
6.25% sales tax _____

RI residents add
7% sales tax _____

TX residents add
8.25% sales tax _____

Shipping _____

Total _____

Please send this order form to:
IDG Books Worldwide, Inc.
7260 Shadeland Station, Suite 100
Indianapolis, IN 46256

Allow up to 3 weeks for delivery.
Thank you!